D1196878

ALSO BY FRANK BIDART

Golden State

The Book of the Body

The Sacrifice

In the Western Night: Collected Poems 1965–90

Desire

Star Dust

Watching the Spring Festival

Metaphysical Dog

AS EDITOR   *The Collected Poems of Robert Lowell*

(with David Gewanter)

HALF-   LIGHT

FARRAR STRAUS GIROUX   **NEW YORK**

HALF- LIGHT

COLLECTED POEMS

1965– 2016

FRANK BIDART

Farrar, Straus and Giroux
18 West 18th Street, New York 10011

Grateful acknowledgment is made for permission to reprint
excerpts from *Existence: A New Dimension in Psychiatry and
Psychology* by Rollo May, copyright © 1958. Reprinted by
permission of Basic Books, a member of The Perseus Books Group.

Library of Congress Cataloging-in-Publication Data
Names: Bidart, Frank, 1939– author.
Title: Half-light : collected poems 1965–2016 / Frank Bidart.
Description: First edition. | New York : Farrar, Straus and Giroux, 2017.
Identifiers: LCCN 2015038552 | ISBN 9780374125950 (hardcover) |
    ISBN 9780374715182 (ebook)
Subjects: BISAC: POETRY / American / General.
Classification: LCC PS3552 .I33 2017 | DDC 811/.54—dc23
LC record available at http://lccn.loc.gov/2015038552

Designed by Quemadura

Our books may be purchased in bulk for promotional, educational, or
business use. Please contact your local bookseller or the Macmillan
Corporate and Premium Sales Department at 1-800-221-7945, extension
5442, or by e-mail at MacmillanSpecialMarkets@macmillan.com.

www.fsgbooks.com
www.twitter.com/fsgbooks
www.facebook.com/fsgbooks

10 9 8 7 6 5 4 3 2 1

Contents

STAR DUST (2005)

I. MUSIC LIKE DIRT

WATCHING THE SPRING FESTIVAL (2008)

METAPHYSICAL DOG (2013)

ONE

THIRST (NEW POEMS, 2016)

PART ONE

PART TWO

IN THE

WESTERN

NIGHT:

POEMS

1965–90

IN THE

WESTERN

NIGHT

(1990)

To the Dead

What I hope (when I hope) is that we'll
see each other again, —

. . . and again reach the VEIN

in which we loved each other. . .
It existed. *It existed.*

There is a NIGHT within the NIGHT, —

. . . for, like the detectives (the Ritz Brothers)
in *The Gorilla,*

once we'd been battered by the gorilla

we searched the walls, the intricately carved
impenetrable paneling

for a button, lever, latch

that unlocks a secret door that
reveals at last the secret chambers,

CORRIDORS within WALLS,

(the disenthralling, necessary, dreamed structure
beneath the structure we see,)

that is the HOUSE within the HOUSE. . .

There is a NIGHT within the NIGHT,—

. . . there were (for example) months when I seemed only
to displease, frustrate,

disappoint you—; then, something triggered

a drunk lasting for days, and as you
slowly and shakily sobered up,

sick, throbbing with remorse and self-loathing,

insight like ashes: clung
to; useless; hated. . .

This was the viewing of the power of the waters

while the waters were asleep:—
secrets, histories of loves, betrayals, double-binds

not fit (you thought) for the light of day. . .

There is a NIGHT within the NIGHT,—

. . . for, there at times at night, still we
inhabit the secret place together. . .

Is this wisdom, or self-pity?—

The love I've known is the love of
two people staring

not at each other, but in the same direction.

Dark Night

(JOHN OF THE CROSS)

In a dark night, when the light
    burning was the burning of love (*fortuitous*
    night, fated, free,—)
    as I stole from my dark house, dark
    house that was silent, grave, sleeping,—

by the staircase that was secret, hidden,
    safe: disguised by darkness (*fortuitous*
    night, fated, free,—)
    by darkness and by cunning, dark
    house that was silent, grave, sleeping—;

in that sweet night, secret, seen by
    no one and seeing
    nothing, my only light or
    guide
    the burning in my burning heart,

night was the guide
    to the place where he for whom I
    waited, whom I had long ago chosen,
    waits: night
    brighter than noon, in which none can see—;

night was the guide
      sweeter than the sun raw at
      dawn, for there the burning bridegroom is
      bride
      and he who chose at last is chosen.

            •

As he lay sleeping on my sleepless
      breast, kept from the beginning for him
      alone, lying on the gift I gave
      as the restless
      fragrant cedars moved the restless winds, —

winds from the circling parapet circling
      us as I lay there touching and lifting his hair, —
      with his sovereign hand, he
      wounded my neck —
      and my senses, when they touched that, touched nothing. . .

In a dark night (*there where I*
      lost myself, —) as I leaned to rest
      in his smooth white breast, everything
      ceased
      and left me, forgotten in the grave of forgotten lilies.

In the Western Night

1. *The Irreparable*

First, I was there where unheard
harmonies create the harmonies

we hear—

then I was a dog, sniffing
your crotch.

I asked you why you
were here; your answer was your beauty.

I said I was in need. You said
that the dead

rule and confuse our steps—

that if I helped you cut your skin
deeply enough

that, at least, was IRREPARABLE. . .

This afternoon, the clouds
were moving so swiftly—

massed above the towers, rushing.

2. In My Desk

Two cigarette butts—
left by you

the first time you visited my apartment.
The next day

I found them, they were still there—

picking one up, I put my lips where
yours had been. . .

●

Our not-love is like a man running down
a mountain, who, if he dares to try to stop,

falls over—
my hands wanted to touch your hands

because we had hands.

●

I put the two cigarette butts
in an envelope, carefully

taping shut the edges.
At first, the thin paper of the envelope

didn't stop

the stale smell of tobacco. . .
Now the envelope is in my desk.

3. Two Men

The man who does not know himself, who
does not know his affections that his actions

speak but that he does not
acknowledge,

who will SAY ANYTHING

and lie when he does not know that he is
lying because what he needs to believe is true

must indeed
be true,

THIS MAN IS STONE. . . NOT BREAD.

STONE. NOT CAKE. NOT CHEESE. NOT BREAD. . .

The man who tries to feed his hunger
by gnawing stone

is a FOOL; his hunger is

fed in ways that he knows cannot satisfy it.

4. *Epilogue: A Stanza from Horace*

At night in dreams I hold you
     and now I pursue you
fleeing through the grass of the Campus Martius,
you, through the waters (you are cruel) fleeing.

BERKELEY, CALIFORNIA; 1983.

Poem in the Stanza of the "Rubaiyat"

1. *Spirit*

The present and the future are the past
now that her body cannot wake, nor, lost
     between the kitchen and the wilderness,
rest—haunted by ghosts, now become a ghost.

2. *Reading the "Rubaiyat"*

Because she loved it even as a girl,
she taught her child to love it—as he still
     does, hearing as he reads beneath his voice
her voice. . . past Waste, the gorgeous, trickling Well.

3. *Christmas Eve in Harvard Square*

Child, when you learn that the laughing ghosts who live
shadowing your steps in forty years give
     substancelessness to stone, is this night one
more thing you'll try to kill in you to live?

In the Ruins

1. *Man is a MORAL animal.*

2. *You can get human beings to do anything, — IF
   you convince them it is moral.*

3. *You can convince human beings anything is moral.*

• • •

Oh Night, —

   . . . THE SUN IS DEAD.
          What we dream moves
across our sky by

day, is a CORPSE, —

that sun's day is not the *real* day —;
that day's light is not the *real* light —;

FOR THE SUN IS DEAD. . .

     Now when I learned this,

I knew the injunction placed upon me.
Before the corpse, I heard: —

     RETURN THE DEAD TO LIFE.

Guilty of Dust

up or down from the infinite C E N T E R
B R I M M I N G *at the winking rim of time*

the voice in my head said

LOVE IS THE DISTANCE
BETWEEN YOU AND WHAT YOU LOVE

WHAT YOU LOVE IS YOUR FATE

●

then I saw the parade of my loves

those PERFORMERS *comics actors singers*

forgetful of my very self so often I
desired to die to myself to live in them

then my PARENTS *my* FRIENDS *the drained*
SPECTRES *once filled with my baffled infatuations*

love and guilt and fury and
sweetness for whom

nail spirit yearning to the earth

•

then the voice in my head said

WHETHER YOU LOVE WHAT YOU LOVE

OR LIVE IN DIVIDED CEASELESS
REVOLT AGAINST IT

WHAT YOU LOVE IS YOUR FATE

1984.

THE

SACRIFICE

(1983)

. . . the speculative Good Friday in place of the historic Good Friday. Good Friday must be speculatively re-established in the whole truth and harshness of its Godforsakenness.

— HEGEL

The War of Vaslav Nijinsky

Still gripped by the illusion of an horizon;
overcome with the finality of a broken tooth;
suspecting that habits are the only salvation,

—the Nineteenth Century's
guilt, *World War One*,

was danced

by Nijinsky on January 19, 1919.

     •   •   •

. . . I am now reading *Ecce Homo*. Nietzsche
is *angry* with me—;

he hates "the Crucified One."

But he did not live through War—;
when the whole world painted its face

with blood.

Someone must expiate the blood.

     •   •   •

No. Let what is past
be forgotten. Let even the blood

be forgotten—; there *can be no* "expiation."

Expiation is not necessary.

Suffering has made me what I am,—

I must not regret; or judge; or
struggle to escape it

in the indifference of (the ruthless
ecstasy of)
                    CHANGE; "my endless RENEWAL"; BECOMING.

—That is Nietzsche.

He wants to say *"Yes"* to life.

I am not Nietzsche. I am the bride of Christ.

•   •   •

He was planning a new and original ballet. It was to be a picture
of sex life, with the scene laid in a *maison tolérée*. The chief char-
acter was to be the owner—once a beautiful *cocotte*, now aged and
paralyzed as a result of her debauchery; but, though her body is a

wreck, her spirit is indomitable in the traffic of love. She deals with all the wares of love, selling girls to boys, youth to age, woman to woman, man to man.

When he danced it, he succeeded in transmitting the whole scale of sex life.

•   •   •

—Many times Diaghilev wanted me
to make love to him

as if he were
a woman—;

I did. I *refuse* to
regret it.
          At first, I felt humiliated for him,—

he saw this. He got angry
and said, "I enjoy it!"

Then, more calmly, he said,

"Vatza, we must not *regret* what we *feel*."

—I REGRETTED

          what I FELT. . . Not

making love, but that since the beginning
I wanted to *leave* him. . .

That I stayed

out of "GRATITUDE,"—

and *FEAR OF LIFE*,—

and AMBITION. . .

That in my soul,

I did *not* love him.

Now my wife wants to have
a second child. I am frightened;

the things a human being must learn,—
the things a child

must *learn* he FEELS,—

frighten me! I know people's faults

because in my soul,

I HAVE COMMITTED THEM.

The man who chops wood for us
was speaking, this morning, in the kitchen,

to my wife. As I passed in the hallway
I heard

whispering—; and LISTENED.

He said that as a child
in his village at Sils Maria

he worked for the writer, *Nietzsche*—;
he felt he must tell her

that just before the "famous man"
was taken away,

INSANE, he acted and looked

as I
do now.

I can choose *"life"* for myself;—

but must I, again, again,
AGAIN,—
              for *any other* creature?

      •   •   •

The Durcals arrived in St. Moritz, and were invited to tea. Asked
what he had been doing lately, Vaslav put on a worldly air, leaned
back on the sofa and said,
    "Well, I composed two ballets, I prepared a new program for
the next Paris season, and lately—I have played a part. You see, I

am an artist; I have no troupe now, so I miss the stage. I thought it would be rather an interesting experiment to see how well I could act, and so for six weeks I played the part of a lunatic; and the whole village, my family, and even the physicians apparently believed it. I have a male nurse to watch me, in the disguise of a *masseur*."

Romola was overcome, torn between anger and relief. She was confirmed in her supposition that her fears had been groundless when the male nurse came, after ten days, to assure her from his long experience that her husband was completely sane.

•   •   •

—Let me explain to you
what *"guilt"* is. . .

When I joke with my wife, and say,
"I think I will go back to Russia
and live as a peasant—"

she jokes back, and says,
"Do as you like! I will
divorce you, and marry
                                        a manufacturer. . ."

She looks at me, and I look at her.

What is terrible

is that I am serious—; and *she* is serious. . .

She is right, of course,—
                              I do *not* have the right

to make her live differently, without servants,
rich friends, elegant clothes—
without her good and sane *habits*;

do not have the right even to try
to *re-make* her. . .

But does *she* then have the right
to make *me* live like this, JUDGED, surrounded by
those who cannot understand or *feel* me,—
                                    like a manufacturer?. . .

She is angry, as I am angry.

We both are *right*—; and both angry. . .

Soon, she feels guilty, feels that she
has failed me—;
                    and I too
feel guilty. . .

The *GUILT* comes from *NOWHERE*.

Neither of us had done wrong!

But I am a good actor—and reassure her
that I love her; am indeed happy; and that
nothing will change. . .

I *want* to be a *good husband.*

Still, I am guilty.

       . . . Why am I guilty?

My life is *FALSE.*

     •   •   •

I know the psychology of lunatics;
if you don't contradict them, they like you.

But I am not insane.

My brother was insane. He died
in a lunatic asylum.

The reason I *know* I am *NOT* insane
is because, unlike my brother,

I *feel guilt.*

The insane do not feel guilt.

My brother was a dancer. He was older than I,
but still in the *corps* when I became
a soloist. He was ashamed, and jealous;

he went insane.

When the doctors questioned him, he showed
astonishing courage, —
                              he thought that everyone
in the company was paid

by the secret police, to gather
evidence against our family. . .

He displayed cunning, and stoic
fortitude, under the questions.

Even when he thought he faced death,
he lied
to protect my mother.

When he was taken away,
she cried, and cried. . .
                              She cried
visiting him, —

but that didn't make him feel GUILTY. . .

My wife thought because
I wore a large *cross* on my neck in the village,—

and told her certain dishes
served at our table were poisoned,—

I was insane.

But I *knew* that my actions
frightened her—; and I suffered.

Nietzsche was insane. He knew
we killed God.

                    . . . This is the *end* of the story:

though He was dead, God was clever
and strong. God struck back,—

AND KILLED US.

If I *act* insane people will call me
"mad clown," and forgive
                              even the truth—;

the insane feel anxiety and horror,

but are RELEASED
from GUILT. . .

I only want to know
things I've learned like this,—

these things I cannot *NOT* know.

·   ·   ·

His other ballet remained unfinished. It was his own life put into
a choreographic poem: a youth seeking truth through life, first as
a pupil, open to all artistic suggestions, to all the beauty that life
and love can offer; then his love for the woman, his mate, who suc-
cessfully carries him off.

He set it in the period of the High Renaissance. The youth is a
painter; his Master one of the greatest artists of the period, part
Genius and part Politician, just as Diaghilev seemed to him to be.
This Master advances him, and defends his daring work from the
attacks of colleagues, as long as he is a student; then he falls in
love, and the Master bitterly rejects not only him but his work.

·   ·   ·

—Last night, once again, I nearly
abandoned my autobiographical ballet. . .

The plot has a good beginning
and middle,—
                    THE PUZZLE

is the end. . .

The *nights* I spend—

                    reading and improving
Nietzsche, analyzing and then abandoning

my life, working on the *Great Questions*

like WAR and GUILT and GOD
and MADNESS,—

I rise from my books, my endless, fascinating
researches, notations, projects,

dazzled.
          —Is this happiness?. . .

I have invented a far more
accurate and specific notation for dance;

it has taken me two months
to write down the movement in my ten-minute

ballet, *L'Après-midi d'un Faune*. . .

There is a MORAL here

about how LONG you must live with
the consequences of a SHORT action,—

but I don't now feel
MORAL.
                Soon I shall begin

Le Sacre du Printemps —; which
is longer. . .

I can understand the pleasures of War.

In War—
                where *killing* is a virtue: *camouflage*
a virtue: *revenge* a virtue:
pity a weakness—
                        the world rediscovers

a *guiltless* PRE-HISTORY

"civilization" condemns. . .

In 1914, I was assured the War would
end in six weeks;

the Germans, in the summer, thought
they would enter Paris by the fall.

But the War
                was *NOT* an accident.

C U S T O M, and his Children,—

Glory. Honor. Privilege. Poverty.
Optimism. "The Balance of Power,"—

for four years

dug a large, long hole
(—a *TRENCH*—)

                   in the earth of Europe;

when they approached the hole
to pin medals

on the puppets
they had thrown there,

they slipped in

blood—; AND FELL IN.

Poverty and *Privilege*
alone survived,

of all the customs of the past. . .

—Should the World
regret the War? Should I

REGRET MY LIFE?

. . . Let our epitaph be:

In Suffering, and Nightmare,
I woke at last

to my own nature.

•   •   •

One Sunday we decided to sleigh over to Maloja.

Kyra was glad and Vaslav was very joyful that morning.

It took us about three hours to get there; Kyra and I got very hungry during the long drive.

The road was extremely narrow during the winter, because it needed cleaning from the heavy snows, and in certain parts there was always a space to await the sleighs coming from the opposite direction.

Vaslav was as a rule a careful and excellent driver, but on this particular Sunday he did not wait, but simply *drove on into* the oncoming sleighs.

We were in danger of turning over; the horses got frightened.

The coachmen of the other sleighs cursed, but this did not make any difference.

Kyra screamed, and I begged Vaslav to be more careful, but the further we went the more fiercely he drove *against* the other sleighs.

I had to clutch on to Kyra and the sleigh to keep ourselves on.

I was furious, and said so to Vaslav.

He fixed me suddenly with a hard and metallic look which I had never seen before.

As we arrived at the Maloja Inn I ordered a meal.

We had to wait.

Vaslav asked for some bread and butter and macaroni.

"Ah, Tolstoy again," I thought, but did not say a word, and bit my lips.

Kyra was anxiously awaiting her steak, and as it was laid before her and she began to eat, Vaslav, with a quick gesture, snatched the plate away.

She began to cry from disappointment.

I exclaimed, "Now, Vaslav, please don't begin that Tolstoy nonsense again; you remember how weak you got by starving yourself on that vegetarian food. I can't stop you doing it, but I won't allow you to interfere with Kyra. The child must eat properly."

I went with Kyra to the other room to have our solitary lunch.

We drove home very quietly without a word.

● ● ●

—The second part of my ballet
Le Sacre du Printemps

is called "THE SACRIFICE."

A young girl, a virgin, is chosen
to die
so that the Spring will return,—

so that her Tribe (free
from *"pity," "introspection," "remorse"*)

out of her blood
can renew itself.

The fact that the earth's renewal
requires human blood

is unquestioned; a mystery.

She is chosen, from the whirling, stamping
circle of her peers, purely by chance—;

then, driven from the circle, surrounded
by the elders, by her peers, by animal
skulls impaled on pikes,

she dances,—

       at first, in paroxysms
of grief, and fear:—

         again and again, she leaps (—*NOT*

as a ballerina leaps, as if she
loved the air, as if
the air were her element—)

SHE LEAPS

BECAUSE SHE HATES THE GROUND.

But then, slowly, as others
join in, she finds that there is a self

WITHIN herself

that is NOT herself

impelling her to accept,—and at last
to *LEAD*,—

        THE DANCE

that is her own sacrifice. . .

—In the end, exhausted, she falls
to the ground. . .

She dies; and her last breath
is the reawakened Earth's

orgasm,—
        a little upward run on the flutes
mimicking

        (—or perhaps MOCKING—)

the god's spilling
seed. . .

The Chosen Virgin
accepts her fate: without considering it,

she knows that her Tribe,—
the Earth itself,—
                    are UNREMORSEFUL

that the price of continuance
is her BLOOD:—

                    she *accepts* their guilt,—

. . . THEIR GUILT

THAT THEY DO NOT KNOW EXISTS.

She has become, to use
our term,
          a *Saint.*

The dancer I chose for this role
detested it.

She would have preferred to do
a fandango, with a rose in her teeth. . .

The training she and I shared,—

training in the traditional
                    "academic" dance,—

emphasizes the illusion
                of *Effortlessness,*
Ease, Smoothness, Equilibrium...

When I look into my life,
these are not the qualities
                    I find there.

Diaghilev, almost alone
in the Diaghilev Ballet, UNDERSTOOD;

though he is not now, after my marriage
and *"betrayal,"*

INTERESTED in my choreographic ambitions...

Nevertheless, to fill a theatre,
he can be persuaded

to *hire* me as a dancer.

Last night I dreamt

I was slowly climbing
a long flight of steps.

Then I saw Diaghilev
and my wife

arm in arm
climbing the steps behind me. . .

I began to hurry, so that
they would not see me.

Though I climbed
as fast as I could, the space

between us
NARROWED. . .

Soon, they were a few feet behind me,—
I could hear them laughing,

gossiping, discussing CONTRACTS
and LAWSUITS. . .

They understood each other perfectly.

I stopped.

       But they

DIDN'T STOP...

They climbed right past me,—
laughing, chatting,

NOT SEEING ME AT ALL...

—I should have been happy;

yet...
        wasn't.

I watched their backs,
as they happily

disappeared, climbing
up, out of my sight.

●   ●   ●

Our days passed in continuous social activity.

    Then one Thursday, the day when the governess and maid had their day off, I was making ready to take Kyra out for a walk when suddenly Vaslav came out of his room and looked at me very angrily.

    "How dare you make such a noise? I can't work."

    I looked up, surprised.

    His face, his manner were strange; he had never spoken to me like this.

"I am sorry. I did not realize we were so loud."

Vaslav got hold of me then by my shoulders and shook me violently.

I clasped Kyra in my arms very close, then with one powerful movement Vaslav pushed me down the stairs.

I lost my balance, and fell with the child, who began to scream.

At the bottom, I got up, more astounded than terrified.

What was the matter with him?

He was still standing there menacingly.

I turned round, exclaiming, "You ought to be ashamed! You are behaving like a drunken *peasant.*"

A very changed Vaslav we found when we came home, docile and kind as ever.

I did not speak about the incident, either to him or to anybody else.

Then one day we went on an excursion and Vaslav again wore his cross over his sweater.

On our way home, he suddenly began to drive fiercely and the sleigh turned over.

Amazingly, no one was hurt.

I got really angry, and walked home with Kyra.

Of course, he was home ahead of us.

When I entered the house, the servant who worshipped Vaslav opened the door and said, "Madame, I think Monsieur Nijinsky is ill, or perhaps very drunk, for he acts so queerly. His voice is hoarse and his eyes all hazy. I am frightened."

I went to our bedroom.

Vaslav lay fully dressed on the bed, with the cross on, his eyes closed.

He seemed to be asleep.

I turned cautiously towards the door, and then noticed that heavy tears were streaming down his face.

"Vatza, how are you feeling? Are you angry with me?"

"It is nothing; let me sleep; I am tired."

•   •   •

Each night now I pray,
                    Let this cup

pass from me!. . .

But it is not a cup. It is my life.

I have *LEARNED*

                    my *NATURE. . .*

I am insane,—
. . . or evil.

Today I walked out into the snow.

I said to myself:

THREE TIMES
YOU TRIED TO HARM YOUR WIFE AND CHILD.

I said:

*LIE DOWN IN THE SNOW
AND DIE. YOU ARE EVIL.*

I lay down in the snow.

I tried to go to sleep.
My HANDS

began to get cold, to FREEZE.

I was lying there a long, long time.

I did not feel cold any more.

Then, God said to me:

*GO HOME
AND TELL YOUR WIFE YOU ARE INSANE.*

I said:

*Thank you, thank you, God!
I am not evil. I am insane.*

I got up. I wanted to go home, —
and tell this news

to my wife.

Then, I said to God:

> *I am insane,—*
> *my wife will suffer. I am guilty.*

Forgive me for being insane.

God said:

> *GOD MADE YOU. GOD DOES NOT CARE*
> *IF YOU ARE "GUILTY" OR NOT.*

I said:

> *I CARE IF I AM GUILTY!*

I CARE IF I AM GUILTY!. . .

God was silent.

> Everything was SILENT.

I lay back down in the snow.

I wanted again to go to sleep, and die.

But my BODY did not want to die.
My BODY spoke to me:

There is no answer to your life.
You are insane; or evil.

There is only one thing that you can do:—

You must join YOUR GUILT

> *to the WORLD'S GUILT.*

I said to myself:

I must join MY GUILT

> *to the WORLD'S GUILT.*

I got up out of the snow.
. . . What did the words mean?

Then I realized what the words meant.

I said to myself:

You must join YOUR GUILT

> *to the WORLD'S GUILT.*

There is no answer to your life.
You are insane; or evil.

. . . Let this be the Body

through which the War has passed.

•   •   •

Nijinsky invited guests to a recital at the Suvretta House Hotel.

When the audience was seated, he picked up a chair, sat down on it, and stared at them. Half an hour passed. Then he took a few rolls of black and white velvet and made a big cross the length of the room. He stood at the head of it, his arms opened wide. He said: "Now, I will dance you the War, which you did not prevent and for which you are responsible." His dance reflected battle, horror, catastrophe, apocalypse. An observer wrote: "At the end, we were too much overwhelmed to applaud. We were looking at a corpse, and our silence was the silence that enfolds the dead."

There was a collection for the Red Cross. Tea was served. Nijinsky never again performed in public.

•   •   •

—The War is a *good* subject. . .

The audience, yesterday, liked
my dance.

The public does not understand *Art*;
it wants to be astonished.

I know how to astonish.

The War allowed me
to project,—
                    to EMBODY,—

an ultimate *"aspect"* of the *"self"*...

A member of the audience told me
I had always been able

"to smell a good subject."

God, on the other hand,—

                    who at times
has responded to my predilection

for *ACTIONS*

that are *METAPHYSICAL EXPERIMENTS*,—

perhaps felt threatened, or even
coerced—;

he perhaps felt that though he could
agree with me

that expiation *IS* necessary,—

he had to agree with
Nietzsche

that expiation is *NOT* possible. . .

In any case, he has chosen, — as
so often, —
        camouflage.

Now that the War has been over
two months, at times I almost
doubt if it existed —;

in truth,
       it never existed, —

. . . BECAUSE IT HAS NEVER BEEN OVER.

Twenty years ago, a boy of nine
was taken by his mother

to the Imperial School of Ballet,

to attempt to become a pupil;

the mother was poor, and
afraid of life; his father

had abandoned the family when the boy was four.

Even then, he had a good jump—;
he was admitted.

He had been taught by the priests
that because of Adam and Eve, all men were born
in *Original Sin*,—

                      that all men wcre,
BY NATURE, guilty.

In his soul, he didn't believe it.

He was a good boy. His mother loved him.

He believed
in his essential innocence,—

he thought his nature "good."

He worked hard. He grew thinner,—
and started

        "dancing like God". . .

Everyone talked about it.

But then,—
        he LEARNED SOMETHING.

He learned that

All life exists

at the expense of other life.

When he began to succeed,
he saw that he was AMBITIOUS,—

                                        JEALOUS

of the roles that others won. . .

Then his brother
got sick—.

THE ROCK
            THAT GIVES SHADE TO ONE CREATURE,—

FOR ANOTHER CREATURE

                        JUST BLOCKS THE SUN.

. . . This is a problem of *BEING.*
                                        I can imagine no

SOLUTION to this. . .

At sixteen, he met a Prince. He loved the Prince,—
but after a time,

the Prince
grew tired of him.

Then he met a Count, whom
he *didn't* love.

The Count gave him a piano.

He had heard of Diaghilev. Diaghilev
invited him
            to the *Hotel Europe*,—

he went to seek his luck.

He found
his luck.

At once, he allowed Diaghilev
to make love to him.

Even then, he disliked Diaghilev
for his too *self-assured* voice. . .

He always had thought he was essentially
different from the people
                in books of history,—

with their lives of *betrayals*; *blindness*;
greed; and *miseries*. . .

He saw, one day, that this illusion,—
this FAITH,—

        had, imperceptibly,

vanished—;

        he was *NOT* different—;

he did not understand *WHY* he did
what he did, nor were his instincts

"good"...

Then, I said to myself:

        "History
IS human nature—; to say I AM GUILTY

is to accept
implication in the human race..."

—Now, for months and months,
I have found

ANOTHER man in me:—

        HE is *NOT* me—; *I*

am afraid of him. . .

He hates my wife and child,—
and hates Diaghilev;

because he thinks *"goodness"* and *"being"*
are incompatible,—

. . . *HE WANTS TO DESTROY THE WORLD.*

Destroy it,—
                or redeem it.

Are they the *SAME?*. . .

As a child, I was taught, by the priests,
to crave the Last Judgment:—

when the *earth* will become a *stage*,—

and WHAT IS RIGHT and WHAT IS WRONG

will at last show *clear*, and *distinct*,
and *separate*,—

and then,—

                THE SLATE IS WIPED CLEAN. . .

—Even now, I can see the World
wheeling on its axis. . . I

shout at it: —

          CEASE.
                    CHANGE,—
                              OR CEASE.

The World says right back: —

I must chop down the tree of life
to make coffins.

Tomorrow, I will go to Zurich —
to live in an asylum.

MY SOUL IS SICK,—
                    NOT MY MIND.

I *am* incurable. . . I did not
live long.

Death came
unexpectedly,—
                for I wanted it to come.

Romola. Diaghilev.

. . . I HAVE EATEN THE WORLD.

My life is the expiation for my life.

Nietzsche understood me.

When *he* was sick, — when his *SOUL*
was sick, —
>   he wrote that he would have

much preferred to be a *Professor* at Basel

than *God*—;
>   but that he did not dare to carry

his egotism
so far as to neglect the creation of the world.

•   •   •

In 1923, Diaghilev came to see him. Vaslav by now got out of bed
in a strange fashion. First of all he went on all-fours; then crawled
around the room; and only then stood upright. In a general way,
he seemed attracted by the floor, to feel a need to be as low down
as possible (his bed was almost on a level with the floor) and to
grab hold of something. As he walked he leaned forward and felt
at his ease only when lying down.

This was the first time Diaghilev had set eyes on him since they
had parted in wrath in Barcelona six years before. "Vatza, you are

being lazy. Come, I need you. You must dance again for the Russian Ballet and for me."

Vaslav shook his head. "I cannot because I am mad."

•   •   •

Frightened to eat with a new set of teeth;
exhausted by the courage the insane have shown;
uncertain whether to REDEEM or to DESTROY THE EARTH,

—the Nineteenth Century's
guilt, *World War One,*

was danced

by Nijinsky on January 19, 1919.

For Mary Ann Youngren

1932–1980

Mary Ann, as they handed you the cup
near the black waters of Lethe,

(the cup of *Forgetfulness*,
the waters of *Obliteration*,)

did you reach for it greedily—

just as, alive, you abruptly needed

not to answer the phone for days: ballet tickets
unused: awake all night: pacing

the apartment: untouchable: chain-smoking?

Dip a finger into the River of Time,—
it comes back
        STAINED.

     •

No, that's *not* enough,—
not true, wrong—

dying of cancer, eager to have the whole thing
over, you nonetheless waited

for your sister to arrive from California
before you died,—

you needed to bring up your cruelest, worst
adolescent brutality, asking:

DO YOU FORGIVE ME?

Then: WILL YOU MISS ME?

At the Resurrection of the Dead,
the world will hear us say

The phone is plugged in, please call,
I will answer it.

Catullus: Odi et amo

I hate *and* love. Ignorant fish, who even
wants the fly while writhing.

Confessional

Is she dead?

Yes, she is dead.

Did you forgive her?

No, I didn't forgive her.

Did she forgive you?

No, she didn't forgive me.

What did you have to forgive?

She was never mean, or willfully
cruel, or unloving.

When I was eleven, she converted to Christ—

she began to simplify her life, denied
herself, and said that she and I must struggle

"to divest ourselves
of the love of CREATED BEINGS,"—

and to help me to do that,

one day

     she hanged my cat.

I came home from school, and in the doorway
of my room,

my cat was hanging strangled.

She was in the bathroom; I could hear
the water running.

—I shouted at her;

                she wouldn't
come out.

     She was in there
for hours, with the water running. . .

Finally, late that night,
she unlocked the door.

She wouldn't look at me.

She said that we must learn to rest
in the LORD,—

and not in His CREATION. . .

Did you forgive her?

Soon, she had a breakdown;
when she got out of the hospital,

she was SORRY. . .

For years she dreamed the cat
had dug
its claws into her thumbs:—

in the dream, she knew, somehow,
that it was dying; she tried

to help it,—

TO PUT IT OUT OF ITS MISERY,—

so she had her hands around its
neck, strangling it.

Bewildered,
it looked at her,

KNOWING SHE LOVED IT—;

and she *DID* love it, which was
what was
so awful. . .

All it could do was
hold on,—
. . . AS
SHE HELD ON.

Did you forgive her?

I was the center of her life,—
and therefore,
of her fears and obsessions. They changed;

one was money.

. . . DO I HAVE TO GO INTO IT?

Did you forgive her?

Standing next to her coffin, looking down
at her body, I suddenly
knew I hadn't—;

          over and over
I said to her,

        I didn't forgive you!
        I didn't forgive you!

I *did* love her. . . Otherwise,

would I feel so guilty?

        What did she have to forgive?

She was SORRY. She *tried*
to change. . .

She loved me. She was generous.

I pretended
that I had forgiven her—;

            and she pretended
to believe it,—

she needed desperately to believe it. . .

SHE KNEW I COULD BARELY STAND TO BE AROUND HER.

      Did you forgive her?

I *tried*—;
       for years I almost
convinced myself I did. . .

But no, I didn't.

—Now, after I have said it all, so I can
rest,

      will you give me ABSOLUTION,—

. . . and grant this
          "created being"

FORGIVENESS?. . .

      Did she forgive you?

I think she tried—;
         but no,—
she *couldn't* forgive me. . .

WHY COULDN'T SHE FORGIVE ME?

Don't you understand even now?

No! Not—not really. . .

Forgiveness doesn't exist.

II

She asked,—

> and I could not, WOULD NOT give. . .

—That is the first of two sentences
I can't get out of my head.

They somehow contain what happened.

The second is:—

THERE WAS NO PLACE IN NATURE WE COULD MEET.

> *Can you explain them?*

—Augustine too
had trouble with his mother,—

. . . *listen.* Confessor
incapable of granting *"rest"* or *"absolution,"*

. . . *listen.*

> *Why are you angry?*

Augustine too
had trouble with his mother,—

. . . but the story of Augustine and Monica
is the *opposite* of what happened

between me and my mother.

We couldn't meet in Nature,—
. . . AND ALL WE HAD WAS NATURE.

How do you explain it?

The scene at the window at Ostia
in Book Nine of the *Confessions*

seems designed to make non-believers
sick with envy.

—You are listening to a soul
that has *always* been

SICK WITH ENVY. . .

How do you explain it?

As a child I was (now, I
clearly can see it)

predatory:—

pleased to have supplanted my father
in my mother's affections, and then

pleased to have supplanted my stepfather. . .

—I assure you, though I was a *"little boy,"*
I could be far more charming, sympathetic,
full of sensibility, *"various,"* far more
an understanding and feeling
ear for my mother's emotions, needs, SOUL

than any man, any man she met,—

I know I *wanted* to be: WANTED
to be the center, the focus of her life. . .

I was her ally against my father;
and then, after the first two or three

years, her ally against my stepfather. . .

—Not long before she died,
she told me something
                    I had never heard:—

when I was nine or ten, early
in her second marriage,

she became pregnant; she said she
wanted to have the child. . .

She said that one day, when my stepfather
was playing golf, she was out walking the course

with him, and suddenly

a man fell from one of the huge trees
lining the fairways. . .

A group of men had been cutting limbs;
she saw one of them fall,
                              and for a long time

lie there screaming.

Later that day, she had a miscarriage.

After saying all this, she
looked at me insistently and said,

"I wanted to have the child."

But as she was telling me the story,
I kept thinking

THANK GOD THE MAN FELL,
THANK GOD SHE SAW HIM FALL AND HAD A MISCARRIAGE

AND THE CHILD DIED. . .

—I felt sick. I knew I was *GLAD*
the man fell, *GLAD* she saw him fall

and the child died. . .

When I was nine or ten, if she
had had a child—; if

she and a child and my stepfather
had made a FAMILY

from which I *had* to be closed off,
the remnant of a rejected, erased past,—

(I never had anything in common with,
or even *respected*, my stepfather,—)

I would have gone crazy. . .

How could she have *BETRAYED*
ME in that way?

      How do you explain it?

I felt sick. I felt ill at how
predatory I was,—

(my feelings *still* were, —)

at the envy and violence I could
will NOT to feel,

but *couldn't* not feel. . .

—Augustine has the temerity, after
his mother dies,

to admit he is GLAD
she no longer wanted to be buried

next to her husband. . .

He thanks God
for ridding her of this "vain desire."

Why are you angry?

In the words of Ecclesiastes: —

"Her loves, her hates, her jealousies, —

these all

have perished, nor will she EVER AGAIN

TAKE PART
in whatever is done under the sun. . ."

My mother, —
   . . . *just died.*

The emotions, the "issues" in her life
didn't come out somewhere, reached no culmination,
climax, catharsis, —

                    she *JUST DIED.*

She wanted them to: —
                    how can I talk about

the way in which, when I was young,

we seemed to be engaged in an ENTERPRISE
together, —

          the enterprise of "figuring out the world,"
figuring out her life, my life, —

THE MAKING OF HER SOUL,

                         which somehow, in our "enterprise"
together, was the making of my soul, —

. . . it's a kind of *craziness*, which some mothers
drink along with their children
                    in their *MOTHER'S-MILK.* . .

Why are you angry?

THERE WAS NO PLACE IN NATURE WE COULD MEET.

I've never let anyone else
in so deeply.

But when the predatory complicit co-conspirator
child

was about twenty, he of course wanted his *"freedom,"*—

and then found

that what had made his life
possible, what he found so deeply

inside him, had its hands around his neck
strangling him:—

and that therefore, if he were
to survive,

he must in turn strangle, murder,
kill it inside him. . .

TO SURVIVE, I HAD TO KILL HER INSIDE ME.

Why are you angry?

Now that she is dead (that her BODY
is DEAD),

I'm capable of an *"empathy,"*

an *"acceptance"* of the inevitable
(in her, and in myself)

that I denied her, living. . .

I DENIED HER, LIVING.

She asked, and I could
not, *would not* give. . .

—I *did* "will" to forgive her, but

forgiveness

lay beyond the will,—

. . . *and I willed*
NOT *to forgive her:*—

        for "forgiveness" seems to say

Everything is forgotten, obliterated,—

                                  the past

is as nothing, erased. . .

Her plea, her need for forgiveness
seemed the attempt to obliterate

the *actions, angers, decisions*

that MADE ME what I am. . .

To obliterate the *crises, furies, refusals*
that are how I

                came to understand her, me, my life—.

Truly to feel "forgiveness,"
to forgive her *IN MY HEART,*

                            meant erasing *ME.* . .

She seemed to ask it to render me
paralyzed, and defenseless.

—Now that I no longer must face her,
I give her in my mind

the *"empathy"* and *"acceptance"*

I denied her, living.

Why are you angry?

. . . But if, somehow, what we were
didn't have to be understood

by MEMORY,

and THIS EARTH—

. . . Augustine and Monica,

as they lean
alone together standing at a window

overlooking a garden at the center of the house
(in Book Nine of the *Confessions*),

near the time of her death (which time,
Augustine says, GOD knew,

though they did not),—

resting here at Ostia from a long journey
by land,

and preparing for a long sea-journey
back to the Africa which is their home,—

. . . as they stand here sweetly talking together,
and ask

"what the eternal life of the saints could be"

(panting to be sprinkled from the waters of God's fountain
to help them meditate
                    upon so great a matter), —

. . . as they stand alone together
at this window,

            they can FORGET THE PAST

AND LOOK FORWARD

                    TO WHAT LIES BEFORE THEM. . .

—They had much to forget;

in the *Confessions*, Monica's ferocity
is frightening: —

            before Augustine became a Christian,
she saw him as dead—;

she refused to live with him or even
eat at the same table in his house,
shunning and detesting his blasphemies, —

until she had a dream in which she
learned that he would finally convert to Christ. . .

—When he planned to leave Africa for Italy,
she was determined he would take her
with him, or remain at home;

she followed him to the seacoast,
clinging to him, he says, with *"dreadful grief"*;

one night he escaped, and
sailed—;

not long after, she followed. . .

—Finally, of course, he became a Christian;
until then, she
ceaselessly wept and mourned and prayed.

Do you know why you are saying all this?

As Augustine and Monica stood leaning at that
window in Ostia, contemplating

what the saints' possession of God is like,

they moved past and reviewed
(Augustine tells us)

each level of created things,—

each level of CREATION, from this earth
to the sun and moon and stars

shining down on this earth. . .

—Talking, musing, wondering
at creation, but knowing that our life and light

here cannot compare

to the sweetness of the saints' LIGHT and LIFE,—

(here, where he had forced her to *SEEK*
what out of her body she had herself

brought forth,—)

. . . now, self-gathered at last in the purity of their own
being, they ascend higher

still, and together S C A L E   T H E   S T A R S. . .

—And so, Augustine tells us, they came to their own

souls, and then went
past them, to that region of richness

unending, where God feeds ISRAEL forever
with the food of Truth. . .

There LIFE is the WISDOM by which
all things are made, which

itself is *not* made. . .

—While they were thus talking of, straining to comprehend,
panting for this WISDOM, with all the effort

of their heart, for one heartbeat,

they *together* attained to *touch* it—;

. . . then sighing, and leaving the first-fruits
of their Spirit bound there,

they returned to the sound of their own voice,—

to *words*,
which have a beginning and an end. . .

"How unlike," Augustine says, "God's WORD,—
changeless, self-gathered, unmade, yet forever

making all things new. . ."

How do you explain it?

Then they said:—
"If any man could shut his ears

to the tumult of the flesh—;

                if suddenly the cacophony
of earth and sea and air

were S I L E N T, and the voice of the self
died to the self, and so the self

found its way beyond the self,—

beyond the SELF it has made,—

                  silent
our expiations and confessions,
the voice that says: *NO REMISSION OF SINS*
WITHOUT THE SHEDDING OF BLOOD,

the Word that was only given us drenched in blood,—

. . . if to any man

        his self, CREATION itself

(Substance and Accidents and their Relations)

suddenly were S I L E N T,—

                and in that silence, he then

heard creation

        say with one voice: —

We are not our own source, —

        even those of us

who made ourselves, creatures
of the Will, the Mirror, and the Dream,

know we are not our own source, —

. . . if he heard this voice,

        and then

all creation were, even for a second, S I L E N T, —

(this creation in which creatures
of consciousness,

        whose LAW is that they come to be

through change, through
birth, fruition, and death,

know that as they move toward fullness
of being, they move toward ceasing to be, —)

. . . if in this silence,

He whom we *crave* to hear

SPOKE AT LAST—;

spoke not through the veil
of earth and sea and air,

thunder, 'SIGNS AND WONDERS,' the voice
of an angel, the enigma of similitude and of

parable, all

the ALIEN that BESETS us here,—

. . . spoke not by them, but by *HIMSELF*, calling

us to return into that secret place from
which He

        comes forth at last to us,—

. . . just as we two
together reached forth and for one

heartbeat attained to *TOUCH*

the *WISDOM* that is our *SOURCE* and *GROUND*,—

. . . if this could continue, and LIFE
were that one moment of
                    wisdom and understanding

for which we then sighed, —

would not *this* be: ENTER THOU INTO THE JOY OF THY LORD?. . .

And when shall it be? At
the resurrection of the dead, when all
shall rise, but not all shall be changed?

And shall WE then be changed?. . ."

In words like these, but not
exactly these, (Augustine then says,)

they talked together that day—

(just as the words I have given you are
not, of course, exactly Augustine's).

Monica then said,
                    "Son, I no longer hope

for anything from this world.

I wanted to stay alive long enough
to see you a Catholic Christian.

God has granted me this, in
superabundance.

. . . What am I still doing here?"

In five days, she fell into a fever;
nine days later she was dead.

       Why are you angry?

My mother, at the end of her life, was *frightened.*

She was afraid to die
not because she feared an afterlife,

but because she didn't know what her life had been.

Her two marriages were failures,—

she stayed married to my stepfather, but
in despair, without trust in or respect for him, or

visible affection. . .

She had had no profession,—

she had painted a few paintings, and
written a handful of poems, but without the illusion

either were any good, or STOOD FOR HER. . .

She had *MADE* nothing.

I was what she had made. —

She saw that her concern and worry and care
in the end called up in me

protestations of affection
that veiled

       unappeasable anger, and remorse.

UNDOING THIS was beyond me. . .

She felt she was here for some reason, —
. . . but never found it.

    Man needs a metaphysics;
    he cannot have one.

The Sacrifice

When Judas writes the history of SOLITUDE,—
. . . let him celebrate

Miss Mary Kenwood; who, without
help, placed her head in a plastic bag,

then locked herself
in a refrigerator.

                        •

—Six months earlier, after thirty years
teaching piano, she had watched

her mother slowly die of throat cancer.
Watched her *want* to die. . .

What once had given Mary life
in the end didn't want it.

Awake, her mother screamed for help to die.
—She felt

GUILTY. . . She knew that *all* men in these situations felt
innocent—; helpless—; yet guilty.

•

Christ knew the Secret. Betrayal
is necessary; as is woe for the betrayer.

The solution, Mary realized at last,
must be brought out of my own body.

Wiping away our sins, Christ stained us with his blood—;
to offer yourself, yet need *betrayal*, by *Judas*, before SHOULDERING

THE GUILT OF THE WORLD—;
. . . *Give me the courage not to need Judas.*

•

When Judas writes the history of solitude,
let him record

that to the friend who opened
the refrigerator, it seemed

death fought; before giving in.

Genesis 1–2:4

In the beginning, God made HEAVEN and EARTH.

The earth without form was waste.

DARKNESS was the face of the deep.
His spirit was the wind brooding over the waters.

·

In darkness he said,
    LET THERE BE LIGHT.

There was light.

In light he said, IT IS GOOD.

God, dividing darkness from light,
named light DAY and darkness NIGHT.

Night and day were the first day.

·

God said,
    LET THE FIRMAMENT

ARC THE EARTH.

The waters opened.

        The ARC above the earth
divided the waters above from the waters below.

God named the arc, HEAVEN.

Night and day were the second day.

     •

God said,
        LET THE WATERS BELOW THE FIRMAMENT

RECEDE, REVEALING THE GROUND.

The waters opened, and receded.
What lay beneath the waters was the ground.

God named the dry ground, EARTH.
He named the waters surrounding the earth, OCEAN.

God looked.
        He said, IT IS GOOD.

God said,
        LET THE BARE EARTH

BREAK OPEN, HEAVY WITH SEED.

The earth broke open.
                      Numberless PLANTS filled

with seed spread over the ground, and TREES
boughed with fruit heavy with seed.

God looked.
              He said, IT IS GOOD.

Night and day were the third day.

          •

God said,
           LET GREAT LIGHTS IN THE FIRMAMENT

ORDER AND ILLUMINATE THE EARTH.

God placed great lights shining in the firmament,

the GREATER LIGHT to dominate the day,
the LESSER LIGHT to dominate the night,

and STARS.

God looked. He said,
                 LET THEM BE FOR SIGNS.

Dividing darkness from light, the shining
made seasons, days, years.

God said, IT IS GOOD.

Night and day were the fourth day.

·

God said,
      LET THE MOVING WATERS LIVE

WITH TEEMING, LIVING CREATURES.

God said,
      LET THE EMPTY FIRMAMENT LIVE

WITH TEEMING, LIVING CREATURES.

God made the creatures of the deep,
BEASTS and MONSTERS, all those

swarming within it. God made the winged creatures
moving across the face of the firmament.

God looked.
      He said, IT IS GOOD.

God blessed them, saying,
      INCREASE. MULTIPLY.

FILL THE WATERS.
      ARCING THE EARTH,

FILL THE FIRMAMENT.

They increased and multiplied.

Night and day were the fifth day.

    •

God said,
    LET THE EARTH BRING FORTH

LIVING CREATURES BOUND TO THE EARTH.

God made the beasts of the earth,
cattle, each according to its kind.

He made the creatures that crawl on the earth,
reptiles, each according to its kind.

God looked.
    He said, IT IS GOOD.

God said,
    LET US MAKE MAN

LIKE US, IN OUR IMAGE AND LIKENESS.

God said,

      LET THEM DOMINATE THE EARTH

AND THE CREATURES OF THE EARTH.

God made MAN in his own image,
in the image of God

he made him,

      MAN and WOMAN
he made them.

Of one likeness

      MALE FE MALE
two he made.

God blessed them, saying,

      INCREASE. MULTIPLY.

DOMINATE THE EARTH

AND THE CREATURES OF THE EARTH.

God looked. He said,

      YOUR MEAT SHALL BE

PLANTS, SEEDS, FRUIT.

God said to the man and woman
and all the creatures on the earth,

YOUR MEAT SHALL BE THE EARTH,

NOT THE CREATURES OF THE EARTH.

God looked.
                He said, IT IS VERY GOOD.

Night and day were the sixth day.

•

God rested. On the seventh day

God rested. He looked at HEAVEN and EARTH,
and ceased.

Heaven and earth with all their panoply
were made.

God blessed the seventh day, God made
the seventh day a holy day,

because on the seventh day God rested, God ceased.

•

This was the creation of the world.

THE BOOK
OF THE BODY

(1977)

The Arc

When I wake up,
> I try to convince myself that my arm
isn't there—
> to retain my sanity.

Then I try to convince myself it is.

•   •   •

INSTRUCTIONS

1. Always bandage *firmly*. The pressure should be constant over the entire stump with greatest pressure near the tip to attempt to make the stump cone-shaped.

2. If stump starts to *throb*, remove the bandage at once. Leave bandage off for one hour and rebandage the stump as before, *firmly*. Inspect the skin of your stump daily for any blisters, spots or sores and report them.

3. Wash bandage with mild soap in luke warm water. DO NOT WRING! Squeeze the waters out gently and place the bandage over the shower rod to dry thoroughly. DO NOT STRETCH OR IRON!!

4. Change the stump sock daily. Wash the sock daily with mild
soap in luke warm water. DO NOT WRING! Squeeze the water
out gently—place the sock on a flat surface to dry.

●　　　　●　　　　●

I used to vaguely perceive the necessity
of coming to terms with the stump-filled, material world,—

things, bodies;
                    CRAP—

a world of accident, and chance—;

but after
the accident, I had to understand it

not as an accident—;

                    the way my mother,
years before locked in McLean's,

believed the painting of a snow-scene above her bed
had been placed there by the doctor to make her feel cold.

How could we *convince* her it had no point?. . .

It had no point,—
                    it was there

without relation to my mother; by chance; by
CHANCE the car swerved when a yellow car

came at us—; and the next
minute, when I looked down

all I saw was a space below the elbow
                                        instead of my arm. . .

The police still can't figure out exactly what happened.

I tell myself:
"Insanity is the insistence on meaning."

              •   •   •

He asked me if I wanted to get undressed, but I'm
embarrassed to take my shirt off,

so I told him to go ahead and take all his clothes off.

His body looked small and white lying on top of the dark bedspread.

I said I wanted to watch him wash
his prick.
            He got up and walked
to the washbasin against the wall,

then I went up, and started to wash
it with mild soap in luke warm water.
I squeezed it.
                    He laughed,

and after drying off, went back to the bed.

I asked if he had a job.
                              "Drove a truck for a while,
but about a week ago—I got laid off."

He looked uneasy, almost scared.
                              "When I was in Vietnam,
my wife met someone else, and divorced me.
I have a little daughter three years old."

He got his wallet and showed me the little girl's picture.

"I don't blame my wife—I was gone
a long time, and like everybody
else in Vietnam I did a lot of fucking around."

He looked frightened and embarrassed, seeming to want
me to reassure him. . .
                    I asked him to tell me about Vietnam.

"Anything you touched might explode. I know guys
just kicked a rock, and got killed. . .
                              Once a buddy of mine

was passing a hut, when a gook motioned to him to come inside.
Inside a woman was lying on her back, with
a pile of cigarettes next to her. He threw
some cigarettes on the pile, got on top of her,
and shoved in his prick.
                              He screamed.
She had a razor blade inside.

The whole end of his thing was sliced in two. . .

They fixed it up;
                              but what can he tell his wife?"

When he asked me what kind of sex I wanted,
I suddenly

forgot why

a body can make me feel horny—;

I wanted to leave.
                    But afraid
leaving might insult him, I asked him to masturbate.

"Sure."
        He closed his eyes. For several minutes
his arm and hand with great energy
worked, as his contorted face tried to concentrate.

I stared at him, wishing
I could know
the image in his mind when at last he came.

•   •   •

The person I can't forget on my mother's ward
I don't know the name of.
                              She still stands there
in my mind,—

                  though it is summer, and hot,
she is wearing a heavy terry-cloth robe,
sweating, with a thin metal chain around her neck:

that's all—
                  she is assuring me
she wears nothing under the robe,

that to wear anything
would *limit* her, that the doctors tell her
to have an "identity"
                              she must wear something—

"But I don't want an identity!

This way I'm *free*. . . Everybody else
has a medal on their chain, with a picture

or name on it, but I don't—
this way
I'm not bound down. . ."

With two hands
she begins to work the chain
around and around her neck, she soon gets
franticly excited,
                    and finally the attendant leads her away. . .

I only saw her once; that's
her identity in my mind,—

and even in my mind,

sweating
she wears a body

        •   •   •

In Michelangelo's drawing *The Dream*, a man,

his arms lightly touching the globe,
all the masks at last lying dead beneath him,

is wakened by an angel
                    hovering above him,

the angel's trumpet directed by the angel's arms,
the two figures connected by the trumpet,

wakened to the World ranged round him,
which is his dream, as well as Sin:

Sex. Identity. History. Family.
Affection. Obsession. Chance.

                              —the seven
Deadly Sins, spirit
implicating itself in matter, only able to know itself
by what it has done in Time,—

are all ranged round him, the angel
waking him to himself. . . his arms lightly touching the globe.

                •   •   •

In Paris, on the footbridge between the Ile St. Louis
and the Ile de la Cité,

about six months after the accident,
I had an illumination:

the *solution* was to forget
that I had ever had an arm.

                       The lost arm had never existed.

Since the accident,
I had gotten more and more obsessed: the image
of what I had been,
                        the anticipations,
demands and predilections of a two-armed man
haunted me—

I was no longer whole; proportioned; inviolate. . .

In a store, I found a "memorial album":
birth date, death date, place
of rest, visitors to the coffin—
                        I could clearly see
an obituary:
            On a certain date, in a certain place,
            he lost his arm.

Twice I dreamed the cone of my stump
was a gravestone:
                I saw it:
                        the whole of my life
was a kind of arc
stretching between two etched, ineradicable dates. . .

I had to escape that arc—

even notions like *career* and *marriage* (all those things
which because they
have a beginning, must end—)
                        seemed to suffocate. . .

I went to Paris. My family's sympathy,
the vivid scenes of my former life

whispered that my body was bound by two iron dates. . .

One day, leaving my hotel on the Ile St. Louis,
I saw a black dog and a young boy madly running.

Nothing unusual—
                    except the dog only had one
front leg. He seemed without consciousness
of what he lacked;
                    free of memory as a vegetable.

Looking at each other, they happily jogged along,
started to cross the bridge, and I followed—

then, as I crossed it, suddenly
I felt that I too must erase my past,
that I could, *must* pretend (almost
as an experiment) I had never had more
than one arm, that the image
faced in the mirror
was the only, the inevitable image. . .

—For a time, it worked;
                    I *was* happy;

without a past, I seemed not to exist
in time at all,—

I only remember a sense of release, ease,
proportion—
            I am now one, not less than one. . .

Then, after about two weeks, imperceptibly
everything I saw became

cardboard. . .

Even the things I touched—
                        I couldn't allow myself to remember
the vivid associations
which gave dimension to what I
                        touched, saw, smelt,—

the resonance of every image
I had to try to cut from my brain, it had been felt
by someone with two hands and two arms. . .

I had to try to cut from my brain
                        my phantom hand
which still gets cramps, which my brain still
recognizes as real—

            and now, I think of Paris,

how Paris is still the city of Louis XVI and
Robespierre, how blood, amputation, and rubble

give her dimension, resonance, and grace.

Happy Birthday

Thirty-three, goodbye—
the awe I feel

is not that you won't come again, or why—

or even that after
a time, we think of those who are dead

with a sweetness that cannot be explained—

but that I've read the trading-cards:
RALPH TEMPLE CYCLIST CHAMPION TRICK RIDER

WILLIE HARRADON CYCLIST
THE YOUTHFUL PHENOMENON

F. F. IVES CYCLIST
100 MILES 6 H. 25 MIN. 30 SEC.

—as the fragile metal of their
wheels stopped turning, as they

took on wives, children, accomplishments, all those
predilections which also insisted on ending,

they could not tell themselves from what they had done.

Terrible to dress in the clothes
of a period that must end.

They didn't plan it that way—
they didn't plan it that way.

Elegy

I. Belafont

"He seemed to have gotten better—

Tuesday, for the first time
in a week, he went out
into the front yard, and
pottied by lifting his leg—

which he hadn't had

the strength to do. So we left him

just for an hour—

the vet says
somebody must have
got to him again, in
that hour—

one in the morning, he started to
cough, throw up, and Floyd
stayed with him
all night—

at six, he called the vet, and at ten
he died.

He had a *good* life—

        you feel so guilty, even though you
        did all you could—

                I talked
                to my doctor, and

        he says you
        always feel that way, though you
        did all you
        humanly could—all you
        humanly could—"

(*pause*) "He had a *good* life—"

                My mother's dog is dead;
                as truly as I am, he was her son;
                we used to laugh at the comparison.

"When your father was drunk one night,
he started to hit me; you were only five, but
stood up to him, and said:
                    'If you ever
try to hit mommy again, I'll kill you.'

I knew then I *had* to leave.

When we came to the city,
you were a real toughie—
                        I'll never forget the first
day of kindergarten, you were sent home because
you called the lady teacher a 'sonofabitch'!

—You'd only been around cowboys;
but later, you only wanted to be with me.

I had to *push* you away—

we were always
more like each other than anyone else."

                    We used to laugh at the comparison.

"I insisted they bury him here, in the garden: Floyd
made a box: we wrapped him

in one of our best
white sheets." —Was it his fault

they loved him
more than each other? Or their fault

their love
forbade him in his nine years

from even licking his genitals?
She got him

the year before I went away to school,
"to take your place,"

she kidded. She used to laugh
at poodles on the street—clipped, manicured,

clung to.
But what was she to do—

change, or have another child?

      Belafont, I saw you in a dream tonight,
      reaching toward me to kiss me

      but carefully avoiding the mouth, as
      taught,

      yet constantly, defiantly skirting it—
      then plunging into a pile of old, empty shoeboxes

      to come up with the strap
      I wear on my weak

      left wrist
      exercising each night, remaking

the embarrassing
soft overfed unloved body

I try to blame on the past—;
tilting your head, the strap

hanging from one side of the mouth,
you look at me with your

daring, lawless
stare—

and begin to chew.

II. Pruning

"I'd rather die than let them
take off a breast. I'd rather die
than go through cobalt again."

She means it, —
                            but I can't help but remember
her at least fifteen years earlier,

standing in the doorway, shrieking at me
when I wanted to be a priest:
                            "It's just as well!

You had mumps—; they went down—; you'll never,
gelding, have kids!"
                            twisting her last knife

to save me from the Church, the Church
which called her marriage adultery. . .

—She is saying: "If the cancer
pops out somewhere else, I won't let them operate.
I'd rather die.
            They just
butcher you. . . Besides, it never works."

III. Lover

"I'll be right over."
"Give me a few minutes: I'm still

in my pajamas."
"Don't get out of your pajamas."

"Don't get out of my pajamas?"
"—Don't get out of your pajamas!"

And so we learned how to make two lovers
of friends; now,

caught "between a rock and a hard place—" (after
the hospital, after

"gestation" was "interrupted") we still
when we call even say we love each other. . .

Too bad two people don't have to "love each other"
more, to make a child.

IV. Light

I am asleep, dreaming a terrible dream, so I awake,
and want to call my father to ask if, just
for a short time, the dog can come to stay with me.

But the light next to my bed won't light:
I press and press the switch. Touching the phone,
I can't see to dial the numbers. Can I learn how to keep

the dog in my apartment? In the dark, trying
a second light, I remember
I always knew these machines would fail me.

          Then I awake,

remember my father and the dog are dead,
the lights in that room do not go on.

V. Lineage

"I went to a mausoleum today, and found
what I want. Eye-level.
Don't forget:
I want to be buried in a mausoleum at eye-level."

She feels she never quite recovered
from her mother's, my grandmother's, death.

Her mother died by falling from a
third floor hospital window.

"—I'm *sure* she didn't want to kill herself;

after the stroke, sometimes she got confused, and
maybe she thought
                    she saw grandpa at the window. . .

She wanted to be at home. After the stroke,
we *had* to put her in a nursing home,—

she hated it, but you couldn't
get help to stay with her, and she needed
someone twenty-four hours a day,—

she begged me to take her out;
                              the cruel,
unreasonable things she said to me! Her doctor

told me I was doing the right thing, but
what she said
                almost drove me crazy. . .

it's astonishing how clearly I can still hear her voice.

I still dream I can see her falling
three stories, her arms stretching out. . .

For forty years, she counted
on grandpa, —
                after he died, she still
talked to him.

I know I made a lot of
mistakes with you, but I couldn't count on anyone —

I had to be both father *and* mother. . ."

As the subject once again changes from my grandmother

to my father, or the dog —
to my stepfather, or me —
                her obsessive, baffled voice

says that when she allowed herself to love

she let something into her head which will
never be got out —;

> which could only betray her
or *be* betrayed, but never appeased—;
whose voice

> death and memory have made
into a razor-blade without a handle. . .

"Don't forget:
I want to be buried in a mausoleum at eye-level."

Envoi

"If it resists me, I know it's real—"
a friend said. I thought of you. . . When I said,
"I feel too much. I can't stand what I feel"

I meant, as always, facing you.—You're real;
and smile at me no *less* woundedly, dead.
If it resists me, I know it's real.

Now no act of Mind,—or Will,—can reveal
the secret to *un-say* all we once said. . .
I feel too much. I can't stand what I feel.

The only way we stumbled to the Real
was through failure; outrage; betrayals; dread.
If it resists me, I know it's real.

Is the only salvation through what's real?
But each book. . . reads me—; who remains unread.
I feel too much. I can't stand what I feel.

Mother, I didn't forgive you. Conceal
unreal forgiving. Show me your face in fury—; not dead.
If it resists me, I know it's real.
I feel too much. I can't stand what I feel.

The Book of the Body

Wanting to cease to feel—;

since 1967,
so much blood under the bridge,—

the deaths of both my parents,
(now that they have no
body, only when I have no body

can we meet—)

my romance with Orgasm,

exhilaration like Insight, but without
content?—

the NO which is YES, the YES which is NO—

Daphnis,
astonished at the unaccustomed threshold of heaven,

in his whiteness
sees beneath his feet the clouds and stars. . .

—So many
infatuations guaranteed to fail before they started,

terror at my own homosexuality,

terror which somehow
evaporated slowly with "Gay Liberation"

and finding that I had fathered a child—;

. . . All those who loved me
whom I did not want;

all those whom I loved
who did not want me;

all those whose love I reciprocated

but in a way somehow
                    unlike what they wanted. . .

—Blindness. Blankness.
A friend said, "I've hurt so many. . ." And

for what?
            to what *end*?—

An adult's forgiveness of his parents
born out of increasing age and empathy

which really forgives nothing,—
but is loathing, rage, revenge,

yet forgiveness as well—;

Sex the type of all action,

reconciliation with the body that is
annihilation of the body,

My romance with pornography,

watching it happen, watching

two bodies trying to make it happen,
however masterful or gorgeous, helpless

climbing the un-mappable mountain
of FEELING, the will

in sweat, hurt, exhaustion, accepting
limits of will,

the NO which is YES, the YES which is NO.

1974.

Ellen West

I love sweets,—
                    heaven
would be dying on a bed of vanilla ice cream. . .

But my true self
is thin, all profile

and effortless gestures, the sort of blond
elegant girl whose
                    body is the image of her soul.

—My doctors tell me I must give up
this ideal;
                    but I
WILL NOT. . . cannot.

Only to my husband I'm not simply a "case."

But he is a fool. He married
meat, and thought it was a wife.

       •   •   •

Why am I a girl?

I ask my doctors, and they tell me they
don't know, that it is just "given."

But it has such
implications—;
             and sometimes,
I even feel like a girl.

· · ·

Now, at the beginning of Ellen's thirty-second year, her physical condition has deteriorated still further. Her use of laxatives increases beyond measure. Every evening she takes sixty to seventy tablets of a laxative, with the result that she suffers tortured vomiting at night and violent diarrhea by day, often accompanied by a weakness of the heart. She has thinned down to a skeleton, and weighs only 92 pounds.

· · ·

About five years ago, I was in a restaurant,
eating alone
             with a book. I was
not married, and often did that. . .

—I'd turn down
dinner invitations, so I could eat alone;

I'd allow myself two pieces of bread, with
butter, at the beginning, and three scoops of
vanilla ice cream, at the end,—

                              sitting there alone
with a book, both in the book
and out of it, waited on, idly
watching people,—

                    when an attractive young man
and woman, both elegantly dressed,
sat next to me.
                    She was beautiful—;

with sharp, clear features, a good
bone structure—;
                    if she took her make-up off
in front of you, rubbing cold cream
again and again across her skin, she still would be
beautiful—
                    more beautiful.

And he,—
          I couldn't remember when I had seen a man
so attractive. I didn't know why. He was almost

a male version
          of her,—

I had the sudden, mad notion that I
wanted to be his lover. . .

—Were they married?
                    were *they* lovers?

They didn't wear wedding rings.

Their behavior was circumspect. They discussed
politics. They didn't touch. . .

—How could I discover?

                              Then, when the first course
arrived, I noticed the way

each held his fork out for the other

to taste what he had ordered. . .

                              They did this
again and again, with pleased looks, indulgent
smiles, for each course,
                    more than once for *each* dish—;
much too much for just friends. . .

—Their behavior somehow sickened me;

the way each *gladly*
put the *food* the other had offered *into his mouth*—;

I knew what they were. I knew they slept together.

An immense depression came over me. . .

—I knew I could never
with such ease allow another to put food into my mouth:

happily *myself* put food into another's mouth—;

I knew that to become a wife I would have to give up my ideal.

      •   •   •

Even as a child,
I saw that the "natural" process of aging

is for one's middle to thicken—
one's skin to blotch;

as happened to my mother.
And her mother.
                I loathed "Nature."

At twelve, pancakes
became the most terrible thought there is. . .

I shall *defeat* "Nature."

In the hospital, when they
weigh me, I wear weights secretly sewn into my belt.

      •   •   •

January 16. The patient is allowed to eat in her room, but comes readily with her husband to afternoon coffee. Previously she had stoutly resisted this on the ground that she did not really eat but devoured like a wild animal. This she demonstrated with utmost realism. . . . Her physical examination showed nothing striking. Salivary glands are markedly enlarged on both sides.

January 21. Has been reading *Faust* again. In her diary, writes that art is the "mutual permeation" of the "world of the body" and the "world of the spirit." Says that her own poems are "hospital poems. . . weak—without skill or perseverance; only managing to beat their wings softly."

February 8. Agitation, quickly subsided again. Has attached herself to an elegant, very thin female patient. Homo-erotic component strikingly evident.

February 15. Vexation, and torment. Says that her mind forces her always to think of eating. Feels herself degraded by this. Has entirely, for the first time in years, stopped writing poetry.

●   ●   ●

Callas is my favorite singer, but I've only
seen her once—;

I've never forgotten that night. . .

It was in *Tosca*, she had long before
lost weight, her voice
had been, for years,
                    deteriorating, half itself. . .

When her career began, of course, she was fat,

enormous—; in the early photographs,
sometimes I almost don't recognize her. . .

The voice too then was enormous—

healthy; robust; subtle; but capable of
crude effects, even vulgar,
                                        almost out of
high spirits, too much health. . .

But soon she felt that she must lose weight,—
that all she was trying to express

was obliterated by her body,
buried in flesh—;
                                abruptly, within
four months, she lost at least sixty pounds. . .

—The gossip in Milan was that Callas
had swallowed a tapeworm.

But of course she hadn't.

                                The *tapeworm*
was her *soul*. . .

—How her soul, uncompromising,
insatiable,
   must have loved eating the flesh from her bones,

revealing this extraordinarily
mercurial; fragile; masterly creature. . .

—But irresistibly, nothing
stopped there; the huge voice

also began to change: at first, it simply diminished
in volume, in size,
    then the top notes became
shrill, unreliable—at last,
usually not there at all. . .

—No one knows *why*. Perhaps her mind,
ravenous, still insatiable, sensed

that to struggle with the *shreds* of a voice

must make her artistry subtler, more refined,
more capable of expressing humiliation,
rage, betrayal. . .

—Perhaps the opposite. Perhaps her spirit
loathed the unending struggle

to *embody* itself, to *manifest* itself, on a stage whose

mechanics, and suffocating customs,
seemed expressly designed to annihilate spirit. . .

—I know that in *Tosca*, in the second act,
when, humiliated, wounded by Scarpia,
she sang *Vissi d'arte*
                    —"I lived for art"—

and in torment, bewilderment, at the end she asks,
with a voice reaching
                    harrowingly for the notes,

"Art has *repaid* me LIKE THIS?"

                                I felt I was watching
autobiography—
                    an art; skill;
virtuosity

miles distant from the usual soprano's
athleticism,—
                    the usual musician's dream
of virtuosity *without* content. . .

—I wonder what she feels, now,
listening to her recordings.

For they have already, within a few years,
begun to date. . .

Whatever they express
they express through the style of a decade
and a half—;
                a style *she* helped create. . .

—She must know that now
she probably would *not* do a trill in
exactly that way,—
                that the whole sound, atmosphere,
dramaturgy of her recordings

have just slightly become those of the past. . ,

—Is it bitter? Does her soul
tell her

that she was an *idiot* ever to think
anything
                material wholly could satisfy?. . .

—Perhaps it says: *The only way*
to escape
the History of Styles

is not to have a body.

•   •   •

When I open my eyes in the morning, my great
mystery
                stands before me. . .

—I *know* that I am intelligent; therefore

the inability not to fear food
day-and-night; this unending hunger
ten minutes after I have eaten. . .
                                    a childish
dread of eating; hunger which can have no cause,—

half my mind says that all this
is *demeaning*. . .

                Bread
for days on end
drives all real thought from my brain. . .

—Then I think, No. The ideal of being thin

conceals the ideal
not to have a body—;
                        which is NOT trivial. . .

This wish seems now as much a "given" of my existence

as the intolerable
fact that I am dark-complexioned; big-boned;

and once weighed
one hundred and sixty-five pounds. . .

—But then I think, *No*. That's too simple,—

without a body, who can
know himself at all?
Only by
acting; choosing; rejecting; have I
made myself—
discovered who and what *Ellen* can be. . .

—But then again I think, NO. This *I* is anterior

to name; gender; action;
fashion;
MATTER ITSELF,—

. . . trying to stop my hunger with FOOD
is like trying to appease thirst
with ink.

●   ●   ●

March 30. Result of the consultation: Both gentlemen agree com-
pletely with my prognosis and doubt any therapeutic usefulness
of commitment even more emphatically than I. All three of us are
agreed that it is not a case of obsessional neurosis and not one of
manic-depressive psychosis, and that no definitely reliable therapy
is possible. We therefore resolved to give in to the patient's demand
for discharge.

• • •

The train-ride yesterday
was far *worse* than I expected. . .

                              In our compartment
were ordinary people: a student;
a woman; her child;—

they had ordinary bodies, pleasant faces;
                              but I thought
I was surrounded by creatures

with the pathetic, desperate
desire to be *not* what they were:—

the student was short,
and carried her body as if forcing
it to be taller—;

the woman showed her gums when she smiled,
and often held her
hand up to hide them—;

the child
seemed to cry simply because it was
small; a dwarf, and helpless. . .

—I was hungry. I had insisted that my husband
not bring food. . .

After about thirty minutes, the woman
peeled an orange

to quiet the child. She put a section
into its mouth—;
                    immediately it spit it out.

The piece fell to the floor.

—She pushed it with her foot through the dirt
toward me
several inches.

My husband saw me staring
down at the piece. . .

—I didn't move; how I wanted
to reach out,
                    and as if invisible

shove it in my mouth—;

my body
became rigid. As I stared at him,
I could see him staring

at me,—
            then he looked at the student—; at the woman—; then
back to me. . .

I didn't move.

—At last, he bent down, and
casually
           threw it out the window.

He looked away.

—I got up to leave the compartment, then
saw his face,—

his eyes
were red;
           and I saw

—*I'm sure I saw*—

disappointment.

•   •   •

On the third day of being home she is as if transformed. At break-
fast she eats butter and sugar, at noon she eats so much that—for
the first time in thirteen years!—she is satisfied by her food and
gets really full. At afternoon coffee she eats chocolate creams and
Easter eggs. She takes a walk with her husband, reads poems, lis-
tens to recordings, is in a positively festive mood, and all heaviness
seems to have fallen away from her. She writes letters, the last one
a letter to the fellow patient here to whom she had become so at-

tached. In the evening she takes a lethal dose of poison, and on the following morning she is dead. "She looked as she had never looked in life—calm and happy and peaceful."

●　　●　　●

Dearest.—I remember how
at eighteen,
　　　　　on hikes with friends, when
they rested, sitting down to joke or talk,

I circled
around them, afraid to hike ahead alone,

yet afraid to rest
when I was not yet truly thin.

You and, yes, my husband,—
you and he

have by degrees drawn me within the circle;
forced me to sit down at last on the ground.

I am grateful.

But something in me *refuses* it.

—How eager I have been
to compromise, to kill this *refuser*,—

but each compromise, each attempt
to poison an ideal
which often seemed to *me* sterile and unreal,

heightens my hunger.

I am crippled. I disappoint you.

Will you greet with anger, or
happiness,

the news which might well reach you
before this letter?

Your *Ellen.*

GOLDEN STATE

(1973)

PART ONE

Herbert White

"When I hit her on the head, it was good,

and then I did it to her a couple of times,—
but it was funny,—afterwards,
it was as if somebody else did it. . .

Everything flat, without sharpness, richness or line.

Still, I liked to drive past the woods where she lay,
tell the old lady and the kids I had to take a piss,
hop out and do it to her. . .

The whole buggy of them waiting for me
                            made me feel good;
but still, just like I knew all along,
                     she didn't move.

When the body got too discomposed,
I'd just jack off, letting it fall on her. . .

—It sounds crazy, but I tell you
sometimes it was *beautiful*—; I don't know how
to say it, but for a minute, *everything* was possible—;
and then,
then,—
       well, like I said, she didn't move: and I saw,
under me, a little girl was just lying there in the mud:

and I knew I couldn't have done that,—
somebody *else* had to have done that,—

standing above her there,
                    in those ordinary, shitty leaves. . .

—One time, I went to see Dad in a motel where he was
staying with a woman; but she was gone;
you could smell the wine in the air; and he started,
real embarrassing, to cry. . .
                              He was still a little drunk,
and asked me to forgive him for
all he hadn't done—; but, What the shit?
Who would have wanted to stay with Mom? with bastards
not even his own kids?

                    I got in the truck, and started to drive,
and saw a little girl—
who I picked up, hit on the head, and
screwed, and screwed, and screwed, and screwed, then

buried,
        in the garden of the motel. . .

—You see, ever since I was a kid I wanted
to *feel* things make sense: I remember

looking out the window of my room back home,—
and being almost suffocated by the asphalt;

and grass; and trees; and glass;
just *there*, just *there*, doing nothing!
not saying anything! filling me up—
but also being a wall; dead, and stopping me;
—how I wanted to see beneath it, cut

beneath it, and make it
somehow, come alive. . .

      The salt of the earth;
Mom once said, 'Man's spunk is the salt of the earth. . .'

—That night, at that Twenty-nine Palms Motel
I had passed a million times on the road, everything

fit together; was alright;
it seemed like
     everything *had* to be there, like I had spent years
trying, and at last finally finished drawing this
        huge circle. . .

—But then, suddenly I knew
somebody *else* did it, some bastard
had hurt a little girl—; the motel
     I could see again, it had been
itself all the time, a lousy
pile of bricks, plaster, that didn't seem to
have to be there,—but *was*, just by chance. . .

—Once, on the farm, when I was a kid,
I was screwing a goat; and the rope around his neck
when he tried to get away
pulled tight;—and just when I came,
he *died*. . .

        I came back the next day; jacked off over his body;
but it didn't do any good. . .

Mom once said:
'Man's spunk is the salt of the earth, and grows kids.'

I tried so hard to come; more *pain* than anything else;
but didn't do any good. . .

—About six months ago, I heard Dad remarried,
so I drove over to Connecticut to see him and see
if he was happy.

        She was twenty-five years younger than him:
she had lots of little kids, and I don't know why,
I felt shaky. . .

        I stopped in front of the address; and
snuck up to the window to look in. . .

            —There he was, a kid
six months old on his lap, laughing
and bouncing the kid, happy in his old age
to play the papa after years of sleeping around,—
it twisted me up. . .

        To think that what he wouldn't give me,
        he *wanted* to give them. . .

I could have killed the bastard. . .

—Naturally, I just got right back in the car,
and believe me, was determined, determined,
to head straight for home. . .

                         but the more I drove,
I kept thinking about getting a girl,
and the more I thought I shouldn't do it,
the more I had to—

                  I saw her coming out of the movies,
saw she was alone, and
kept circling the blocks as she walked along them,
saying, 'You're going to leave her alone.'
'You're going to leave her alone.'

                        —The woods were scary!
As the seasons changed, and you saw more and more
of the skull show through, the nights became clearer,
and the buds,—erect, like nipples. . .

—But then, one night,
nothing *worked*. . .
                Nothing in the sky
would blur like I wanted it to;
and I couldn't, *couldn't*,

get it to seem to me
that somebody *else* did it. . .

I tried, and tried, but there was just me there,
and her, and the sharp trees
saying, 'That's you standing there.

You're. . .

just you.'

I hope I fry.

—Hell came when I saw

MYSELF. . .

and couldn't stand

what I see. . ."

Self-Portrait, 1969

He's *still* young—; thirty, but looks younger—
or does he?. . . In the eyes and cheeks, tonight,
turning in the mirror, he saw his mother,—
puffy; angry; bewildered. . . Many nights
now, when he stares there, he gets angry:—
something *unfulfilled* there, something dead
to what he once thought he surely could be—
Now, just the glamour of habits. . .
                                    Once, instead,
he thought insight would remake him, he'd reach
—what? The thrill, the exhilaration
unraveling disaster, that seemed to teach
necessary knowledge. . . became just jargon.

Sick of being decent, he craves another
crash. What *reaches* him except disaster?

PART TWO

PART TWO

California Plush

The only thing I miss about Los Angeles

is the Hollywood Freeway at midnight, windows down and
radio blaring
bearing right into the center of the city, the Capitol Tower
on the right, and beyond it, Hollywood Boulevard
blazing

—pimps, surplus stores, footprints of the stars

—descending through the city
                    fast as the law would allow

through the lights, then rising to the stack
out of the city
to the stack where lanes are stacked six deep

                and you on top; the air
                now clean; for a moment weightless

                        without memories, or
                        need for a past.

The need for the past

is so much at the center of my life
I write this poem to record my discovery of it,
my reconciliation.

                    It was in Bishop, the room was done
in California plush: we had gone into the coffee shop, were told
you could only get a steak in the bar;
                                  I hesitated,
not wanting to be an occasion of temptation for my father

but he wanted to, so we entered

a dark room, with amber water glasses, walnut
tables, captain's chairs,
plastic doilies, papier-mâché bas-relief wall ballerinas,
German memorial plates "bought on a trip to Europe,"
Puritan crosshatch green-yellow wallpaper,
frilly shades, cowhide
booths—

I thought of Cambridge:

                the lovely congruent elegance
                of Revolutionary architecture, even of

ersatz thirties Georgian

seemed alien, a threat, sign
of all I was not—

to bode order and lucidity

as an ideal, if not reality—

not this California plush, which

        also

I was not.

And so I made myself an Easterner,
finding it, after all, more like me
than I had let myself hope.

        And now, staring into the embittered face of
        my father,

again, for two weeks, as twice a year,
    I was back.

        The waitress asked us if we wanted a drink.
Grimly, I waited until he said no. . .

Before the tribunal of the world I submit the following
document:

        Nancy showed it to us,
in her apartment in the motel,

as she waited month by month
for the property settlement, her children grown
and working for their father,
at fifty-three now alone,
a drink in her hand:

>
> as my father said,
"They keep a drink in her hand":

> *Name* Wallace Du Bois
> *Box No* 128   *Chino, Calif.*
> *Date* July 25 ,19 54

Mr Howard Arturian

   I am writing a letter to you this afternoon while I'm in the mood
of writing. How is everything getting along with you these fine
days, as for me everything is just fine and I feel great except for the
heat I think its lot warmer then it is up there but I don't mind it
so much. I work at the dairy half day and I go to trade school the
other half day Body & Fender, now I am learning how to spray
paint cars I've already painted one and now I got another car to
paint. So now I think I've learned all I want after I have learned
all this. I know how to straighten metals and all that. I forgot to say
"Hello" to you. The reason why I am writing to you is about a job,
my Parole Officer told me that he got letter from and that you
want me to go to work for you. So I wanteded to know if its truth.
When I go to the Board in Feb. I'll tell them what I want to do and
where I would like to go, so if you want me to work for you I'd
rather have you sent me to your brother John in Tonapah and
place to stay for my family. The Old Lady says the same thing in

her last letter that she would be some place else then in Bishop, thats the way I feel too. and another thing is my drinking problem. I made up my mind to quit my drinking, after all what it did to me and what happen.

This is one thing I'll never forget as longs as I live I never want to go through all this mess again. This sure did teach me a lot of things that I never knew before. So Howard you can let me know soon as possible. I sure would appreciate it.

P. S   From Your Friend
I hope you can read my   Wally Du Bois
writing. I am a little nervous yet

—He and his wife had given a party, and
one of the guests was walking away
just as Wallace started backing up his car.
He hit him, so put the body in the back seat
and drove to a deserted road.
There he put it before the tires, and
ran back and forth over it several times.

When he got out of Chino, he did,
indeed, never do that again:
but one child was dead, his only son,
found with the rest of his family
immobile in their beds with typhoid,
next to the mother, the child having been
dead two days:

he continued to drink, and as if it were the Old West
shot up the town a couple of Saturday nights.

"So now I think I've learned all I want
after I have learned all this: this sure did teach me a lot of things
that I never knew before.
I am a little nervous yet."

It seems to me
an emblem of Bishop—

For watching the room, as the waitresses in their
back-combed, Parisian, peroxided, bouffant hairdos,
and plastic belts,
moved back and forth

I thought of Wallace, and
the room suddenly seemed to me
   not uninteresting at all:

   they were the same. Every plate and chair

   had its congruence with

   all the choices creating

   these people, created

by them—by me,

for this is my father's chosen country, my origin.

Before, I had merely been anxious, bored; now,
I began to ask a thousand questions. . .

He was, of course, mistrustful, knowing I was bored,
knowing he had dragged me up here from Bakersfield

after five years

of almost managing to forget Bishop existed.

But he soon became loquacious, ordered a drink,
and settled down for
an afternoon of talk. . .

He liked Bishop: somehow, it was to his taste, this
hard-drinking, loud, visited-by-movie-stars town.
"Better to be a big fish in a little pond."

And he was: when they came to shoot a film,
he entertained them; Miss A——, who wore
nothing at all under her mink coat; Mr. M——,
good horseman, good shot.

"But when your mother
let me down" (for alcoholism and
infidelity, she divorced him)
"and Los Angeles wouldn't give us water any more,
I had to leave.

We were the first people to grow potatoes in this valley."

When he began to tell me
that he lost control of the business
because of the settlement he gave my mother,

because I had heard it
many times,

in revenge, I asked why people up here drank so much.

He hesitated. "Bored, I guess.
—Not much to do."

And why had Nancy's husband left her?

In bitterness, all he said was:
"People up here drink too damn much."

And that was how experience
had informed his life.

"So now I think I've learned all I want
after I have learned all this: this sure did teach me a lot of things

that I never knew before.
I am a little nervous yet."

Yet, as my mother said,
returning, as always, to the past,

"I wouldn't change any of it.
It taught me so much. Gladys
is such an innocent creature: you look into her face
and somehow it's empty, all she worries about
are sales and the baby.
Her husband's too good!"

It's quite pointless to call this rationalization:
my mother, for uncertain reasons, has had her
bout with insanity, but she's right:

the past in maiming us,
makes us,
fruition
          is also
destruction:

          I think of Proust, dying
in a cork-lined room, because he refuses to eat
because he thinks that he cannot write if he eats
because he wills to write, to finish his novel

—his novel which recaptures the past, and
with a kind of joy, because
in the debris
of the past, he has found the sources of the necessities

which have led him to this room, writing

—in this strange harmony, does he will
for it to have been different?

                And I can't *not* think of the remorse of Oedipus,

who tries to escape, to expiate the past
by blinding himself, and
then, when he is dying, sees that he has become a Daimon

—does he, discovering, at last, this cruel
coherence created by
                "the order of the universe"

—does he will
anything reversed?

           I look at my father:
as he drinks his way into garrulous, shaky
defensiveness, the debris of the past
is just debris—; whatever I reason, it is a desolation
to watch. . .

must I watch?
He will not change; he does not *want* to change;

every defeated gesture implies
the past is useless, irretrievable. . .
—I want to change: I want to stop fear's subtle

guidance of my life—; but, how can I do that
if I am still
afraid of its source?

1966–67.

Book of Life

I once knew a man named Snake.

He killed
All our snakes.

    One day one bit him.

"Ha-ya feelin', Snake?"
I asked when he returned.

He said,
"My name is Walter."

      The brown house
      on the brown hill
      reminds me of my parents.

Its memory is of poverty,
not merely poverty of means,
but poverty of history, of awareness of
the ways men have found to live.

    My stepfather was from Texas.

"Niggers, you know they're different from us,
they go mad when they make love,
we white men have to watch out or women

won't have anything to do with us."

(*pause*) "Back in McKinney, there's a spot on the pavement
where they caught a nigger who'd raped a white woman,
right there they tied him down,
poured gasoline on him, and
lit him afire.
—You can still see the mark."

Illuminated by the lore of the past, justified
by the calluses on his hands,
—won walking round and round
a wheel digging a water
well fourteen hours a day—
he was happy with himself.

                    Before my mother married him, she was
                    free for several years, proposed to
                    by several men we may call,
                    in this context,

                    "educated"

(a lawyer; a doctor; unconfident men
sharing a certain unmistakable
humaneness)

and later, she often asked herself

why she married him.

She would laugh, and say, "I always liked the horse's asses!"

(*pause*) "My mother never told me about these things."

Its memory is of poverty,
not merely poverty of means,
but poverty of history, of awareness of
the ways men have found to live.

My father
"was the handsomest man in Kern County."

When they met, he was eight years older, and

driving a truck for a bootlegger.

He had had a dance studio in Hollywood,
gone broke, and

was back. "He introduced me to a fast, drinking crowd; my God,

we smoked—! And I wore lipstick: Olive and I promised each other

we would never do that."

So he went back into farming, as he had done as a child
when his father died, and
"was a genius."

"Your father, on our wedding night, told me
he had ninety-two thousand dollars in the bank. His first
potato crop. He didn't have a dime the year before."

But he
spent all the afternoons in the cool bars.
"He always was a sucker for a no-good
bum with a slick line and a good story.
How an intelligent man like that—"

Soon he
was an alcoholic, and unfaithful; unfaithful
many times; which fact was, as it were,
brought home to her, by
detectives. She would shake her head:

"How an intelligent man like that—"

(*bitterly*) "He never would have made us a real home,
the way decent men do."

In her own illness, when she began to
try to turn brass and tin into gold
by boiling them in a large pot full of
soap, cat's fur, and orange rinds,

she was following

the teachings of the Rosicrucians,

the secrets of the past, the mysteries of the

pyramids.

      Later, as she began
      to be well, she would ask,

"Why did it happen?

          It seems to
say something awful about
everything I've done.
          Does it make everything wrong?
I knew so little
all along!"

(*pause*) "Why did it happen to *me*—at

forty-eight?"

Its memory is of poverty,
not merely poverty of means,
but poverty of history, of awareness of
the ways men have found to live.

For men are not
children, who learn
not to touch the burner; men,

unlike Walter,
cannot simply revert

to their true names.
                        The brown clapboard house,
in spite of its fine pioneer tradition,
because of the absence of the knowledge in its
lines of other architecture, because of the
poverty of its

brown, barren hill,

reminds me of my parents.

1966.

Golden State

I

To see my father
lying in pink velvet, a rosary
twined around his hands, rouged,
lipsticked, his skin marble. . .

My mother said, "He looks the way he did
thirty years ago, the day we got married, —
I'm *glad* I went;
I was afraid: now I can remember him
like that. . ."

Ruth, your last girlfriend, who wouldn't sleep with you
or marry, because you wanted her
to pay half the expenses, and "His drinking
almost drove me crazy —"
                              Ruth once saw you
staring into a mirror,
in your ubiquitous kerchief and cowboy hat,
say:
    "Why can't I look like a cowboy?"

You left a bag of money; and were
the unhappiest man
I have ever known well.

II

It's in many ways
a relief to have you dead.

                          I have more money.
Bakersfield is easier: life isn't so nude,
now that I no longer have to
face you each evening: mother is progressing
beautifully in therapy, I can almost convince myself
a good analyst would have saved you:

for I *need* to believe, as
always, that your pervasive sense of disappointment

proceeded from
trivial desires: but I fear
that beneath the wish to be a movie star,
cowboy, empire builder, all those
cheap desires, lay
radical disaffection

                        from the very possibilities
of human life. . .

Your wishes were too simple:
                    or too complex.

III

I find it difficult to imagine you
in bed, making love to a woman. . .

By common consensus, you were a *good* lover:
and yet,
mother once said: "Marriage would be better
if it weren't mixed up with sex. . ."

Just after the divorce, — when I was
about five, — I slept all night with you

in a motel, and again and again
you begged me
to beg her to come back. . .

I said nothing; but she went back
several times, again and again
you would go on a binge, there would be
another woman,
mother would leave. . .

You always said,
"Your mother is the only woman I've ever loved."

IV

Oh Shank, don't turn into the lies
of mere, neat poetry. . .

I've been reading Jung, and he says that we can
never get to the bottom
of what is, or was. . .

But *why* things were as they were
obsesses; I know that you
the necessity to contend with you
your *helplessness*
before yourself,
              —has been at the center
of how I think my life. . .

                    And yet your voice, raw,
demanding, dissatisfied,
saying over the telephone:

        "How are all those bastards at Harvard?"

remains, challenging: beyond all the
patterns and paradigms
                    I use silence and stop it.

V

I dreamed I *had* my wish:
                    —I seemed to see
the conditions of my life, upon
a luminous stage: how I could change,
how I could not: the root of necessity,
and choice.
                The stage was labelled
"Insight".
                The actors there
had no faces, I cannot remember
the patterns of their actions, but
simply by watching,

I knew that beneath my feet
the fixed stars
governing my life

had begun to fall, and melt. . .
                    —Then your face appeared,

laughing at the simplicity of my wish.

VI

Almost every day
I take out the letter you wrote me in Paris.
. . . Why?

It was written
the year before you married Shirley; Myrtle,
your girlfriend, was an ally of mine
because she "took care of you,"
but you always
made it clear
she was too dumpy and crude to marry. . .

In some ways "elegant,"
with a pencil-thin, neatly clipped moustache,
chiselled, Roman nose, you were
a millionaire
and always pretended
you couldn't afford to go to Europe. . .

When I was a child,
you didn't seem to care if I existed.

Bakersfield, Calif
July 9, 1961

Dear Pinon.
    Sorry I haven't wrote to you sooner but glad to hear that you are
well and enjoying *Paris*.

I got you fathers day wire in the hospital where I put in about twelve days but I am very well now. I quit the ciggeretts but went through ten days of hell quitting and my back had been giving me hell.

It had been very hot here but the last few days has been very nice. Emily just got out of the hospital yesterday. She had her feet worked on. I guess she will tell you about it. Glad to hear you are learning some French.

We are just about through with potatoes. Crop was very good but no price at all whitch made it a poor year. Cattle are cheap too. It look like a bad year for all farmer's.

I don't know anything else to tell you. Take care of your self and enjoy it. Maybe you will never have another chance for another trip. I don't think I'll ever get the chance to go, so if you run into a extra special gal between 28 & 35 send her over here to me as all I know over here don't amount to mutch. Well I guess I'll close now as I am going over to see Emily.

Hoping to hear from you right away.

This address is 4019 Eton St. be sure and get it straight. Myrtle would like to know how much that watch amounts to. Let us know

Will close now and write soon.

Love 'Shank'

P.S. Excuse this writing as its about 30 years since I wrote a letter.

VII

How can I say this?
                    I think my psychiatrist
likes me: he knows
the most terrible things I've done, every stupidity,
inadequacy, awkwardness,
ignorance, the mad girl I screwed
because she once again and again
teased and rejected me, and whose psychic incompetence
I grimly greeted as an occasion for revenge;
he greets my voice

with an interest, and regard, and affection,
which seem to signal I'm worth love;

—you finally
forgave me for being your son, and in the nasty
shambles of your life, in which you had less and less
occasion for pride, you were proud
of me, the first Bidart
who ever got a B.A.; Harvard, despite
your distrust, was the crown;—but the way
you eyed me:
                    the *bewilderment,* unease:
the somehow always
tentative, suspended judgment. . .

—however *much* you tried (and, clearly,
you *did* try)
            you could not remake your
taste, and like me: could not remake
yourself, to give me

the grace
needed to look in a mirror, as I often can
now, with some equanimity. . .

VIII

When did I begin to substitute
insight, for prayer?. . .

        —You believed in neither:
but said, "My life is over,"
after you had married Shirley,
twenty-five years younger, with three
small children, the youngest
six months old; she was unfaithful
within two months, the marriage was simply
annulled. . .
        A diabetic, you didn't
take your insulin when you drank, and
almost managed to die
many times. . .
        You punished Ruth
when she went to Los Angeles for a weekend, by
beginning to drink; she would return home
either to find you in the hospital,
or in a coma on the floor. . .

        The exacerbation
of this seeming *necessity*
for connection—;
        you and mother taught me
there's little that's redemptive or useful
in natural affections. . .

I must *unlearn*; I must believe

you were merely a man—
with a character, and a past—;

                                        you wore them,
                                        unexamined,
like a nimbus of
furies

round your
greying, awesome head. . .

IX

What should I have done? In 1963,
you wanted to borrow ten thousand dollars
from me, so that we could buy cattle
together, under the name "Bidart and Son,"—
most of your money was tied up
in the increasingly noxious "Bidart Brothers,"
run by your brother, Johnny. . .

I said no,—
that I wanted to use the money
for graduate school; but I thought
if you went on a binge, and as had happened
before, simply threw it away. . .

The Bidarts agreed
you were *not* to be trusted; you accepted
my answer, with an air
of inevitability I was shocked at. . .

I didn't *want* to see your self-disgust;
—somehow, your self-congratulation
had eroded more deeply, much
more deeply, than even I had wished,—

but for *years*, how I had wished!. . .

I have a friend who says
that he has never felt a conflict

between something deeply wished or desired,
and what he thought was "moral"...

Father, such innocence
surely is a kind of *Eden*—; but,
somehow, I can't regret that we
are banished from that company—;
in the awareness, the
history of our contradictions and violence,
insofar as I am "moral" at all,
is the beginning of my moral being.

X

When I began this poem,
                    to see myself
as a piece of history, having a past
which shapes, and informs, and thus inevitably
limits —
            at first this seemed sufficient, the beginning of
freedom. . .
                The way to approach freedom
was to acknowledge necessity: —
I sensed I had to become not merely
a speaker, the "eye," but a character. . .

And you had to become a character: with a past,
with a set of internal contradictions and necessities
which if I could *once* define, would at least
begin to release us from each other. . .

But, of course, no such knowledge is possible; —
as I touch your photographs, they stare back at me
with the dazzling, impenetrable, glitter of mere life. . .

You stand smiling, at the end of the twenties,
in a suit, and hat,
cane and spats, with a collie at your feet,
happy to be handsome, dashing, elegant: —

and though I cannot connect this image

with the end of your life, with the defensive
gnarled would-be cowboy,—

you seem happy at that fact, happy
to be surprising; unknowable; unpossessable. . .

You say it's what you always understood by freedom.

1968–69.

PART THREE

PART THREE

Vergil Aeneid 1.1–33

Arms and the man I sing, the man and hero, who
driven by fate, by the gods' mere force and Juno's hate,
found Italy, found Latium, the man and hero
battered on land and sea, who founded our city,
brought us gods and lineage,
even to this, garlanded walls of substantial Rome.
　　　Muse, make me mindful of the causes, load upon me
knowledge of her sorrows, she whom men call the queen of the gods
but driven to drive the most earnest of men
to such misfortunes. After foundering Troy,
what human being would not have been satisfied?
　　　An ancient city, held by farmers, fronting Italy
and the mouth of the Tiber, then
magnificent in elegance, rich in courage:
such was Carthage—it is said, the city of Juno, and loved
by her even above Samos, seat of her shrine.
She wanted this new home of her weapons and chariot
first among men. But the fates did not so spin:
bathed in the faded pageant of Troy, in rue and despair,
a race was to come to rule over men,
merciless in war, graceful in victory.
She had heard that beloved Carthaginian Libya
would soon be a level plain.
Within her mind the resistless past returned:
scenes of burning Troy, herself as chief of destruction—
and deeper, to the causes in insult and wounded love

and proper mother's pride, Paris's
judgment, the bastard
founding of the city, Ganymede snatched above her own daughter:
out of this the Trojans must wander, must wander in error
seeking over the world's seas
what the remnant left by the Greeks and merciless Achilles
may never enjoy through the will of the queen of the gods:
how heavy the burden, to found the Roman race.

After Catullus

The day was calm. . . For the usual reason
I had gone into the country, and indeed
there seemed peace. Understanding friend:
with whom only
I can be frank; can even you
receive this as I received it?

I walked down into a field. The lions were in bloom,
crocus, hyacinth, coxcombs,
shouting to be so full of sun and seed.
I said to myself: "I must lie down."
They touched my face. I
could not see the sun.

In this darkness then: a sound became clear,
half-moaning
half-delight
of a girl—twelve?—lying
not five feet from me
with her legs spread apart. Above her in jeans

a boy maybe younger worked away. . . He was good!
But he didn't see me standing staring with blind eyes
in the sun. She resisted: his arms held her arms
firmly down

as the open front of his jeans disappeared
under her dress. I
put him to the sword!

With my prick.

To My Father

I walked into the room.
There were objects in the room. I thought I needed nothing
from them. They began to speak,
but the words were unintelligible, a painful cacophony. . .
Then I realized they were saying
                              the name
of the man who had chosen them, owned them,
ordered, arranged them, their deceased cause,
the secret pattern that made these things order.
I strained to hear: but
the sound remained unintelligible. . .
senselessly getting louder, urgent, deafening.

Hands over my ears, at last I knew
                              they would remain
inarticulate; your name was not in my language.

Another Life

"—In a dream I never *exactly* dreamed,
but that is, somehow, the quintessence
of what I *might* have dreamed,

                   Kennedy is in Paris

again; it's '61; once again
some new national life seems possible,
though desperately, I try to remain unduped,
even cynical. . .

             He's standing in an open car,

brilliantly lit, bright orange
next to a grey de Gaulle, and they stand
not far from me, slowly moving up the Champs-Elysées. . .

Bareheaded in the rain, he gives a short
choppy wave, smiling like a sun god.

—I stand and
look, suddenly at peace; once again mindlessly

moved,
       as they bear up the fields of Elysium

the possibility of Atlantic peace,

reconciliation between all the power, energy,
optimism,—
        and an older wisdom, without
illusions, without force, the austere source
of nihilism, corrupted only by its dream of Glory. . .

But no—; as I
watch, the style is

          not quite right—;

                  Kennedy is *too* orange. . .

And de Gaulle, white, dead
white, ghost white, not even grey. . .

            As my heart
began to grieve for my own awkwardness and
ignorance, which would never be
soothed by the informing energies
           of whatever
wisdom saves,—

      I saw a young man, almost
my twin, who had written

'MONSTER'
in awkward lettering with a crayon across
the front of his sweat shirt.

He was gnawing on his arm,

in rage and anger gouging up
pieces of flesh—; but as I moved to stop him, somehow
help him,
         suddenly he looked up,

and began, as I had, to look at Kennedy and de Gaulle:

and then abruptly, almost as if I were seeing him
through a camera lens, his figure
split in two,—
         or doubled,—

and all the fury
         drained from his stunned, exhausted face. . .

But only for a moment. Soon his eyes turned down
to the word on his chest. The two figures
again became one,

and with fresh energy he attacked the mutilated arm. . .

—Fascinated, I watched as this
pattern, this cycle,
         repeated several times.

Then he reached out and touched me.

—Repelled,
            I pulled back. . . But he became
frantic, demanding that I become
the body he split into:
                        'It's harder
to manage *each* time! Please
give me your energy; —*help me!'*

                        —I said it was impossible,
there was *no part* of us the same:
we were just watching a parade together:
(and then, as he reached for my face)
                        leave me *alone!*

He smirked, and said
I was never alone.

            I told him to go to hell.

He said that this was hell.

                        —I said it was impossible,
there was *no part* of us the same:
we were just watching a parade together:
                        when I saw

Grief, avenging Care, pale
Disease, Insanity, Age, and Fear,

                —all the raging desolations

which I had come to learn were my patrimony;
the true progeny of my parents' marriage;
the gifts hidden within the mirror;

—standing guard at the gate of this place,
triumphant,
          striking poses
               eloquent of the disasters they embodied. . .

—I took several steps to the right, and saw
Kennedy was paper-thin,
              as was de Gaulle;
mere cardboard figures
whose possible real existence
lay buried beneath a million tumbling newspaper photographs. . .

—I turned, and turned, but now all that was left
was an enormous
          fresco;—on each side, the unreadable
                fresco of my life. . ."

THE FIRST
HOUR OF
THE NIGHT

(1990)

Now In Your Hand

1. Victor Hugo: Preface to Les Misérables, *1862*

SO LONG AS, on this earth, in our civilization, fixed there by its laws and its customs, HELL EXISTS—A DAMNATION MADE BY MEN over and above the fate all men must face;

SO LONG AS the three great violations of our age,

> *men debased by the nature of their work*
> *women devoured by their hunger*
> *children stunted by night without light*

are unsolved, and even unseen;

SO LONG AS the world human beings have made is a world where we cannot breathe;

IN SUM, SO LONG AS ALL THAT IS AT HOME ON THIS EARTH ARE IGNORANCE AND MISERY WITHOUT RECOURSE OR VOICE,

books such as the one now in your hand will not, I think, be, perhaps, useless.

2.

when

once, pursuing the enslaving enemies and enslaving protectors
of our civilization, but encountering
only the unthinkable, a blank screen, banal
interiority, commas multiplying ad infinitum, in
short, the appearance in his consciousness of the consciousness
of the appearance of himself

when he doubted he ever believed they exist

he found that they destroyed enemies and friends

using the means in which he believed,
this system in which in every sentence you can insert not

You remain...

You remain, bride whose recourse has been silence, and absence:—
you appear under the names *arena*, *stage*, but your essence

always is other and elsewhere, your gift
the voices of the dead filled and emptied by the future.

Protect against those who entering
the orifices of this house

seek to control it—

Muse, Autodidact, Collector,
renew its inmate dedicated to you.

By These Waters

What begins in recognition, —
. . . ends in obedience.

The boys who lie back, or stand up,
allowing their flies to be unzipped

however much they charge
however much they charge

give more than they get.

When the room went dark, the screen lit up.

By these waters on my knees I have wept.

Long and Short Lines

You who call me to weep afresh love's long since cancelled woe,—
. . . mock me

with you—

hypocrisy's thirst somewhere if you're anywhere must
now make you again pave someone's road to hell.

Toward that design cut long ago by your several divided nature
and mine,

. . . learn I too
twist, unchanged.

1989.

Book of Night

After the sun
fell below the horizon of the west,

THE SUN-GOD

(according to words carved
on the sarcophagus of the pharaoh Seti I)

each night, during the twelve hours of the night, must
journey through
    THE WORLD THAT IS BENEATH THE WORLD,—

        . . . must

meet, once again, the dead.

The hour that must follow the eleventh hour

is blank within my eye:—
I do not know what will make the sun rise again.

With a light placed
inside it, the sarcophagus carved out of alabaster

is transparent:—

here is the beginning of our night.

The First Hour of the Night

"This happened about twelve years before I died.

●

What I have to tell you

is the narrative of an evening and night, little more than
a succession of dreams, one
anxiety following another, —

the whole, somehow, for me (at least) *wound* and *balm*.

●

The friend I had been closest to throughout
my life, three years earlier, suddenly

was dead —;
for three years, his son

had invited me to visit the family home, —
. . . the family 'seat,'

a 'GREAT HOUSE'

inherited by my friend in his twenties at his
father's death, inherited now by his only son. . .

•

What use to return? —

During his life, both of us often insisted that our
philosophical discussions, ebullient
arguments, hydra-headed analyses of
the motivations, dilemmas that seemed to block
and fuel our lives,

                     were central, crucial: —

but after his death, all I now could see

was the self-generating *logic* of his life, its distant,
inaccessible self-sufficiency. . .

He had been a storm
at sea, seen from land.

•

What use to return? —

As I imagined standing again within that house,
—within that world he had been
given, but had so
transformed by his affections, curiosity, shifting
enthusiasms, care: —

walking up the central staircase, then, after
twenty feet, entering his study—;

its obscure, *ARBITRARY*
finality stopped my breath.

                    •

Three years (to the day) after this first death of
a friend my own age, his son

wrote that I would do his father's only child

a great kindness
if once again I came to stay, even for a night. . .

The house was of course changed.

I suppose I had expected
a *museum* to my friend:—

instead, I found the embodiment of
different interests,
                    as well as incomprehension
of, or even the desire to ERASE, to BLUR

what in his father had seemed bold
or witty or coherent:—

an unsymmetrical, fragile Indonesian rocker
had been sold, because 'uncomfortable';—

curtains obscured the high bare rectangles of
windows whose light or blackness once
was shut out only by recessed, seldom-used shutters. . .

Half the books were stored,—
. . . or sold.

After dinner, we went into the study.

Neither of us sat in his father's chair.

Highbacked, winged, it still stood
at an angle, right of the fire,—and I sat

facing it, on
the left, where I had always sat. . .

The couch to my right was still there,—
he slumped at its far end.

The small coal fire, as always, burned one's face;
and failed to heat the dark, huge room.

He put his hands to his temples, making
a kind of hood over his eyes; I couldn't

see his eyes. Then he spoke:—

●

I can neither SELL this house, nor
LIVE in it. If father had a favorite horse, you and I could

sacrifice and eat it

next to his grave—; then set up its head on a stake
driven directly into the grave. . .

That's how Harva says the Tartars
convince the dead to STAY DEAD.

They seldom succeed. If a dead man's widow and children
grow sick

the shaman knows the dead are eating them.

You've known me since I was born:

you know that I wasn't
waiting for father to die. I had my own

work, friends, income (I admit that I've always been
a spendthrift, but I wasted

my own money, not his—). . .

The prerogatives that descended upon me at his death

—'position'; much more money; the freedom
implicit in the demands now
placed upon me—

I didn't connive, or even will: they came
in the course of things,—

                    . . . BECAUSE HE WAS NOT HERE.

But I enjoy them; and even, now, expect them.

. . . Again and again I dream

                         father has come back:—

he is standing in the hallway, as I
descend the staircase.

He looks up at me, tired, relieved to be home.

He is whole: WELL: not changed,—

                              but even as I
rush down the steps to embrace him

(even as the irreparable
fact that drained and diminished the world

isn't fact,—)

I know that I don't want him to have come back.

All this is HIS, not MINE —; I am
again what his death made me no longer. . .

Before I reach him, an elated circle of servants and friends
surrounds him, and leads him off.

As they disappear,
his head turns back to look at me.

—Then I know that each object that father
chose for this house, but absent now from it
                                says that everything ever

unresolved clearly FOREVER
is unresolvable between us.

For though I
must give it all back, I CAN'T

give it all back: I've already
spent too much money!. . .

Thus, though I know that no creature
possesses anything on this earth, sweating

I wake up
terrified that father has returned to it: —

baffled, and appalled
to find that what I want is his death.

        ●

Then he stopped. There was a long silence.

The voice
I heard as he said all this
            —in a sudden

intonation, a passing phrase, in the pervasive
self-wounding relentlessness of its logic,—

was his father's.

The fist at the center of my chest

refused to unclench until he and I, the furniture we
sat on, the room, the house, the very

world itself

cracked apart, then SELF-COMBUSTED, self-
consumed by our own self-contradictions.

        ●

I told him that when I was a child I had a pony

who was, for a period, my
life —;
     . . . even now, if I close
my eyes, and look into his face

I am a boy again, looking into the face of a neurasthenic
panicked *mute* creature like himself, in secret

alliance forged
half-against what we lacked: —
         WORDS, a world that demonstrated its

mastery over us
by coercive involuted adult human speech. . .

He was a high-strung, intelligent miniature colt,
my size: —
     . . . the prize of my sixth birthday.

    •

Perhaps time and retrospect have improved our mutual absolute
trust, delight, connection: —
        but this was the first of those passionate

attachments, passionate
judgments that *here* like-*answers*-like, soul-*answers*-soul

which since my childhood, whether in relation to
animal, friend, an artist or
performer I've discovered, or work of art

                              (except where feeling has been
bewildered by the desire for
the reciprocation of erotic desire)

have never betrayed me, never when I have
encountered again in body or memory

                              WHAT I LOVED

seemed then stupid, ill-founded, grounded
merely in willfulness, more illusion. . .

              •

At nine, I was sent to boarding school.

The approach of this cataclysm held no allure for me,
rather I felt

rage and a sense of betrayal—;

but in fact, within a few weeks
books, the desire to dominate the attention of
my teachers, and even wary camaraderie with my peers

for the first time
                swallowed me. . .

When I, un-
willingly, arrived home on our first holidays,

I was told that several horses had come down with
a fever, including mine; *that my horse was dying.*

The next day he was carted off.

                        THERE WAS NO GRAVE.

Perhaps my earliest memory that is absolutely
fixed in scene and time

is the black horse flies big as thumbs
covering and clinging to his body, the weird unseasonable

blood-red sunset saturating the world

while I *knew* his body was being carried off but
howling I was held back within the house.

                •

Much later, when I was twelve, thirteen, fourteen,
in my dreams
                my little horse again and again

came back—;

he wanted to play, for me once again to mount
him and ride.

But I had no time: what I now was
interested in were friends, school, my studies,—

. . . besides, as I stood
next to him,

HE WAS TOO SMALL—;

I had grown, and he was now
TOO SMALL to ride—;

with a shiver, a stamp and sound of
torment, he seemed to take this in. . .

I told my friend's son that what he had felt in his dream
was nothing so simple as 'greed' or 'selfishness'—;

that later, in my
thirties, again I had known very similar emotions after

other deaths—; that there seemed to be something
STRUCTURAL in human relations

making what we had felt, well, 'impersonal.'

●

Though he thanked me for my generosity and
candor, and said that he felt not only

exhausted but somewhat
better, as I mounted the stairs to my room that night

what I felt was
woe, unameliorated, unappeased.

II

Now follows my

    'DREAM OF THE HISTORY OF PHILOSOPHY,'—

. . . for that night, in my room, as I threw off
my clothes, seeking in sleep only
oblivion, erasure of the throbbing but
irremediably ignorant *I*,

—angry at I did *NOT* know what,—

        above my bed I saw, again,
what since my
   first visit had hung there,

Volpato's fine
etching of Raphael's

'SCHOOL OF ATHENS'. . .

I remembered, with a sudden and flooding
access of pleasure, the first time I had seen, in

Rome, Raphael's fresco:—

here, under the image of the many-breasted
Goddess of Philosophy

(in a medallion in the ceiling)

flanked by two angels
announcing

'KNOWLEDGE OF THE CAUSES OF THINGS,'—

. . . at the center of the high arch of the fresco itself,

framed there by a vast, symmetrical,
seemingly stable but
essentially (at least according to
some writers) unbuildable architecture,—

. . . their two heads isolated by three great
descending central arches
that, dreamlike, open to the sky,—

. . . calmly presiding over an 'ideal' assembly of the great
philosophers of Antiquity

                         (not only metaphysicians and
scientists, but students, a soldier,
the leaning, listening figure of
Averroës, commentator, representative of Islam, —)

PLATO and ARISTOTLE

                      by their *parallel* but *opposite*

gestures (Aristotle
pointing downward, Plato upward, —)

                      DIVIDE and ORDER

this debating, brooding, teaching, writing, nearly
disharmonious multitude. . .

On the side of Aristotle, representatives of the 'exact'
sciences (Euclid, Ptolemy), with 'speculative'
thinkers (Heraclitus, Pythagoras) on the side of Plato. . .

Opposite gestures that, *JANUS-LIKE*, show
us where to seek the causes of things.

       •

In this 'ideal' community of the spirit, — the social

world as the social world
never is, —

       Death, Rage, and *Eros*

have receded to adorn recesses in the architecture: —

. . . on the left, under a yielding, even
voluptuous Apollo holding his lyre, an aging
triton seizes the breast of a resisting sea nymph —;

. . . on the right, Medusa's severed
face, mouth frozen open in an *O* of horror, from
Athena's victorious shield stares

powerless: —
       Athena, Goddess of Wisdom, protector of
the *Home, Family, Reason, Civilization. . .*

      •

When I first saw this scene (—the title
'School of Athens' a misapprehension

imposed on it in the eighteenth century, —)

I was largely ignorant of the intricate
iconography
       connecting the room's four walls and ceiling: —

'*Philosophy*' looks across at '*Theology*,'

                       while '*Poetry*'

faces '*Jurisprudence*,'—each

itself divided: 'Canon
Law' and 'Civil Law'. . .

—In the interrelations and elegant
distinctions informing its walls and ceiling,
this is a compendium, even synthesis of

Renaissance speculative, religious, aesthetic thinking:—

an 'ideal' Renaissance TEMPLE OF THE HUMAN MIND. . .

Its premise,—
                the Neo-Platonic Christian-Humanist
confidence that the world's obdurate
contradictions, terrifying
unintelligibility, can be tamed by
                      CLASSIFICATION,—

time now has effaced.

       •

This room,—
                intended as the site of the Pope's personal

library, then where he signed, before assembled
dignitaries of the highest Papal
tribunals, bulls and official documents,—

was the first of the rooms that Raphael
painted for the Pope:—

                 only twenty-five, with
little reputation, he had been summoned from
Florence to Rome
                at the suggestion of his
patron, Bramante, architect of the new St. Peter's. . .

Decoration of the room was already
begun—;
         but no one is certain how much

Sodoma, six years Raphael's
senior, had completed:—

for when the Pope saw Raphael's sketches

(*there is never enough wall space
here, at the center of power,—*)

he ordered everything that Sodoma had painted destroyed.

          •

In the fresco, next to Raphael's own
self-portrait, is the face of
                              Sodoma—;

both stand behind Euclid (geometry is
central to the painter's skill at perspective,—)

'Euclid' has the head of Bramante. . .

Raphael, without
illusions, looks out at us—;
                              Sodoma
smiles,—
            without rancor or humiliation
absorbed in the conversation before him.

      •

In this 'ideal' COMMUNITY OF THE SPIRIT,

Socrates and Aristotle are modelled on
antique busts, but Plato

has the features of Leonardo:—

Heraclitus (self-enclosed but
writing), the short, hooded, stonecutter's
smock of a *pensieroso*
                              Michelangelo. . .

'The Apollo who

          SHARES REIGN

                    with Athena here

is the god, not of reason, but P O E T R Y,—'

I said to myself as I began to fall asleep;

and then,
fixing the arc of the fresco before my mind:—

'Here,—everyone feels it,—
the gesture of PLATO and the gesture of ARISTOTLE

are O N E. . .'

Knowing that I loved it, my friend once had
placed the 'School of Athens'

above my bed. Smiling, now I
remembered this. . . *'Now I*

must sleep.'

                   •

Then, to my humiliation and shame,

                        I was *IN* it,—

that tumultuous, perished world (now
NOT perished,—)
                          lay before me:—

out of estrangement I had gained or been given
entrance: privilege

in no way earned—;

above me, past the Temple's
multitudinous, strangely empty rising steps,

                                   Ptolemy still
held aloft
the green-and-blue *GLOBE OF THE EARTH*,—

. . . then (as I turned to crouch, or
hide—)
           from the distance on either side I saw a long

row of men, dressed in the varied
garments of succeeding

centuries, approach the steps where I stood.

          •

When each figure
passed me, for a moment looking into my eyes

full-face, I tried to recognize him:—

there (just as I had imagined
them in the light of their portraits)

was BRUNO, one button missing

on his long black scholar's gown, still
smelling of sulphur from the fires of the Inquisition—

he held a book titled *Feast of Ashes*;—

DESCARTES, priestlike

in devotion to his self-made
revolution: heavy-lidded, as if worn out by
thought, or lessons at dawn for the Queen of Sweden;—

HEGEL and SCHELLING, walking

hand-in-hand, as in the morning of their young
collaboration, before distance, fame, silence.

●

. . . These, and so many others (*each*

alive as his voice on the page:—

each body now inseparable from its

fate, yet with the unachieved,
purposeful will of the living—)

ascended the steps, and,
                    WITHOUT
BARRIER,
            began to listen and mix and speak

in earnest debate, yet strangers' courteous deference,
with the philosophers of Antiquity. . .

Irrational happiness seized me:—
not at the absence of discord (discord

will come) but to see

this that at last lies before
me is as I have known real.

After chimeras of CONTINGENCY and resistless
SELF-ESTRANGEMENT,—

. . . to see chimeras of the real.

                    •

Then, something happened which I did
not expect
            even in a dream:—

as if compelled or drawn by inner
necessity, DIVIDING they rushed to join themselves

into GROUPS:—
                    groups that, now, I saw

had been there, though I had never seen them

(—but my words are mere
summary, for what I remembered when I

woke, seemed the faithless shadow of what I had seen).

                    •

First the movement pressed to the right, where
next to Ptolemy (wearing on his
gown a resplendent globe of the heavens)
                                        Archimedes

leaning down to the stone beneath them drew his circles:—

here, around these
two figures,

          gathered *Materialists, Mathematical
Naturalists, Positivists*

                    (I recognized Hobbes—; Comte
arguing with Descartes—; then, restlessly circling at

the edges of the group,
                         D'Alembert, whose ironic smile

seemed to mock the dreams of the metaphysicians)

. . . all those thinkers who see
within the indecipherable, furious
cataract of life, within bewildering, annihilating

FLUX, a great *intelligible* P R O C E S S:—

measurable, universal Nature,—
                              impartial, non-censorious,

whose unbreakable chain of unvarying, coherent Laws

frees us from the prison-house of human
superstition, religious dogma, hallucination. . .

Here 'mind' and 'consciousness' are
body—; 'free-will,'
darkness still-undispelled by science.

Now Comte,—
                systematizer of
Positivism, standing as if confident that he is

heir to the immense authority (confirming its
insight into reality) conferred on science

by its transformation of the world,—

announces to devoted, listening
thinkers from all nations

(*his face flushed, eyes shrewd but credulous*)

a new CLERGY: a scientific-industrial
elite henceforth translating to

expectant, hungry Society

'*invariable laws*' new-found by fecund science. . .

•

As he spoke, Descartes (abruptly
once again the French
cavalier, setting forth with bold stride)

disengaged himself from

all these figures, turning his gaze
irresistibly toward
the center of the Temple:—

to a *second* GROUP, which had

assembled, arranged itself
as if magnetized

around SOCRATES as its center:—

with an old,

god-like Plato and
young Aristotle
each writing down his words at his feet.

Here the conviction that Mind, Spirit, Consciousness
are merely an *interpolation*

in the immense text of the physical universe

was *reversed*:—

as Socrates spoke (among those listening

I saw Plotinus; Cicero; Christian
theologians: Augustine held the *Confessions*;
Thomas Aquinas distractedly
fingered strands of straw from a crown of straw on his head,—)

as he explained that through *DIALECTIC*,

dialogue, argument by

CONTRADICTION proceeding to the reconciliation of
contradiction (for only contradiction

impels *thought*, and what is *thought*

but the silently-occurring internal dialogue
of the soul with itself?—)

(pugnosed and pugnacious, Socrates
yet made me feel that he had seen in
spirit what he struggled to express in words—)

. . . as he explained that through dialectic, our power of
reason,
>we can make our way to an order

past the delusions of custom, self-deception, desire,—

and can then, by an act of
choice,
>CHANGE,—correct our lives:—

suddenly, from behind his
voice, blending with his voice,

was a woman's voice:—

(I moved slightly to the left, to see its
source)

>. . . there, with the seated figures of
Dante and Sappho (who grasped
disintegrating pages of a book in her hand)
>>rapt, silent before her,

was S C H E H E R A Z A D E,—

                         seated on an embroidered
pillow, wearing transparent
silks, plucking an instrument,—

whose wizard songs (I have known them since
my youth)
            beguile the sword that hangs above her.

        •

Troubled, excited voices
soon broke my attention; turning back, I saw

the circle of listeners now had divided into
disputing factions:—

                while Augustine, standing
to one side, stared out at them. . .

—What one thinker confidently
asserted, another spurned as illusion—;

what one human being
flew from, another sought—;

some struggled to reconcile the wisdom of
Greece
        with Christ's revelation—

while other, melancholy voices
doubted the free sufficient autonomy of

reason and the *human will*

faced with our confusion, weak and isolated
organs of perception, helplessness. . .

The abrupt arrival of Descartes
                                    (for the first time, I noticed
that the hair thickly
growing beneath his lower

lip, on one side, was *shaved off*—)

                              then, later, of the stooped,

slightly built Kant, with his
cane and three-cornered hat, his features
hardened as if by the strain of thought,

brought brief ORDER to this spectacle:—

                              . . . but Augustine, pushing
past all this with a gesture of
revulsion that seemed to rise from an intuition
indistinguishable from himself,

—his hands now
empty,—

already had abandoned the scene before him, turning to

a third, *final* GROUP, gathered at
the left of the temple, whose center was

Pythagoras and Heraclitus. . .

      ●

From this milling, mercurial crowd
                    (—Hegel now looked
at one moment like
Bismarck, at another like Shelley—)

words emerge: —

        Master and Slave. Predestination. Preservation of
the Species. God immanent in
Nature. Race. Blood.
            Stages of absolute mind. Progress. Class.
The inexorable laws of History, the Psyche, the Age.
                    Logos. The world
as will and idea. The One. The inescapable
society of the dead and the living, who have made us what we are. . .

Here the Materialists have been, as it were,
turned on their heads: —

now S P I R I T, —
        immanent, transcendent, or unknowable, —

is *ground* of body, *governs* body:—

... the single human psyche
powerless within the immeasurable
power of its laws, goals, will.

●

Reached by daring to contemplate in a calm spirit
COHERENCE (or by hard, practiced
submission)

        'freedom' here is to *accept* NECESSITY—;

or else, when intolerable existence
wholly becomes the snake that swallows its own
tail, *to smash the head of the snake.*

Here ceaseless human choices, decisions, dilemmas,
mortality itself

is illusion:—
        the cunning used upon us to
silence the voice
within that says, *Someone else led my life.*
I am an onlooker on my own life. . .

●

Then, among those listening to
Schopenhauer, I saw my dead friend, —

. . . I am *certain* that I saw him, though

when I approached him, standing
just behind him, —
                   when he
turned at my touch, —

                        his head was a C L O U D

dispersed into discrete
atoms; as if I had drawn too close to a painting
made out of discrete spots of separate color,

HE was no longer *THERE*. . .

                   •

Inheritor inheriting inheritors, he had worked to
transform an inheritance

transformed
in its turn: —
                   as if the soul, delivered over unconscious and

defenseless not only to this world of
things, but to its own DARKNESS, —

. . . flinging itself into the compensations that the world
and its own self

offer it, but finding the light of *self-knowledge*
only through
                    mediation, through WORKS and SIGNS,—

. . . seeing and remaking itself within that broken
mirror made by all the things that it has
inherited and remade,—

. . . in the end, alienates its being in them.

                         •

The spectral E M P T I N E S S became only
emptier before me

as I advanced toward him,—

. . . until at last, surrounded by
nothing, with resignation

turning I drew back.—

Not before Augustine,
                         engaged in animated

argument with Spinoza and Bruno, was embraced by
Luther: appalled, recoiling, he fled.

•

Now, as I lay
dreaming in the house of my dead friend,

finally I saw the THREE GROUPS
in one view: —

            I was exhausted, I wanted to
stop, at last to have reached *bottom*: —

. . . but busy figures ceaselessly rushed
between the groups, trying to

mediate: —
            for all these conflicting intuitions

surely were grounded in the nature of the universe: —

in the relationship between the impenetrable,
immeasurable

UNIVERSE that lies *WITHIN* as well as beyond us

and the solitary, finite
perceiving mind: —

            •

. . . indeed, I felt pain at this scene: —to see

PHILOSOPHY itself

divided, torn
into three, or even more directions—;

. . . the unity of my being torn,

for I had felt recognition
before the truth that united *each* group in its turn. . .

●

But as I strove for
unity of thought, in vain the mediators

hastened to and fro among the groups:—

. . . now a hostile
alienation envelops them, the distance between them

increases, the ground

DISAPPEARS
beneath their bewildered, desperate feet. . .

●

The Temple itself, then, collapsed.

As the ground engulfed, swallowed all that I had seen,

(—this *'tradition'* that I cannot
THINK MY LIFE

without, nor POSSESS IT within—;)

the frozen facial mask of
Medusa, hung on Athena's shield, suddenly

smiled. *Smirked.*

III

Then I wanted to shout at this destruction, this
ruin, not only

in pain, but in relief:—

> *Whenever human beings have felt*
conviction that what they possess is indeed

'KNOWLEDGE OF THE CAUSES OF THINGS,'—

. . . whenever this conviction has been
shared by, animated a whole
society, or significant group within society,—

the ancient hegemony of POWER *and* PRIESTHOOD
is reconstituted:—

  implicit within each
vision of cause, a structure of power:—

  an imagination not only of
where power resides, but should, must reside. . .

•

At the end of the First Crusade,
  when their goal
JERUSALEM
  fell at last before the Crusaders,

Christian troops running through the streets
stabbed, mutilated, slew
  everyone they saw:—

the savagery of the massacre
perhaps *unexampled* (these
facts, I assure you, a matter of record,—)

in the history of wars fought mainly for *gain* or *glory:—*

. . . in the narrow lanes, rivers of blood carrying headless
bodies and fragments of bodies

reached the horses' hocks —;

. . . the Jewish community, huddling for safety in
the central synagogue,
                    was barricaded

in by the Crusaders, and burnt alive —;

after two days, when, gone like
snow on the lawn in a hot sun,

the frenzy of RIGHTEOUS ANGER and REVENGE

had passed, the few thousand still
alive from a population that before numbered forty thousand

were assembled
near the gates, and sold as slaves.

— Damascus and Baghdad
were shocked at the fate of the Holy City, vowing

recompense.

                    •

The *'moral law within'*

                    (for Kant, the ground
of the moral life itself, certain, beautiful, fixed

like the processional of stars above our heads)

is near to MADNESS—; everything terrible
but buried in human motivation
                                    released, justified

by self-righteousness and fanaticism. . .

                    •

Then, as I struggled to find words
to *punish* confidence in the possession of truth,

I had the sick sensation of
falling, the stones were

cracking, giving way beneath my

feet, and suddenly, *at the same time,*
I knew that nothing that I,—
                                    heir
to the ages,—

                    might reach or understand or grasp

will lodge safe
in *unhistorical* existence—; safe

within the hungry blankness of a culture WITHOUT
WISDOM, its wisdom the negative
wisdom embraced by exhaustion after
centuries of the Wars of Religion. . .

●

Thus, infected with the desolation of
history's
            leprosy,—leprosy of SPIRIT,—
                                    the stones

breaking, disappearing as my working legs
flailed in air,—

I woke.
            Despair was what I felt.
                                    At last, after fitful, thrashing

sleeplessness, again I slept, and for
a final time that night, dreamt:—

●

. . . A brown, wide, desolate, broken only by
scars and protuberances, dun landscape

stretched without boundary before me.

Then, stooping, staring
out into this barrenness,

I realized that on my back I was carrying

—*had* carried
all my life,—

        the ENTRAILS of my horse—;

secret, familiar
weight, either chosen or thrust upon me too long ago

now to put down, or often remember.

        ●

What at one moment looked parched, dun, desolate,
the next moment was
        ochre, glowing, burnished:—

as I walked, what first had seemed
scars, as if the earth were WOUNDED too

deeply to heal without visible
mark, now I saw

were deep PITS dug by men and women who
slowly carried
        the earth dug

out of the pits, heaping it up to make
the hill next to each hole.

Other women and men

filled in other pits, leveling these hills.

Two signs stood against the horizon: —

THE GREAT ACT OF BURYING

THE GREAT ACT OF DIGGING UP

Because these human beings seemed
concentrated, *absorbed*, —

at moments anxious, even

tormented, at others earnest, eager
as if *answering their nature*, —

. . . I could not tell whether this work was
freedom, or servitude.

•

Then suddenly entangling my feet were
dozens of just-born

lambs, stretching their necks to reach their

mothers next to them: —

hungry, sucking mouths
stretched toward swollen, distended
udders that I saw must be

painful *unless* sucked—;

                    Reciprocity! I thought,—

Not the chick within the egg, who by eating its way
out, must destroy the egg to become itself.

          ●

Then, as I reached to steady the entrails
on my back,
          I bent down to watch more closely:—

. . . hypnotized, I saw eager lambs
                 suck the paps of an

at-one-moment
yielding, relieved, even voluptuously

satisfied, but at-the-next-moment
sleepy, withdrawing, now
              indifferent, *hostile* Nature. . .

I felt again that
PENETRATION OF KNOWLEDGE that is almost like

illness, an invading sickness:—

envious, yet afraid of
getting kicked in the head, I wanted

to live against a ewe's
breathing, sleeping side.

●

—When at last both ewes and lambs
slept,
    I walked to the edge of a pit:—

. . . there, standing
at the bottom, looking up at me,

                           was my little horse:—

I was *afraid*—; had he forgiven what
must have seemed to him, unfaithfulness?

—WAS unfaithfulness?—

I worked my way down the steep, loose,
yielding sides of the pit.

When I reached bottom, as I lay his
entrails before him,
            I saw that they had become

my color, after years of carrying them—;

. . . slowly, he bent down his
head, sniffed, then

        ATE the entrails—;

expectant, he
looked up at me:—

       as I climbed on his

back, startled once again by his
animal warmth as I clung to him,

                —now
somehow *NEITHER*
NOT the same size, nor the same size,—

we rose
out of the pit, and I woke.

Though I had no impulse to relate this dream to
the categories and figures dreamt earlier,—

though I had no evidence whether it issued from
the gate of *Ivory* or the gate of *Horn*,—

(from which gate *true* dreams come, and which
false, frankly

       I've never been able to remember,—)

as I retell it, the *ashheap* begins to GLOW AGAIN:—

. . . for I woke
with a sense of

beneficence: an emotion which, though it did *not*
erase, transformed
              what earlier had overwhelmed

consciousness lying sleepless between dream and dream."

       •

This is the end of the first hour of the night.

DESIRE

(1997)

I

As the Eye to the Sun

To Plotinus what we seek is VISION, what
wakes when we wake to desire

as the eye to the sun

It is just as if you should fall in love with
one of the sparrows which fly by

when we wake to desire

But once you have seen a hand cut off, or
a foot, or a head, you have embarked, have begun

as the eye to the sun

The voyage, such is everything, you have not come to
shore, but little children and their sports and

when we wake to desire

Poor spirits carrying about bodies of the dead,
for bodies give way but the spirit will not give way

as the eye to the sun

You know that every instrument, too, vessel, mere
hammer, if it does that for which it was made

when we wake to desire

Is well, yet he who made it is not there, is dead:
so, unaverted, one, not one, to NOTHING you ask

as the eye to the sun

May I be made into the vessel of that which
must be made

when we wake to desire

Certain what you have reached is not shore you
shall disappear in that which produced you

as the eye to the sun

But once you have seen a hand cut off you have begun

Love Incarnate

(DANTE, *Vita Nuova*)

To all those driven berserk or humanized by love
this is offered, for I need help
deciphering my dream.
When we love our lord is LOVE.

When I recall that at the fourth hour
of the night, watched by shining stars,
LOVE at last became incarnate,
the memory is horror.

In his hands smiling LOVE held my burning
heart, and in his arms, the body whose greeting
pierces my soul, now wrapped in bloodred, sleeping.

He made him wake. He ordered him to eat
my heart. He ate my burning heart. He ate it
submissively, as if afraid, as LOVE wept.

Overheard Through the Walls
of the Invisible City

. . . telling those who swarm around him his desire
is that an appendage from each of them
fill, invade each of his orifices, —

repeating, chanting,
Oh yeah   Oh yeah   Oh yeah   Oh yeah   Oh yeah

until, as if in darkness he craved the sun, at last he reached
consummation.

—Until telling those who swarm around him begins again

(we are the wheel to which we are bound).

Adolescence

He stared up into my eyes with a look
I can almost see now.

He had that look in his eyes
that bore right into mine.

I could sense that he *knew* I was
envious of what he was doing—; and *knew* that I'd

always wish I had known at the time
what he was doing was something I'd always

crave in later life, just as he did.

He was enjoying what he was doing.
The look was one of pure rapture.

He was gloating. He knew.

I still remember his look.

Catullus: Excrucior

I hate and—love. The sleepless body hammering a nail nails itself, hanging crucified.

Borges and I

We fill pre-existing forms and when we fill them we change them and are changed.

The desolating landscape in Borges' "Borges and I"—in which the voice of "I" tells us that its other self, Borges, is the self who makes literature, who in the process of making literature falsifies and exaggerates, while the self that is speaking to us now must go on living so that Borges may continue to fashion literature—is seductive and even oddly comforting, but, I think, false.

The voice of this "I" asserts a disparity between its essential self and its worldly second self, the self who seeks embodiment through making things, through work, who in making takes on something false, inessential, inauthentic.

The voice of this "I" tells us that Spinoza understood that everything wishes to continue in its own being, a stone wishes to be a stone eternally, that all "I" wishes is to remain unchanged, itself.

With its lonely emblematic title, "Borges and I" seems to be offered as a paradigm for the life of consciousness, the life of knowing and making, the life of the writer.

The notion that Frank has a self that has remained the same and that knows what it would be if its writing self did not exist—like all assertions about the systems that hold sway beneath the moon, the opposite of this seems to me to be true, as true.

When Borges' "I" confesses that Borges falsifies and exaggerates it seems to do so to cast aside falsity and exaggeration, to attain an entire candor unobtainable by Borges.

This "I" therefore allows us to enter an inaccessible magic space, a hitherto inarticulate space of intimacy and honesty earlier denied us, where voice, for the first time, has replaced silence.

— Sweet fiction, in which bravado and despair beckon from a cold panache, in which the protected essential self suffers flashes of its existence to be immortalized by a writing self that is incapable of performing its actions without mixing our essence with what is false.

Frank had the illusion, when he talked to himself in the clichés he used when he talked to himself, that when he made his poems he was changed in making them, that arriving at the order the poem suddenly arrived at out of the chaos of the materials the poem let enter itself out of the chaos of life, consciousness then, only then, could know itself, Sherlock Holmes was somebody or something before cracking its first case but not Sherlock Holmes, ACT is the cracked mirror not only of motive but self, *no other way*, tiny mirror that fails to focus in small the whole of the great room.

But Frank had the illusion that his poems also had cruelly replaced his past, that finally they were all he knew of it though he knew they were not, everything else was shards refusing to make a pattern and in any case he had written about his mother and father until the poems saw as much as he saw and saw more and he only saw what he saw in the act of making them.

He had never had a self that wished to continue in its own being, survival meant ceasing to be what its being was.

Frank had the illusion that though the universe of one of his poems seemed so close to what seemed his own universe at the second of writing it that he wasn't sure how they differed even though the paraphernalia often differed, after he had written it its universe was never exactly his universe, and so, soon, it disgusted him a little, the mirror was dirty and cracked.

Secretly he was glad it was dirty and cracked, because after he had made a big order, a book, only when he had come to despise it a little, only after he had at last given up the illusion that this was what was, only then could he write more.

He felt terror at the prospect of becoming again the person who could find or see or make no mirror, for even Olivier, trying to trap the beast who had killed his father, when he suavely told Frank as Frank listened to the phonograph long afternoons lying on the bed as a kid, when Olivier told him what art must be, even Olivier insisted that art is a mirror held up by an artist who himself needs to see something, held up before a nature that recoils before it.

We fill pre-existing forms and when we fill them we change them and are changed.

Everything in art is a formal question, so he tried to do it in prose with much blank white space.

Homo Faber

Whatever lies still uncarried from the abyss within
me as I die dies with me.

In Memory of Joe Brainard

the remnant of a vast, oceanic
bruise (wound delivered early and long ago)

was in you purity and
sweetness self-gathered, CHOSEN

•

When I tried to find words for the moral sense that unifies
and sweetens the country voices in your collage *The Friendly Way,*

you said *It's a code.*

You were a code
I yearned to decipher.—

In the end, the plague that full swift runs by
took you, broke you;—

> *in the end, could not*
> *take you, did not break you—*

you had somehow erased within you not only
meanness, but anger, the desire to punish
the universe for everything

not achieved, *not* tasted, seen again, touched—;

. . . the undecipherable
code unbroken even as the soul

learns once again the body it loves and hates is
made of earth, and will betray it.

The Yoke

don't worry   I know you're dead
but tonight

turn your face again
toward me

when I hear your voice there is now
no direction in which to turn

I sleep and wake and sleep and wake and sleep and wake and

but tonight
turn your face again

toward me

see   upon my shoulders is the yoke
that is not a yoke

don't worry   I know you're dead
but tonight

turn your face again

Lady Bird

Neither an invalid aunt who had been asked to care for a sister's
little girl, to fill the dead sister's place, nor the child herself

did, could: not in my Daddy's eyes—nor
should they;

        so when we followed that golden couple into the White House

I was aware that people look at
the living, and wish for the dead.

If I Could Mourn Like a Mourning Dove

It is what recurs that we believe,
your face not at one moment looking
sideways up at me anguished or

elate, but the old words welling up by
gravity rearranged:
two weeks before you died in

pain worn out, after my usual casual sign-off
with *All my love*, your simple
solemn *My love to you, Frank.*

The Return

As the retreating Bructeri began to burn their own
possessions, to deny to the Romans every sustenance but
ashes,

      a flying column sent by Germanicus
commanded by Lucius Stertinius

routed them;
         and there, discovered amid plunder and the dead,

was the Eagle of the nineteenth
legion, lost with Varus.

      •

The Romans now
brought to the land of the Bructeri,—to whatever lay
between the river Ems and the river Lippe,
to the very edge of their territory,—
           devastation;

until they reached at last

the Teutoburgian Wood,
      in whose darkness

Varus and the remains of his fifteen thousand men,
it was said, lay unburied.

•

Germanicus then conceived a desire
to honor with obsequies these unburied warriors whose
massacre once filled Augustus himself with rage and
shame,—
      with hope or fear every corner of the Empire,—

while the least foot soldier, facing alien
terrain, was overcome with pity when he

thought of family, friends, the sudden
reversals of battle, and shared human fate.

•

First Caecina and his men
entered,—
      ordered to reconnoitre the dismal

treacherous passes, to attempt to build bridges and
causeways across the uneven, sodden marshland,—

then the rest of the army, witness to scenes
rending to sight and memory of sight.

•

Varus' first camp, with its wide sweep and deployment
of ordered space in confident dimension,
testified to the calm labors of three legions;—

then a ruined half-wall and shallow ditch
showed where a desperate remnant had
been driven to take cover;—

                              on the open ground between them

were whitening bones, free
from putrefaction,—

                      scattered where men had been struck down
fleeing, heaped up

where they had stood their ground before slaughter.

Fragments of spears and horses' limbs lay
intertwined, while human

                              skulls were nailed

like insults to the tree-trunks.

Nearby groves held the altars
on which the savage Germans
sacrificed the tribunes and chief centurions.

•

Survivors of the catastrophe slowly began, at last,
to speak, —
                    the handful who had escaped death or slavery

told their fellow soldiers where the generals
fell, how the Eagles and standards were seized; —

one showed where Varus received his first wound, and
another, where he died by his own melancholy hand; —

those thrown into crude pits saw
gibbets above them,
                    as well as the platform from which Arminius

as if in delirium harangued
his own victorious troops, —

fury and rancor so joined to his
joy, the imprisoned men thought they would soon be butchered, —

until desecration of the Eagles at last satisfied
or exhausted his arrogance.

•

And so, six years after the slaughter,
a living Roman army had returned
to bury the dead men's bones of three whole legions, —

no man knew whether the remains that he had
gathered, touched perhaps in consigning to the earth, were

those of a stranger or a friend: —

all thought of all
as comrades and
bloodbrothers; each, in common rising

fury against the enemy, mourned at once and hated.

●

When these events were reported to Rome

Cynics whispered that *thus* the cunning State
enslaves us to its failures and its fate. —

Epicureans saw in the ghostly mire
an emblem of the nature of Desire. —

Stoics replied that life is War, ILLUSION
the source, the goal, the end of human action.

●

At the dedication of the funeral
mound, Germanicus laid the first earth, —

thereby honoring the dead, and choosing to demonstrate
in his own person his
heartfelt share in the general grief.

He thereby earned the disapproval of Tiberius,—

perhaps because the Emperor interpreted
every action of Germanicus unfavorably; or he may have felt

the spectacle of the unburied dead
must give the army less alacrity for battle and more
respect for the enemy—
                              while a commander belonging to

the antique priesthood of the Augurs
pollutes himself by handling
objects belonging to the dead.

       •

          on the open ground

whitening bones scattered where men had been struck down
fleeing

      heaped up

where they stood their ground

Varus' first camp with its
wide sweep

　　　　across the open ground

the ruined
half-wall and shallow ditch

　　　　　　　　on the open ground between them

whitening bones scattered where men had been struck down
fleeing

　　　　heaped up

where they stood their ground

I have returned here a thousand times,
though history cannot tell us its location.

　　　　•

Arminius, relentlessly pursued by
Germanicus, retreated into pathless country.

(AFTER TACITUS, *ANNALS*, I, 60–63)

A Coin for Joe, with the Image of a Horse; c350–325 B.C.

COIN

chip of the closed, — L O S T *world, toward whose unseen grasses*

this long-necked emissary horse

               eagerly still
               stretches, to graze

•

                          World; Grass;

stretching Horse; — ripe with hunger, bright circle
of appetite, risen to feed and famish us, from exile underground. . . for

you   chip of the incommensurate
closed world   *A n g e l*

II

The Second Hour of the Night

On such a night

> after the countless

assemblies, countless solemnities, the infinitely varied
voyagings in storm and in calm observing the differences

among those who are born, who live together, and die,

●

On such a night

> *at that hour when*

slow bodies like automatons begin again to move down

into the earth beneath the houses in which they
live bearing the bodies they desired and killed and now

bury in the narrow crawl spaces and unbreathing abrupt
descents and stacked leveled spaces these used

bodies make them dig and open out and hollow for new
veins whose ore could have said *I have been loved* but whose

voice has been rendered silent by the slow bodies whose descent
into earth is as fixed as the skeletons buried within them

 ●

On such a night

 at that hour in the temple of

delight, when appetite
feeds on itself, —

 ●

On such a night, perhaps, Berlioz wrote those pages

in his autobiography which I first read when my mother
was dying, and which to me now inextricably
call up

 not only her death but her life: —

"A sheet already covered her. I drew it back.

Her portrait, painted in the days of
her splendor,

 hung beside the bed—

I will not attempt to describe the grief that possessed me.

It was complicated by something, *incommensurate,*
tormenting, I had always found hardest to bear—

a sense of pity.

Terrible, overmastering

pity swept through me at everything she had suffered:—

Before our marriage,
her bankruptcy.

(*Dazed, almost*
appalled by the magnitude of her sudden
and early Paris triumph—as Ophelia, as Juliet—
she risked the fortune fame had brought
on the fidelity of a public without memory.)

Her accident.

(*Just before a benefit*
performance designed to lessen, if not
erase her debts, a broken leg left her
NOT—as the doctors feared—lame, but visibly
robbed of confidence and ease of movement.)

Her humiliating
return to the Paris stage.

*(After Ophelia's
death, which a few years earlier at her debut
harrowed the heart of Paris, the cruel
audience did not recall her to the stage
once, though it accorded others an ovation.)*

Her decision, made voluntarily but forever
mourned, to give up her art.

Extinction of her reputation.

The wounds each of us
inflicted on the other.

Her not-to-be-extinguished, insane JEALOUSY,—
. . . which, in the end, had cause.

Our separation, after eleven years.

The enforced
absence of our son.

Her delusion that she had forfeited the regard of
the English public, through her attachment to France.

Her broken heart.

Her vanished beauty.

Her ruined health. (Corrosive, and growing,
physical pain.)

The loss of speech, —
. . . and movement.

The impossibility of making herself understood in any way.

The long vista of death and oblivion stretching before her
as she lay paralyzed for four years, inexorably dying.

   My brain shrivels in my skull
at the horror, the PITY of it.

Her simple tomb bears the inscription:

   *Henriette-Constance Berlioz-Smithson, born at
   Ennis in Ireland, died at Montmartre 3rd March 1854*

At eight in the evening the day of her death
as I struggled across Paris to notify
the Protestant minister required for the ceremony,

the cab in which I rode, *vehicle
conceived in Hell*, made a detour and

took me past the Odeon: —

it was brightly lit for a play then much in vogue.

There, twenty-six years before, I discovered
Shakespeare and Miss Smithson at the same moment.

Hamlet. Ophelia. There
I saw Juliet for the first and last time.

Within the darkness of that arcade on many
winter nights I feverishly
paced or watched frozen in despair.

Through that door I saw her enter
for a rehearsal of *Othello.*

She was unaware of the existence of
the pale dishevelled youth with
haunted eyes staring after her—

*There I asked the gods to allow her
future to rest in my hands.*

If anyone should ask you, Ophelia, whether the unknown
youth without reputation or position
leaning back within the darkness of a pillar

will one day become your
husband and prepare your last journey—

with your great inspired eyes

answer, *He is a harbinger of woe.*"

•

On such a night, at such an hour

she who still carries within her body the growing
body made by union with what she once loved, and now

craves or
loathes, she cannot say —;

she who has seen the world and her own self and the gods

within the mirror of
Dionysus, as it were —

compelled to labor since birth in care of the care-
needing thing into which she had entered; —

. . . Myrrha, consigning now to

the body heavier and heavier within her
what earlier she could consign only to air,

requests

in death transformation to nothing
human, to be not alive, not dead.

II

Ovid tells the tale: —

     or, rather, Ovid tells us that

Orpheus sang it
in that litany of tales with which he

filled the cruel silence after Eurydice
had been sucked back down into the underworld
cruelly and he driven back cruelly
from descending into it again to save her. . .

He sang it on a wide green plain
without shade,
    but there the trees, as if
mimicking the attending beasts and birds, hearing his song

came to listen: the alder, the yew, the laurel
and pine whose young sweet nut
is dear to the mother of the gods since under it
Attis castrated himself to become her votary and vessel. . .

Beasts; birds; trees; but by his will
empty of gods or men.

    •

In each tale of love he sang, —

Ganymede; Apollo and
Hyacinthus; Pygmalion; Adonis avenged upon
Venus; the apples that Atalanta found irresistible, —

fate embedded in the lineaments of desire

(desire itself helplessly surrounded by what cannot be
eluded, what
even the gods call GIVEN, —)

at last, in bitter or sweet enforcement, finds

transformation (except for the statue
Pygmalion makes human) to an inhuman, un-
riven state, become an element, indelible,
common, in the common, indelible, given world. . .

The story of Myrrha, mother of Adonis, is of all
these tales for good reason the least known.

It is said that Cinyras, her father, had he been
childless, might have died a happy man.

Famed both for his gold and for his beauty, Cinyras
had become King of Cyprus and of Byblus

by marrying the daughter of the king, Myrrha's
mother, whose father had become king by marrying the daughter

of the king, Myrrha's mother's
mother, Paphos,—

. . . child
born from the union of Pygmalion and the statue.

When the eyes of Cinyras
followed, lingered upon her, Myrrha had the sensation
he was asking himself whether, in
another world, she could heal him.

Myrrha was Pygmalion and her father the statue.

He was Pygmalion and Myrrha the statue.

—As a dog whose body is sinking into quicksand
locks its jaws around a branch hanging
above it, the great teeth grasping so fiercely the stable world
they snap the fragile wood,—

. . . Myrrha looped a rope over the beam above her bed

in order to hang herself.

What she wants she does not want.

The night she could no longer NOT tell herself
her secret, she knew that there had never
been a time she had not known it.

It was there like the island

that, night after
night, as she

wished herself to sleep, she embellished
the approach to:—

the story has many beginnings, but one ending—

out of the air she has invented it, air
she did not invent

•

In the earliest version whose making and remaking Myrrha
remembers,
                  she and her father escape from Cyprus

in a small boat, swallowed, protected
by a storm that blackens sea and stars;

he has been stripped of power by advisors of the dead
old king, father of Myrrha's mother, Queen
Cenchreis, and now, the betrayers make Cenchreis

head of state,—

Cinyras in the storm shouts that they have made his
wife their pawn, and Myrrha shouts that many
long have thought
                    they are HERS,—

. . . the storm, after days,
abandons them to face a chartless, terrifying horizon.

Then, the island.

In the version that Myrrha now
tells herself since both her father and mother as
King and Queen insist that with their concurrence

soon, from among the royal
younger sons who daily arrive at court as rivals for
her bed, she must choose a husband—

both for her own natural happiness, and
to secure the succession,—

. . . now she is too violated by the demand that she marry

to invent reasons why the story that she
tells herself to calm herself to sleep begins with
a powerless king standing next to his
daughter in a tiny boat as they stare out at
a distant, yearned-for, dreaded island. . .

On the island, later, she again and again relives
stepping onto the island.

Each of them knows what will happen here: —

. . . she can delay, he can delay
because what is sweet about
deferral is that what arrives

despite it, is revealed as inevitable: —

she is awake
only during the lucid
instant between what she recognizes

must happen, and what happens: —

each of them knows that the coldest eye looking
down at them, here, must look without blame: —

now, the king
hesitates —

      he refuses to place his foot upon the shore: —

. . . the illusion of rescue from what he is, what
she is, soon must recede, once on
land everything
not nature fall away,

as unstarved springs

divide them from all that
divide them from themselves: —

bulls fuck cows they
sired, Zeus himself fathered Dionysus-Zagreus
upon Persephone, his daughter: —

beasts and gods, those
below us and those above us, open
unhuman eyes

when they gaze upon what they desire
unstained by disgust or dread or terror: —

. . . Myrrha, watching him, now once again can close her eyes
upon sleep. She sees him

step onto the island. He has entered her.

●

Grief for the unlived life, grief
which, in middle age or old age, as goad

or shroud, comes to all,

early became Myrrha's
familiar, her narcotic

chastisement, accomplice, master.

What each night she had given with such
extravagance,—

. . . when she woke, had not been given.

Grief for the unlived life, mourning
each morning renewed as Myrrha

woke, was there

and not there, for hours merely
the memory of itself, as if long ago

she told herself
a story (*weird*

dream of enslavement) that seemed
her story, but now she cannot

recollect why listening she could not
stop listening, deaf to any other. . .

But soon she heard the music beneath every other music:—

what she could not transform herself
into is someone

without memory, or need for memory: —

four steps forward then
one back, then three
back, then four forward. . .

Today when Myrrha's father reminded her that
on this date eighteen
years earlier her mother announced that he
was the man whom she would in one month

marry, —

and then, in exasperation, asked what Myrrha
wanted in a husband, unsupplied by the young men cluttering his
court in pursuit of her hand and his throne, —

after she, smiling, replied, "You,"

blushing, he turned
away, pleased. . .

Four steps forward then
one back, then three
back, then four forward: —

today her father, not ten feet from where
once, as a child, she had in
glee leapt upon him surrounded by

soldiers and he, then, pretending to be overwhelmed
by a superior force fell backwards with
her body clasped in his arms as they rolled
body over body down the long slope
laughing and that peculiar sensation of his weight
full upon her and then
not, then full upon her, then not,—

until at the bottom for a half-
second his full weight rested upon her, then not,—

. . . not ten feet from where what
never had been repeated except within
her today after reminding her that today her mother

exactly at her age chose him,—

after she had answered his question
with, "You,"

blushing, he turned
away, pleased. . .

There is a king inside the king that the king
does not acknowledge.

*Four steps forward then
one back, then three
back, then four forward:—*

. . . the illusion of movement without
movement, because you know that what you
move towards

(malignant in the eyes of gods and men)

isn't there:—

       doesn't exist:—

though the sensation of motion without
movement or end offers the hypnotic

solace of making not only each repeated
act but what cannot be repeated

an object of contemplation,—

. . . what by rumor servant girls, and slaves, as well as
a foreign queen

       taste, for Myrrha alone

isn't there, doesn't exist,
malignant in the eyes of gods and men. . .

The gods who made us either
didn't make us,—

. . . or loathe what they have made.

Four steps forward then
one back, then three
back, then four forward:—

. . . but you have lied about your
solace, for hidden, threaded

within repetition is the moment when each step
backward is a step
downward, when what you move toward moves toward

you lifting painfully his cloak to reveal his
wound, saying, *"love answers need"*. . .

Approaching death, for days Myrrha more and more
talked to the air:—

My element is the sea. I have seen

the underside of the surface of the sea, the glittering
inner surface more beautiful than the darkness below it,

seen it crossed

and re-crossed by a glittering ship from which dark eyes
peering downward must search the darkness.

Though they search, the eyes
fix upon nothing.

The glittering ship swiftly,
evenly, crosses and re-crosses.

No hand reaches down from it to penetrate the final
membrane dividing those whose element
is the sea, from those who breathe in the light above it.

The glittering ship captained by darkness
swiftly, evenly, crosses and

re-crosses.

I have seen it. I cannot
forget. Memory is a fact of the soul.

•

Hippolyta, Myrrha's nurse, thanked the gods
she heard the thump of the rope

hitting the wooden beam, the scrape of
the heavy stool moved into place,

and clasped Myrrha's legs
just as they kicked away the light that held them.

—The creature plummeting resistlessly to the sunless
bottom of the sea was
plucked up, and placed upon the shore.

She slept. After a period of indefinite
duration Hippolyta's voice almost uninflected

woke her, saying that now her nurse must
know the reason for her action.

Failure had made her Hippolyta's
prisoner—; she

told her. . .

Head bowed deferentially, Hippolyta
listened without moving.

Hippolyta gathered up the rope, then
disappeared.

Myrrha slept. After a period of indefinite
duration Hippolyta's voice almost uninflected

woke her, saying that she had seen the King and
told the King that she could bring to him tonight a young

girl in love with him who wished to share
his bed, but who must, out of modesty, remain veiled.

Tonight the Festival of Demeter began, during
which the married women of Cyprus in
thanksgiving for the harvest, garlanded
with unthreshed
ears of wheat, robed in white, in secret
purification within the temple for nine days and
nights, abstained from their husbands' now-outlawed beds.

(Each year, Queen Cenchreis fulfilled with ostentatious
ardor the letter of the law.)

Hippolyta told Myrrha that when she
asked the King whether the King will

accept the girl, he asked
her age.

Hippolyta replied, "Myrrha's age."

The King then said, "*Yes.*"

Listening to Hippolyta's words Myrrha
knew that tonight she would allow Hippolyta in
darkness to lead her veiled to her father's chamber.

The door that did not exist

stood open —; she would
step through.

Hippolyta once again
disappeared.

•

In her own room at last Hippolyta fell upon
her knees before her altar to the Furies.

Ten years earlier, when Menelaus and Odysseus
and Agamemnon's herald Talthybius
arrived in Cyprus seeking from the newly-crowned King
(Queen Cenchreis still wore mourning)

help for their expedition to humble Troy,—

. . . Cinyras, giddy not only with unfamiliar
obeisance to his power by men of power, but too much

wine, promised in six months to send sixty ships.

As a gift for Agamemnon, he gave his herald the breastplate
of the still-mourned King, gorgeously
worked with circles of cobalt and gold and tin, with two
serpents of cobalt rearing toward the neck.

Hippolyta and Myrrha overheard the Queen
next morning calmly tell the King that the great families who
chose the King's advisors had no intention of
honoring his drunken
grandiloquent bravado by funding sixty ships—

that if he persisted either the house of her
father must fall, or she would be forced
to renounce him and marry another, ending

the birthright of their daughter.

As a newcomer, a stranger on Cyprus, he owns
no man's loyalty.

—In six months, one ship sent by Cinyras
entered the harbor holding the Greek expedition;

on its deck were fifty-nine clay
ships with fifty-nine clay crews.

Serving on it were Hippolyta's
father and brother.

Cyprians applauded their new King's canny
wit, his sleight-of-hand and boldness; they felt

outrage when Agamemnon, as mere token of
his vengeance, sank the ship, its
crew strapped to its deck. . .

Now before the altar long ago
erected, Hippolyta implores the Furies:—

May the King of the Clay Ships
find the flesh within his bed

clay. Avenge in
torment the dead.

●

As Myrrha is drawn down the dark corridor toward her father

not free not to desire

what draws her forward is neither COMPULSION nor FREEWILL: —

or at least freedom, here *choice,* is not to be
imagined as action upon

preference: no creature is free to choose what
allows it its most powerful, and most secret, release:

I fulfill it, because I contain it—
it prevails, because it is within me—

it is a heavy burden, setting up longer to enter that
realm to which I am called from within. . .

As Myrrha is drawn down the dark corridor toward her father

not free not to choose

she thinks, *To each soul its hour.*

•

Hippolyta carrying a single candle led her through
a moonless night to the bed where
her father waits.

The light disappears.

Myrrha hears in his voice that he is
a little drunk.

She is afraid: she knows that she must not
reveal by gesture or sound
or animal
leap of the spirit that is hers alone, her animal

signature, that what touches him in ways
forbidden a daughter

is his daughter, —

. . . entering his bed, Myrrha must not be
Myrrha, but Pharaoh's daughter come by
law to Pharaoh's bed.

Sweeter than the journey that constantly surprises
is the journey that you will to repeat: —

. . . *the awkward introduction of a foreign object*

which as you prepare to expel
it enters with such insistence

repeatedly that the resistance you have
marshalled against it

failing utterly leaves
open, resistless, naked before it

what if you do NOT *resist it* CANNOT *be reached:—*

you embrace one of the two species of
happiness, the sensation of
surrender, because at the same instant

you embrace the other, the sensation of power:—

. . . the son whose sister is his mother
in secrecy is conceived within
the mother whose brother is her son.

Before leaving the bed of sleeping
Cinyras, Myrrha slowly runs her tongue

over the skin of his eyelid.

•

Cinyras insisted to Hippolyta that his
visitor must return a second night, then

a third—

if this new girl proves
beautiful, he will bind her to him. . .

No warrior, Cinyras is a veteran of the combats in
which the combatants think that what they

win or lose is love:—

at the well of Eros, how often he has
slaked the thirst that is but briefly
slaked—;
          he worries that though he still

possesses stamina, an inborn
grace of gesture, the eye of
command, as well as beautiful hands and feet,

thickenings, frayed edges to what he knows was his
once startling
beauty betray how often. . .

The sharp-edged profile still staring from the coins
stamped to celebrate his marriage

mocks him.

And now this creature who
seems when he is exhausted, is un-
renewable,
        to make love to his skin,—

. . . who touching its surface seems to
adore its surface so that he
quickens as if he is its surface.

—Myrrha was awakened by the bright lamp
held next to her face. It was held there

steadily, in silence.

The lamp was withdrawn, then
snuffed out.

She heard a sword pulled from its sheath.

Before the sheath clattered to the stone floor
she slipped from the bedclothes.

She heard the sword descend and
descend again, the bedclothes

cut and re-cut.

•

The gods, who know what we want not
why, asked who among them

had placed this thing in Myrrha.

Each god in turn denied it. Cupid
indignantly insisted that his arrows abhorred

anything so dire; Venus seconded her son.

Cupid then said that such
implacable events brought to mind the Furies.

The Furies when roused growled that in
a corollary matter they justly again and
again had been beseeched, but upon inspection

exertion by immortals was unneeded.

•

—Sheba's withered
shore. . . Scrub; rocks; deserted coast

facing the sea. Because there is no
landscape that Myrrha's presence does not
offend, she stares at the sea:—

across the sea

she fled Cinyras; encircled by sea
lay the island that she spent childhood
approaching; from Cyprus the sea brought

NOT what she had expected, the King's
minions impelled by the injunction to
shut her, dirt shoved within her mouth, beneath
dirt silenced, exiled forever, —

                    but representatives of
the Queen, informing her of what had
followed her departure: —

                    when Cinyras found Hippolyta
bowing before an altar, he split her with his sword
from the nape to the base of the spine, then after
dragging the body to a parapet overlooking
rocks and sea, with a yell threw it over the edge; —

within hours what
precipitated Myrrha's disappearance was common
gossip; —

within days three warships
appeared in the harbor at Paphos, sent by
Agamemnon, conqueror of Troy.

Word came from them that the people of Paphos could
avoid destruction if, within three days,

Cinyras were delivered to them.

On the third day, as the King's advisors still
debated how to balance honor with prudence,

the King, standing on the parapet from which had
fallen Hippolyta's body,

                              looking out at the ships

leapt. Some said that the cause was
Myrrha; others, Agamemnon.

The eyes of the people of Cyprus
must find offense should Myrrha attempt return. . .

Cyprians are relieved that the Queen, not yet
forty, has decided to accept the unanimous

counsel of her advisors, and remarry.

•

—She still smells the whiff of something
fatuous when Cinyras as a matter of

course accepted her adoration.

Now Myrrha teaches her child by daily
telling her child, listening
within her, the story of Myrrha and Cinyras. . .

She failed because she had poured, *tried
to pour*, an ocean into a thimble.

Whatever lodged *want* within her had seen her
vanity and self-intoxication and married

her to their reflection.

The thimble was a thimble—and she had
wronged it. . .

She grew careless because she allowed
herself to imagine that if he once
saw her he must love what he had seen.

Bewildered, betrayed
eyes wait now to accuse her in death.

Her mother once told her:—

*A queen remains a queen only when
what she desires is what she is*

expected to desire.

She would anatomize the world
according to how the world

anatomizes DESIRE. As a girl she had taught

herself to walk through a doorway as if
what she knows is on the other side is
NOT on the other side, as if her father

were a father as other fathers (though
kings) merely are fathers—;
                          will, calculation

and rage replaced in Myrrha what
others embraced as "nature". . .

Her friends live as if, though what they
desire is entirely what they are
expected to desire, it is they who desire.

Not "entirely"; almost entirely.

—In the final months, when Myrrha again and
again told the child heavier and heavier within her
the story of Myrrha and Cinyras,

she stripped from it words like "ocean" and "thimble."

She was a sentence that he had spoken in
darkness without
knowing that he had spoken it.

She had the memory of taste before she knew
taste itself: *The milk*

that is in all trees. The sweet water that is beneath.

One fruit of all the world's fruit, for
her, tastes—;

she had failed because her fate, like
all fates, was partial.

Myrrha ended each repetition by telling the child
within her that betrayed, bewildered

eyes wait now to accuse her in death.

—Phoenicia; Panchaia; Sheba—

people everywhere lived lives indifferent to the death of
Cinyras—; suffocating, Sheba's
highlands thick with balsam, costmary,
cinnamon, frankincense—;

. . . there is no landscape that her
presence does not offend, so she is free to
prefer this forsaken shore swept by
humid winds, facing the sea.

Her body is dying.

That her body is dying, her labors not yet
finished, her child un-
born, is not what is bitter.

Myrrha addressed the gods:—

Make me nothing
human: not alive, not dead.

Whether I deny what is not in my
power to deny, or by deception

seize it, I am damned.

I shall not rest until what has been
lodged in me is neither

lodged in me,—nor NOT lodged in me.

Betrayed, bewildered eyes
wait for me in death.

You are gods. Release me, somehow, from both
life and death.

The gods granted her request. From her toes roots

sprout; the dirt rises to cover her
feet; her legs of which she never had been

ashamed grow thick and hard; bark like disease
covers, becomes her skin; with terror she
sees that she must
submit, lose her body to an alien
body not chosen, as the source of ecstasy is
not chosen—

      suddenly she is eager to submit: as the change

rises and her blood becomes
sap, her long arms long branches, she cannot bear
the waiting: she bends her face
downward, plunging her face into the rising

tree, her tears new drops glistening everywhere on its surface:—

fixed, annealed within its body
the story of Myrrha and Cinyras:—new
body not alive not dead, story
everywhere and nowhere:—

Aphrodisiac. Embalmers' oil. (Insistence of
sex, faint insistent sweetness of the dead undead.)
Sacred anointment oil: with wine an
anodyne. Precious earth-
fruit, gift fit for the birth and death of

prophets:—no sweet thing without
the trace of what is bitter
within its opposite:—

. . . MYRRH, sweet-smelling
bitter resin.

●

Soon the child, imprisoned within the tree,
sought birth. Lucina, Goddess of Child-Birth, helped

the new tree contort, the bark
crack open, —

> . . . pretty as Cupid in

a painting, from the bitter
vessel of Myrrha and Cinyras Adonis was born.

We fill pre-existing forms, and when
we fill them, change them and are changed: —

day after day Myrrha told the child
listening within her her story. . .

Once grown to a man, beautiful as Cupid were
Cupid a man, Myrrha's son

> by his seductive

indifference, tantalizing
refusals tormented love-sick Venus.

Ovid tells us that upon Venus Myrrha's
son avenged his mother.

His final indifference is
hunting (to Venus' horror) the boar

that kills him. . .

Venus did not, perhaps, in her own person
intervene in the fate of Myrrha and Cinyras,—
but children who have watched their parents'
blighted lives blighted in the service of Venus

must punish love itself.

     •

O you who looking within the mirror discover in
gratitude how common, how lawful your desire,

before the mirror
anoint your body with myrrh

precious   bitter resin

III

On such a night, at such an hour,

when the inhabitants of the temple of
delight assume for each of us one
profile, different of course for each of us,

but for each of us, single:—

when the present avatar of powers not present though
present through him, different for each of us,

steps to the end of the line of other, earlier
inhabitants of the temple of
delight, different for each of us:—

when the gathering turns for its portrait

and by a sudden trick of alignment and light and
night, all I see

the same, the same, the same, the same, the same—

on such a night,

        at such an hour

. . . grace is the dream, half-
dream, half-

light, when you appear and do not answer the question

that I have asked you, but courteously
ask (because you are dead) if you can briefly

borrow, inhabit my body.

When I look I can see my body
away from me, sleeping.

I say *Yes*. Then you enter it

like a shudder as if eager again to know
what it is to move within arms and legs.

I thought, *I know that he will return it.*

I trusted in that none
earlier, none other.

        •

I tasted a sweet taste, I found nothing sweeter.
Taste.
My pleasant fragrance has stripped itself to stink.
Taste.
The lust of the sweetness that is bitter I taste.
Taste.
Custom both sweet and bitter is
the intercourse of this flesh.
Taste.
The milk that is in all trees,

the sweet water that is beneath.
Taste.
The knife of cutting is the book of mysteries.
Taste.
Bitterness sweetness, eat that you may eat.
Taste.
I tasted a sweet taste, I found nothing sweeter.
Taste.
These herbs were gathered at full noon, which was night.
Taste.

●

. . . *bodies carrying bodies*, some to bury in
earth what offended earth by breathing, others

become vessels of the dead, the voice erased
by death now, for a time, unerased.

●

infinite the sounds the poems

seeking to be allowed to S U B M I T, —*that this*

dust become seed

like those extinguished stars whose fires still give us light

●

This is the end of the second hour of the night.

STAR DUST

(2005)

I

USIC

DIRT

For the Twentieth Century

Bound, hungry to pluck again from the thousand
technologies of ecstasy

boundlessness, the world that at a drop of water
rises without boundaries,

I push the PLAY button: —

... *Callas, Laurel & Hardy, Szigeti*

you are alive again, —

the slow movement of K.218
once again no longer

bland, merely pretty, nearly
banal, as it is

in all but Szigeti's hands

●

Therefore you and I and Mozart
must thank the Twentieth Century, for

it made you pattern, form
whose infinite

repeatability within matter
defies matter—

*Malibran. Henry Irving. The young
Joachim.* They are lost, a mountain of

newspaper clippings, become words
not their own words. The art of the performer.

Music Like Dirt

FOR DESMOND DEKKER

I will not I will not I said but as my body turned in the solitary
bed it said But he loves me which broke my will.

music like dirt

That you did but willed and continued to will refusal you
confirmed seventeen years later saying I was not wrong.

music like dirt

When you said I was not wrong with gravity and weird
sweetness I felt not anger not woe but weird calm sweetness.

music like dirt

I like sentences like He especially dug doing it in
houses being built or at the steering wheel.

music like dirt

I will not I will not I said but as my body turned in the solitary
bed it said But he loves me which broke my will.

Young Marx

That man's own life is an object for him. That animals
build nests, build dwellings,

whereas man contemplates himself

in the world that he has created:
That you cannot find yourself in your labor

because it does not belong to your essential being:

That estranged from labor the laborer is
self-estranged, alien to himself:

That your nature is to labor:

That feeling himself fleetingly unbound only when
eating, drinking, procreating, in his dwelling and dressing-up,

man erects means into sole and ultimate ends:

That where he makes what he makes, he is
not: That when he makes, he is not:

Thus the ground of our self-estrangement.

—Marx in 1844, before the solutions that he proposed
betrayed him by entering history, before, like
Jesus, too many sins were committed in his name.

For Bill Nestrick (1940–96)

Out of the rectitude and narrow care of those who
teach in the public schools, —
                              a mother
who would not let her son watch cartoons of
Porky Pig because we must
not laugh at someone who stutters, —

. . . the mystery, your brilliant
appetite for the moment.

•

For Herbert, the aesthetic desideratum is

unpremeditated art, not as "natural" or "spontaneous"
but a speaking of the Spirit as it becomes
conscious, a fidelity to

the moment itself. The only

appropriate gift is discovered to be
inseparable from
the giver, for man can only give himself.

In 1975, the magazine that printed your great essay
announced: *He is writing a book on Herbert.*

•

You lived in the realm where coin of the realm
is a book,

and despite the fact that by the end of
graduate school you
already had published twenty thousand articles

you never published a book.

Against the background of this bitter
mysterious lapse your brilliant
appetite for the moment.

Little Fugue

at birth you were handed a ticket

beneath every journey the ticket to this
journey in one direction

or say the body

is a conveyor belt, moving in one direction
slower or swifter than sight

at birth

you were handed a ticket, indecipherable
rectangle forgotten in your pocket

or say you stand upon a moving walkway

as if all you fear
is losing your

balance moving in one direction

beneath every journey the ticket to this
journey in one direction

Advice to the Players

There is something missing in our definition, vision, of a human being: the need to make.

●

We are creatures who need to make.

●

Because existence is willy-nilly thrust into our hands, our fate is to make something—if nothing else, the shape cut by the arc of our lives.

●

My parents saw corrosively the arc of their lives.

●

Making is the mirror in which we see ourselves.

●

But *being* is making: not only large things, a family, a book, a business: but the shape we give this afternoon, a conversation between two friends, a meal.

•

Or mis-shape.

•

Without clarity about what we make, and the choices that under-
lie it, the need to make is a curse, a misfortune.

•

The culture in which we live honors specific kinds of making
(shaping or mis-shaping a business, a family) but does not under-
stand how central making itself is as manifestation and mirror of
the self, fundamental as eating or sleeping.

•

In the images with which our culture incessantly teaches us, the
cessation of labor is the beginning of pleasure; the goal of work is
to cease working, an endless paradise of unending diversion.

•

In the United States at the end of the twentieth century, the great-
est luxury is to live a life in which the work that one does to earn
a living, and what one has the appetite to make, coincide—by a
kind of grace are the same, one.

•

Without clarity, a curse, a misfortune.

●

My intuition about what is of course unprovable comes, I'm sure, from observing, absorbing as a child the lives of my parents: the dilemmas, contradictions, chaos as they lived out their own often unacknowledged, barely examined desires to make.

●

They saw corrosively the shape cut by the arc of their lives.

●

My parents never made something commensurate to their will to make, which I take to be, in varying degrees, the general human condition—as it is my own.

●

Making is the mirror in which we see ourselves.

●

Without clarity, a curse, a misfortune.

●

Horrible the fate of the advice-giver in our culture: to repeat one-self in a thousand contexts until death, or irrelevance.

●

I abjure advice-giver.

●

Go make you ready.

Stanzas Ending with the Same Two Words

At first I felt shame because I had entered
through the door marked *Your Death*.

Not a valuable word written
unsteeped in your death.

You are the ruin whose arm encircles the young woman
at the posthumous bar, before your death.

The grass is still hungry
above you, fed by your death.

Kill whatever killed your father, your life
turning to me again said before your death.

Hard to grow old still hungry.
You were still hungry at your death.

The Poem Is a Veil

V E I L,—as if silk that you in fury must thrust repeatedly
high at what the eye, your eye, naked cannot see

catches, clinging to its physiognomy.

Luggage

You wear your body as if without
illusions. You speak of former lovers with some

contempt for their interest in sex.
Wisdom of the spirit, you

imply, lies in condescension and poise.

. . . Fucking, I can feel
the valve opening, the flood is too much.

Or too little. I am
insatiable, famished by repetition.

Now all you see is that I am luggage

that smiles as it is moved from here
to there. *We could have had ecstasies.*

In your stray moments, as now in
mine, may what *was not*

rise like grief before you.

Hammer

The stone arm raising a stone hammer
dreams it can descend upon itself.

When the quest is indecipherable, —
. . . what is left is a career.

What once was apprehended in passion
survives as opinion.

To be both author of
this statue, and the statue itself.

Injunction

As if the names we use to name the uses of buildings
x-ray our souls, war without end:

Palace. Prison. Temple. School.
Market. Theater. Brothel. Bank.

War without end. Because to name is to possess
the dreams of strangers, the temple

is offended by, demands the abolition of brothel, now theater, now
school; the school despises temple, palace, market, bank; the bank by

refusing to name depositors welcomes all, though in rage prisoners each
night gnaw to dust another stone piling under the palace.

War without end. Therefore time past time:

Rip through the fabric. Nail it. Not
to the wall. Rip through

the wall. Outside

time. Nail it.

Heart Beat

ear early tuned to hear beneath the call to end
eating flesh, sentient suffering beings (creatures

bred now for slaughter will
then never be bred)   *less life*   *less life*   tuned to hear

still the vow solemn and implacable I made as a kid
walking a sidewalk in Bakersfield

never to have a child, condemn a creature
to this hell   as the prisoner

chorus in wonder is released into the sun, ear early tuned to hear
beneath the melody the ground-bass   *less life*   *less life*

Legacy

When to the desert, the dirt,
comes water

comes money

to get off the shitdirt
land and move to the city

whence you

direct the work of those who now
work the land you still own

My grandparents left home for the American

desert to escape
poverty, or the family who said *You are the son who shall*

become a priest

After Spain became
Franco's, at last

rich enough

to return you
refused to return

The West you made

was never unstoried, never
artless

Excrement of the sky our rage inherits

there was no gift
outright   we were never the land's

Lament for the Makers

Not bird not badger not beaver not bee

Many creatures must
make, but only one must seek

within itself what to make

My father's ring was a B with a dart
through it, in diamonds against polished black stone.

I have it. What parents leave you
is their lives.

Until my mother died she struggled to make
a house that she did not loathe; paintings; poems; me.

Many creatures must

make, but only one must seek
within itself what to make

Not bird not badger not beaver not bee

●

Teach me, masters who by making were
remade, your art.

II

Curse

May breath for a dead moment cease as jerking your

head upward you hear as if in slow motion floor

collapse evenly upon floor as one hundred and ten

floors descend upon you.

May what you have made descend upon you.
May the listening ears of your victims   their eyes   their

breath

enter you, and eat like acid
the bubble of rectitude that allowed you breath.

May their breath now, in eternity, be your breath.

●

Now, as you wished, you cannot for us
not be. May this be your single profit.

Of your rectitude at last disenthralled, you
seek the dead. Each time you enter them

they spit you out. The dead find you are not food.

Out of the great secret of morals, *the imagination to enter the skin of another*, what I have made is a curse.

Knot

After, no ferocity of will could the hand

•

uncurl. One day, she joked, I'll cut it off.

•

OPEN. Her hand replies that flesh insulted by being cannot bear to

•

wake. OPEN. She repeats the word to what once was hers

•

but now not.

Phenomenology of the Prick

You say, Let's get naked. It's 1962; the world
is changing, or has changed, or is about to change;
we want to get naked. Seven or eight old friends

want to see certain bodies that for years we've
guessed at, imagined. For me, not
certain bodies: one. Yours. You know that.

We get naked. The room
is dark; shadows against the windows'
light night sky; then you approach your wife. You light

a cigarette, allowing me to see what is forbidden to see.
You make sure I see it hard.
You make sure I see it hard

only once. *A year earlier, through the high partition between cafeteria*
booths, invisible I hear you say you can get Frank's
car keys tonight. Frank, you laugh, will do anything I want.

You seemed satisfied. This night, as they say,
completed something. After five years of my
obsession with you, without seeming to will it you

managed to let me see it hard. Were you
giving me a gift. Did you want fixed in my brain
what I will not ever possess. Were you giving me

a gift that cannot be possessed. You make sure
I see how hard
your wife makes it. You light a cigarette.

The Soldier Who Guards the Frontier

On the surface of the earth
despite all effort I continued
the life I had led in its depths.

So when you said cuckoo
hello and my heart
leapt up imagine my surprise.

From its depths some mouth
drawn by your refusals of love
fastened on them and fattened.

It's 2004; now the creature
born from our union in 1983
attains maturity.

He guards the frontier.
As he guards the frontier he listens
all day to the records of Edith Piaf.

Heroic risk, Piaf sings. Love
is heroic risk, for what you are impelled
to risk but do not

kills you; as does, of course this voice
knows, risk. He is addicted
to the records of Edith Piaf.

He lives on the aroma, the intoxications
of what he has been spared.
He is grateful, he says, not to exist.

Romain Clerou

When I asked if she was in pain he said
No but that she had in her final minutes showed that panic

he had often seen the faces of the dying show facing the void.

He said this matter-of-factly, as if because he was
a doctor his experience mattered, as if he had known

her and her son long enough not to varnish or lie.

They had gone to high school together and now
because he had become a doctor and then become

her doctor he watched Martha face the void.

Twenty-eight years later, I can hear the way he said
Martha. His name was Clerou: Dr. Romain Clerou.

Hadrian's Deathbed

Flutter-animal
talkative
unthing

soon from all tongue unhoused

where
next

forgotten
voiceless
scared?

Song

You know that it is there, lair
where the bear ceases
for a time even to exist.

Crawl in. You have at last killed
enough and eaten enough to be fat
enough to cease for a time to exist.

Crawl in. It takes talent to live at night, and scorning
others you had that talent, but now you sniff
the season when you must cease to exist.

Crawl in. Whatever for good or ill
grows within you needs
you for a time to cease to exist.

It is not raining inside
tonight. You know that it is there. Crawl in.

Star Dust

Above the dazzling city lies starless
night. Ruthless, you are pleased the price of one

is the other. That night

dense with date palms, crazy with the breath-
less aromas of fresh-cut earth,

black sky thronging with light so thick the fixed

unbruised stars bewildered
sight, I wanted you dazzled, wanted you drunk.

As we lie on our backs in close dark parallel furrows newly

dug, staring up at the consuming sky, light
falling does not stop at flesh: each thing hidden, buried

between us now burns and surrounds us,

visible, like breath in freezing air. *What you ignore or refuse*
or cannot bear. What I hide that I ask, but

ask. The shimmering improvisations designed to save us

fire melts to law. *I touched the hem of your garment. You opened*
your side, feeding me briefly just enough to show me why I ask.

Melancholy, as if shorn, you cover as ever each glowing pyre

with dirt. In this light is our grave. Obdurate, you say: *We are darkness. We are the city*

whose brightness blots the stars from night.

The Third Hour of the Night

When the eye

When the edgeless screen receiving
light from the edgeless universe

When the eye first

When the edgeless screen facing
outward as if hypnotized by the edgeless universe

When the eye first saw that it

Hungry for more light
resistlessly began to fold back upon itself   TWIST

As if a dog sniffing

Ignorant of origins
familiar with hunger

As if a dog sniffing a dead dog

Before nervous like itself but now
weird inert cold nerveless

Twisting in panic had abruptly sniffed itself

When the eye
first saw that it must die   When the eye first

Brooding on our origins you
ask *When* and I say

Then

●

wound-dresser   let us call the creature

driven again and again to dress with fresh
bandages and a pail of disinfectant
suppurations that cannot
heal for the wound that confers existence is mortal

wound-dresser

what wound is dressed   the wound of being

●

Understand that it can drink till it is
sick, but cannot drink till it is satisfied.

It alone knows you. It does not wish you well.

Understand that when your mother, in her only
pregnancy, gave birth to twins

painfully stitched into the flesh, the bone of one child

was the impossible-to-remove cloak that confers
invisibility. The cloak that maimed it gave it power.

Painfully stitched into the flesh, the bone of the other child

was the impossible-to-remove cloak that confers
visibility. The cloak that maimed it gave it power.

Envying the other, of course each twin

tried to punish and become the other.
Understand that when the beast within you

succeeds again in paralyzing into unending

incompletion whatever you again had the temerity to
try to make

its triumph is made sweeter by confirmation of its

rectitude. It knows that it alone
knows you. It alone remembers your mother's

mother's grasping immigrant bewildered

stroke-filled slide-to-the-grave
you wiped from your adolescent American feet.

Your hick purer-than-thou overreaching veiling

mediocrity. Understand that you can delude others but
not what you more and more

now call the beast within you. Understand

the cloak that maimed each gave each power.
Understand that there is a beast within you

that can drink till it is

sick, but cannot drink till it is satisfied. Understand
that it will use the conventions of the visible world

to turn your tongue to stone. It alone

knows you. It does
not wish you well. *These are instructions for the wrangler.*

II

Three Fates. One
fate, with three faces.

Clotho   Lachesis   Atropos

Thread spun by one
from all those forever unspun.

Thread touched by one and in
touching twisted into something

forever unlike all others spun.

Thread touched by one and in
touching withered to nothing.

Atropos   Lachesis   Clotho

Three, who gave us in recompense
for death

the first alphabet, to engrave in stone
what is most evanescent,

the mind. *According to Hesiod, daughters of Night.*

•

"Unless teeth devour it it
rots: now is its season.

My teeth have sunk into firm-skinned
pears so succulent time stopped.

When my wife, dead now

ten years, pulls her dress over her petticoats
and hair, the air crackles, her hair rising

tangles in ecstasy. We are electric ghosts.

●

You hear the strange cricket in the oven
sing, and ask what it sings.

This is what it sings.

Because *Benvenuto* in my native tongue
means *welcome*, write

here lies an artist who did not
recoil from residence on earth—but,
truly named, welcomed it.

But I mis-spoke: not *wife*. Servant: model: mother
of my child, also now dead.

●

In prison, immured in the black pit where the Pope
once fed Benedetto da Foiano less and less each day
until God's will, not the Pope's own hand, killed him,—

where outside my door each day the castellan
repeated that darkness will teach me I am
a counterfeit bat, and he a real one,—

blackness, silence so unremitted
I knew I had survived another day only by the malignant
welcome singsong of his triumphant voice,—

Benvenuto is a counterfeit bat, and I a real one,—

where God had not found me worthy of seeing the sun
even in a dream, I asked the God of Nature
what unexpiated act the suffocation of my senses, such

suffering, served to expiate.

(This was my first prison.)

      ●

For the two murders I had committed,—their just,
free but necessary cause

revenge, however imperfect the justice—

two successive Popes recognized the necessity
and pardoned me. *Absolved* me.

Because my fame as a maker in gold and silver

preceded me, though I was hardly more
than an apprentice, when Pope Clement came into

possession of the second largest diamond in the world

he summoned me from Florence to Rome—called me
into his presence to serve him. To crown the resplendent

glittering vestment covering his surplice, he wanted

a golden clasp big and round as a small
plate, with God the Father in half-relief above the diamond

and cherubs, arms raised, below. *Hurry*, he said,

finish it quickly, so that I may enjoy its
use a little while.

Pope Clement, unlike the great I now serve, was

an excellent, subtle
connoisseur; he approved my design.

Each week he summoned me into the presence

two or three times, eager to inspect my progress.
Then Cecchino, my brother, two years younger than I

and still beardless, died—

was killed, as he tried to avenge the unjust killing of
a comrade by the ruthless guard of the Bargello.

Thus was stolen from him the chance to incise

his presence into the hard, careless surface of the world.
The fool who killed him

in what justice must call self-defense

later proved his nature by
boasting of it.

His boasting enraged, maddened me. In this

great grief the Pope rebuked me: *You act as if
grief can change death.*

Sleepless, eatless, by day I worked at the Pope's

absorbing golden button—and by night, hypnotized
as a jealous lover, I watched and followed

the fatuous creature who murdered my brother.

At last, overcoming my repugnance to an enterprise
not-quite-praiseworthy, I decided

to end my torment. My dagger entered the juncture

of the nape-bone and the neck
so deep into the bone

with all my strength I could not pull it out.

I ran to the palace of Duke Alessandro—for those who
pursued me knew me. The Pope's natural son,

later he became Duke of Florence, before his murder

by his own cousin Lorenzino, whose too-familiar
intimacies and pretensions to power

he not only indulged but openly mocked.

Alessandro told me to stay indoors
for eight days. For eight days I stayed indoors, working

at the jewel the Pope had set his heart on.

For eight days the Pope failed
to summon me. Then his chamberlain, saying that all was

well if I minded my work and kept silent, ushered me

into the presence. The Pope cast so menacing
a glance toward me I trembled.

Examining my work, his countenance cleared,

saying that I had accomplished a vast amount
in a short time. Then he said, *Now that you are*

cured, Benvenuto—change your life.

I promised that I would. Soon after this, I opened
a fine shop, my first; and finished the jewel.

●

As the knife descended (forgive me, O God of
Nature, but *thus* you have arranged it,—)

to my fevered mind
each moment was infinite, and mine.

●

Late one night, in farewell, Michelangelo
turning to me said, *Benvenuto,*

you deliver yourself into their hands.

●

Here I leapt   Here I leapt   Here I leapt   Here I leapt
the shrilling cricket in the shrilling summer evening

sings; as did my father in the sweet years

he served the pleasure of the lords of Florence
as a piper, in the Consort of Pipers.

Imagine my father, no longer young, married, still

childless, an engineer who designs bridges and
battlements for the Duke, but whose

first love is music — the flute. He joined

the Duke's Consort of Pipers. Now his nights
often are spent not bending over charts and plans

but dazzled at the court of Lorenzo, called *The Magnificent* —

the same Lorenzo who once plucked Michelangelo, still
a boy, from among the horde of the merely-talented

bending to copy the masters in the ducal palace.

Lorenzo, with his father's consent, adopted
the boy; fed him at his own table.

Imagine, tonight, the brief concert is over —

the Consort of Pipers (respectable, honorable
amateurs: small merchants, a banker, a scholar)

mingle, slightly awed, with an ambassador, a Cardinal. . .

Suddenly Lorenzo is at my father's ear: *He stood*
not six inches from me.

Not six inches from my father's ear Lorenzo

in a low voice as he begins to move through
the crowd followed by his son Piero

(as now my father must struggle to follow)

tells my father he has painfully and increasingly
remarked that the flute has led my father to neglect

his fine engineering talent and therefore my

father will understand why Piero and the Duke
must dismiss him from the Consort of Pipers.

Lorenzo, entering the private apartments, was gone.

In later years, my father repeated to his
children: *He stood not six inches from me.*

It is a lie. It is a lie that the Medici and you and I

stand on the same earth. What the sane eye
saw, was a lie: —

two things alone cross the illimitable distance

between the great and the rest of
us, who serve them: —

a knife; and art.

•

The emblem of Florence is the lion; therefore
lions, caged but restless and living, centuries ago

began to announce to the Piazza della Signoria

this is the fearsome seat of the free
government of the Republic of Florence.

Duke Cosimo, hating the noise and smell, had them

moved behind the palace. For years, I had known
the old man who fed and tended the lions, —

one day he humbly asked me if I could make a ring

unlike all others for his daughter's wedding.
I said yes, of course; but, as payment for its

rarity, I wanted him to drug the strongest lion

asleep, so that I could
examine, for my art, his body.

He said he knew no art of drugging; such poison

could kill the creature; a week later,
in fury he said yes.

The animal was numbed but not

sleeping; he tried to raise
his great head, as I lay lengthwise against his warm body;

the head fell back. My head

nestling behind his, each arm, outstretched, slowly
descending along each leg, at last with both hands I

pulled back the fur and touched a claw.

This creature whose claw waking could kill me, —
. . . I wore its skin.

●

After the Medici were returned from eighteen years'
banishment, placed over us again not by the will

of Florentines, but by a Spanish army —

my father, though during the republic he regained
his position as piper, ever loyal to the Medici

wrote a poem celebrating his party's victory

and prophesying the imminent
advent of a Medici pope. Then Julius II died;

Cardinal de' Medici, against expectation, was elected;

the new pope wrote my father that he must
come to Rome and serve him.

My father had no will to travel. Then Jacopo

Salviati, in power because married to a Medici,
took from my father his place at the Duke's new court;

took from him his profit, his hope, his will.

Thus began that slow extinguishment
of hope, the self's obsequies for the self

at which effacement I felt not only a helpless

witness, but
cause, author.

He said I was his heart.

I had asked to be his heart
before I knew what I was asking.

Against his mania to make me a musician

at fifteen I put myself to the goldsmith's trade;
without money

or position, he now could not oppose this.

Help the boy—for his father is poor
rang in my ears as I began to sell

the first trinkets I had made. Later, to escape

the plague then raging, he made me
quickly leave Florence; when I returned,

he, my sister, her husband and child, were dead.

These events, many occurring before my birth, I
see because my father described them

often and with outrage.

To be a child is to see things and not
know them; then you know them.

                    •

Despite the malicious
stars, decisive at my birth: despite their

sufficient instrument, *the hand within me that moves*

against me: in the utter darkness of my first prison
God granted me vision:

surrounded by my stinks, an Angel, his beauty

austere, not wanton, graciously
showed me a room in half-light crowded with the dead:

postures blunted as if all promise of change

was lost, the dead
walked up and down and back and forth:

as if the promise of change

fleeing had stolen the light.
Then, on the wall, there was a square of light.

Careless of blindness I turned my eyes

to the full sun. I did not care
to look on anything again but this. The sun

withering and quickening without distinction

then bulged out: the boss
expanded: the calm body of the dead Christ

formed itself from the same

substance as the sun. Still on the cross,
he was the same substance as the sun.

●

The bait the Duke laid
was Perseus. Perseus

standing before the Piazza della Signoria.

My statue's audience and theater, Michelangelo's
David; Donatello's

Judith With the Head of Holofernes. . .

Here the school of Florence, swaggering, says
to the world: *Eat.*

Only Bandinelli's odious *Hercules and Cacus*

reminds one that when one walks
streets on earth one steps in shit.

Duke Cosimo desired, he said, a statue of Perseus

triumphant, after intricate trials able
at last to raise high

Medusa's mutilated head—he imagined,

perhaps, decapitation of the fickle
rabble of republican Florence. . .

I conceived the hero's gesture as more generous:—

Kill the thing that looked
upon makes us stone.

Soon enough, on my great bronze bust of the great

Duke, I placed—staring out from his chest—
Medusa, her head not yet cut, living.

•

Remember, Benvenuto, you cannot bring your
great gifts to light by your strength alone

You show your greatness only through

the opportunities we give you
Hold your tongue   I will drown you in gold

•

As we stared down at the vast square, at
David, at *Judith*—then at *Hercules and Cacus*

approved and placed there by Cosimo himself—

from high on the fortress lookout of the palace,
against whose severe façade so many

human promises had been so cunningly

or indifferently crushed, I told the Duke that I
cannot make his statue. My brief return from France

was designed only to provide for the future of

my sister and six nieces, now without husband
or father. The King of France alone had saved me

from the Pope's dungeon—not any lord of Italy!

At this, the Duke looked at me
sharply, but said nothing.

All Rome knew that though I had disproved

the theft that was pretext for my arrest, Pope Paul
still kept me imprisoned, out of spite—

vengeance of his malignant son Pier Luigi, now

assassinated by his own retainers.
One night at dinner, the King's emissary gave the Pope

gossip so delicious that out of merriment, and about to vomit

from indulgence, he agreed
to free me. I owed King Francis

my art, my service. The same stipend he once paid

Leonardo, he now paid me; along with a house in Paris.
This house was, in truth, a castle. . .

I omitted, of course, quarrels with the King's

mistress, demon who taunted me for the slowness
of my work, out of her petty hatred of art itself;

omitted her insistence to the King that I

am insolent and by example teach
insolence to others. Omitted that I overheard the King

joke with her lieutenant: —

Kill him, if you can find me
his equal in art.

Before the school of Florence I had only been able,

young, to show myself as goldsmith
and jeweler; not yet as sculptor.

Duke Cosimo then announced that all the King of France

had given me, he would surpass: boasting,
he beckoned me to follow him past the public

common galleries, into the private apartments. . .

Dutiful abashed puppet, I followed; I knew
I would remain and make his statue.

·

In the mirror of art, you who are familiar with the rituals of
decorum and bloodshed before which you are

silence and submission

while within stone
the mind writhes

contemplate, as if a refrain were wisdom, the glistening

intrication
of bronze and will and circumstance in the mirror of art.

·

Bandinelli for months insinuated in the Duke's ear
Perseus never would be finished: —

I lacked the art, he said, to move from the small

wax model the Duke rightly praised, to lifesize
bronze whose secrets tormented even Donatello.

So eighteen months after work began, Duke Cosimo grew

tired, and withdrew his subsidy. Lattanzo Gorini,
spider-handed and gnat-voiced, refusing to hand over

payment said, *Why do you not finish?*

Then Bandinelli hissed *Sodomite!* at
me—after my enumeration, to the court's

amusement, of the sins against art and sense

committed by his *Hercules and Cacus*, recital
designed to kill either him or his authority. . . .

The Duke, at the ugly word, frowned

and turned away. I replied that the sculptor of
Hercules and Cacus must be a madman to think that I

presumed to understand the art that Jove in heaven

used on Ganymede, art nobly practiced here on earth
by so many emperors and kings. My saucy speech

ended: *My poor wick does not dare to burn so high!*

Duke and court broke into laughter. Thus was
born my resolve to murder Bandinelli.

●

I'd hurl the creature to hell. In despair at what must
follow—the Duke's rage, abandonment of my

never-to-be-born Perseus—I cast

myself away for lost: with a hundred crowns
and a swift horse, I resolved first to bid

farewell to my natural son, put to wet-nurse in Fiesole;

then to descend to San Domenico, where Bandinelli
returned each evening. *Then, after blood, France.*

Reaching Fiesole, I saw the boy

was in good health; his wet-nurse
was my old familiar, old gossip, now

married to one of my workmen. The boy

clung to me: wonderful in a two-year-old, in
grief he flailed his arms when at last

in the thick half-dusk

I began to disengage myself. Entering the square
of San Domenico on one side, I saw my prey

arriving on the other. Enraged that he still

drew breath, when I reached him
I saw he was unarmed. He rode a small sorry

mule. A wheezing donkey carried a ten-year-old

boy at his side. In my sudden presence, his face
went white. I nodded my head and rode past.

•

I had a vision of Bandinelli surrounded
by the heaped-up works of his hand.

Not one thing that he had made

did I want to have made.
From somewhere within his body

like a thread

he spun the piles surrounding him. Then he
tried to pull away, to release the thread; I saw

the thread was a leash.

He tried and tried to cut it.
At this, in my vision I said out-loud: —

My art is my revenge.

●

When I returned to Florence from Fiesole, after
three days news was brought to me that my little boy

was smothered by his wet-nurse

turning over on him as they both slept.
His panic, as I left; his arms raised, in panic.

●

*from the great unchosen narration you will soon
be released*

Benvenuto Cellini

*dirtied by blood and earth
but now*

you have again taught yourself to disappear

moving wax from arm
to thigh

you have again taught yourself to disappear

here where each soul is its
orbit spinning

sweetly around the center of itself

at the edge of its eye the great
design of virtue

here your Medusa and your Perseus are twins

his triumphant body still furious with purpose
but his face abstracted absorbed in

contemplation as she is

abstracted absorbed
though blood still spurts from her neck

defeated by a mirror

as in concentration you move wax
from thigh to arm

under your hand it grows

•

The idyll began when the Duke reached me a goldsmith's
hammer, with which I struck the goldsmith's

chisel he held; and so the little statues were

disengaged from earth and rust. Bronze
antiquities, newly found near Arezzo, they lacked

either head or hands or feet. Impatient for my

presence, the Duke insisted that I join him each evening
at his new pastime, playing artisan—leaving orders

for my free admittance to his rooms, day or night.

His four boys, when the Duke's eyes were turned,
hovered around me, teasing. One night

I begged them to hold their peace.

The boldest replied, *That we can't do!* I said
what one cannot do is required of no one.

So have your will! Faced with their sons'

delight in this new principle, the Duke and Duchess
smiling accused me of a taste for chaos. . . .

At last the four figures wrought for the four

facets of the pedestal beneath Perseus
were finished. I brought them one evening to the Duke,

arranging them on his worktable in a row:—

figures, postures from scenes that the eye cannot
entirely decipher, story haunting the eye with its

resonance, unseen ground that explains nothing. . . .

The Duke appeared, then immediately
retreated; reappearing, in his right hand

he held a pear slip. *This is for your garden, the garden of*

your house. I began, *Do you mean,* but he cut me off
saying, *Yes, Benvenuto: garden and house now are yours.*

Thus I received what earlier was only lent me.

I thanked him and his Duchess; then both
took seats before my figures.

For two hours talk was of their beauty,—

the Duchess insisted they were too exquisite
to be wasted down there

in the piazza; I must place them in her apartments.

No argument from intention or design
unconvinced her.

So I waited till the next day—entering the private

chambers at the hour the Duke and Duchess
each afternoon went riding, I carried the statues

down and soldered them with lead into their niches.

Returning, how angry the Duchess became! The Duke
abandoned his workshop. I went there no more.

•

The old inertia of earth that hates the new
(as from a rim I watched)

rose from the ground, legion:—

truceless ministers of the great unerasable
ZERO, eager to annihilate lineament and light,

waited, pent, against the horizon:—

some great force (*massive, stubborn, multiform as
earth, fury whose single name is LEGION,—*)

wanted my Perseus not to exist: —

and I must
defeat them.

Then my trembling assistants woke me.

They said all my work
was spoiled.

Perseus was spoiled. He lay buried in earth

wreathed in fragile earthenware veins from the furnace
above, veins through which he still

waited to be filled with burning metal.

The metal was curdled. As I slept, sick,
the bronze had been allowed to cake, to curdle.

Feverish, made sick by my exertions for

days, for months, I slept; while those charged
with evenly feeding the furnace that I had so well

prepared, LARKED —

I thought, *Unwitting ministers of the gorgon
Medusa herself.* The furnace choked with caking, curdling

metal that no art known to man could

uncurdle, must be utterly dismantled—all
who made it agreed this must destroy

the fragile, thirsty mould of Perseus beneath.

But Perseus was not more strong
than Medusa, but more clever:—if he ever

was to exist as idea, he must first exist as matter:—

all my old inborn
daring returned,

furious to reverse

the unjust triumphs of the world's mere
arrangements of power, that seemingly on earth

cannot be reversed. First, I surveyed my forces:—

seven guilty workmen, timid, sullen,
resentful; a groom; two maids; a cook.

I harassed these skeptical troops into battle:—

two hands were sent to fetch from the butcher
Capretta a load of young oak,—

in bronze furnaces the only woods you use

are slow-burning alder, willow, pine: now I needed
oak and its fierce heat. As the oak

was fed log by log into the fire, how the cake began

to stir, to glow and sparkle. Now
from the increased

combustion of the furnace, a conflagration

shot up from the roof: two windows
burst into flame: I saw the violent storm

filling the sky fan the flames.

All the while with pokers and iron rods
we stirred and stirred the channels—

the metal, bubbling, refused to flow.

I sent for all my pewter plates, dishes, porringers—
the cooks and maids brought some two hundred.

Piece by piece, I had them thrown

into the turgid mass. As I watched the metal for
movement, the cap of the furnace

exploded—bronze welling over on all sides.

I had the plugs pulled, the mouths of the mould
opened; in perfect liquefaction

the veins of Perseus filled. . . .

Days later, when the bronze had cooled, when the clay
sheath had been with great care removed, I found

what was dead brought to life again.

●

Now, my second
prison. It began soon after Perseus was unveiled

to acclaim—great acclaim. Perhaps I grew

too glorious. Perseus, whose birth consumed
nine years, found stuck to his pedestal

sonnets celebrating the master's hand that made him. . . .

On the day of unveiling, Duke Cosimo stationed himself
at a window just above the entrance to the palace;

there, half-hidden, he listened for hours to the crowd's

wonder. He sent his attendant Sforza to say
my reward

soon would astonish me.

Ten days passed. At last Sforza appeared and asked
what price I placed on my statue.

I was indeed astonished: *It is not my custom,*

I replied, *to set a price for my work, as if
he were a merchant and I a mere tradesman.*

Then, at risk of the Duke's severe displeasure, I was

warned I must set a price: infuriated, I said
ten thousand golden crowns.

Cities and great palaces are built with ten thousand

golden crowns, the Duke
two days later flung at me in anger.

Many men can build cities and palaces,

I replied, *but not one can make
a second Perseus.*

Bandinelli, consulted by the Duke, reluctantly

concluded that the statue was worth
sixteen thousand.

The Duke replied that for two farthings

Perseus could go to the scrap heap; that would
resolve our differences.

At last, the settlement was thirty-five hundred, one

hundred a month. Soon after, charges were brought
against me, for sodomy —

I escaped Florence as far as Scarperia, but there

the Duke's soldiers caught me and in chains
brought me back.

I confessed. If I had not, I could have been made

to serve as a slave in the Duke's galleys for life.
The Duke listened behind a screen as I was made

publicly to confess, in full court. . . . Punishment

was *four years* imprisonment. Without the Duke's
concurrence, of course, no charges could have been

lodged, no public humiliation arranged

to silence the insolent. *The first Cosimo, founder of Medici*
power, all his life protected Donatello — whose

affections and bliss were found in Ganymede.

After imprisonment one month, Cosimo
finally commuted my sentence to house arrest.

There his magnanimity allowed me to complete

my Christ of the whitest marble
set upon a cross of the blackest.

Now, my Christ sits still packed in a crate

in the Duke's new chapel; my bust of the Duke
is exiled to Elba, there to frighten in open air

slaves peering out from his passing galleys.

Now, after the Duchess and two of their sons
died of fever within two months, Cosimo

grows stranger: he murdered Sforza

by running him through with a spear: —
he does not own

his mind; or will.

When I ask release from his service, he says
that he cannot, that he soon

will have need of me for great projects; no

commissions come. Catherine de' Medici, regent of
the young French king, petitioned that I be allowed

to enter her service. He said I had no will now to work.

In prison I wrote my sonnet addressed
to Fortune: *Fortune, you sow!*

You turned from me because Ganymede

also is my joy. . . . O God of Nature, author
of my nature,

where does your son Jesus forbid it?

When I was five, one night my father
woke me. He pulled me to the basement, making me

stare into the oak fire and see what he just had seen.

There a little lizard was sporting
at the core of the intensest flames.

My father boxed me on the ears, then kissed me—

saying that I must remember this night: —
My dear little boy, the lizard you see

is a salamander, a creature that lives

at the heart of fire. You and I are blessed: no other
soul now living has been allowed to see it.

●

I am too old to fight to leave Florence: —

here, young, this goldsmith and jeweler
began to imagine that

severity, that *chastity* of style

certain remnants of the ancient world
left my hand hungry to emulate: —

equilibrium of ferocious, contradictory

forces: equilibrium whose balance or poise is their
tension, and does not efface them, —

as if the surface of each thing

arranged within the frame, the surface of each
body the eye must circle

gives up to the eye its vibration, its nature.

Two or three times, perhaps,—*you
say where,*—I have achieved it.

•

See, in my great bronze bust of the great
Duke, embedded in the right epaulette like a trophy
an open-mouthed
face part lion part man part goat, with an iron
bar jammed in its lower jaw

rising resistlessly across its mouth.

See, in Vasari's clumsy portrait of me, as I float
above the right shoulder of the Duke, the same face."

•

*As if your hand fumbling to reach inside
reached inside*

*As if light falling on the surface
fell on what made the surface*

*As if there were no scarcity of sun
on the sun*

III

I covered my arm with orchid juice.

With my hatchet I split a mangrove stick
from a tree, and sharpened it.

I covered the killing stick with orchid juice.

We were camping at Marunga Island
looking for oysters. This woman I was about to kill

at last separated herself from the others

to hunt lilies. She walked into the swamp, then
got cold, and lay down on sandy ground.

After I hit her between the eyes with my hatchet

she kicked, but couldn't
raise up.

With my thumb over the end of the killing stick

I jabbed her Mount of Venus until her skin pushed
back up to her navel. Her large intestine

protruded as though it were red calico.

With my thumb over the end of the killing stick
each time she inhaled

I pushed my arm

in a little. When she exhaled, I stopped. Little by little
I got my hand

inside her. Finally I touched her heart.

Once you reach what is
inside it is outside. I pushed the killing stick

into her heart.

The spirit that belonged to that dead woman
went into my heart then.

I felt it go in.

I pulled my arm
out. I covered my arm with orchid juice.

Next I broke a nest of green ants

off a tree, and watched the live ants
bite her skin until her skin moved by itself

downward from her navel and covered her bones.

Then I took some dry mud and put my sweat
and her blood in the dry mud

and warmed it over a fire. Six or eight times

I put the blood and sweat and mud
inside her uterus until there was no trace of her

wound or what I had done.

I was careful none of her pubic hair was left
inside her vagina for her husband to feel.

Her large intestine stuck out several feet.

When I shook some green ants on it, a little
went in. I shook some more. All of it went in.

When I whirled the killing stick with her heart's blood

over her head, her head
moved. When I whirled it some more, she moved

more. The third time I whirled the killing stick

she gasped for breath. She blew some breath
out of her mouth, and was all right.

I said, *You go eat some lilies.* She

got up. I said, *You will live
two days. One day you will be happy. The next, sick.*

She ate some lilies. She walked around, then

came back and slept. When laughing and talking women
woke her she gathered her lilies and returned to camp.

The next day she walked around and played,

talked and made fun, gathering with others oysters
and lilies. She brought into camp what she

gathered. That night she lay down and died.

Even the gods cannot
end death. In this universe anybody can kill anybody

with a stick. What the gods gave me

is *their* gift, the power to bury within each
creature the hour it ceases.

Everyone knows I have powers but not such power.

If they knew I would be so famous
they would kill me.

I tell you because your tongue is stone.

If the gods ever give you words, one night in
sleep you will wake to find me above you.

●

After sex & metaphysics, —
. . . what?

What you have made.

●

Infinite the forms, finite
tonight as I find again in the mirror the familiar appeaseless

eater's face

Ignorant of cause or source or end
in silence he repeats

Eater, become food

All life exists at the expense of other life
Because you have eaten and eat as eat you must

Eater, become food

unlike the burning stars
burning merely to be

Then I ask him how to become food

In silence he repeats that others have
other fates, but that I must fashion out of the corruptible

body a new body good to eat a thousand years

Then I tell the eater's face that within me is no
sustenance, on my famished

plate centuries have been served me and still I am famished

He smirks, and in silence repeats that all life exists
at the expense of other life

You must fashion out of the corruptible
body a new body good to eat a thousand years

Because you have eaten and eat as eat you must
ignorant of cause or source or end

•

drugged to sleep by repetition of the diurnal
round, the monotonous sorrow of the finite,

within   I am awake

repairing in dirt the frayed immaculate thread
forced by being to watch the birth of suns

•

This is the end of the third hour of the night.

WATCHING
THE SPRING
FESTIVAL

(2008)

Marilyn Monroe

Because the pact beneath ordinary life (*If you
give me enough money, you can continue to fuck me—*)

induces in each person you have ever known
panic and envy before the abyss,

what you come from is craziness, what your
mother and her mother come from is

craziness, panic of the animal
smelling what you have in store for it.

Your father's name, your mother said to the child
you, is too famous not to be hidden.

Kicking against the pricks,
she somehow injured her mind.

You are bitter all that releases
transformation in us is illusion.

Poor, you thought being rich is utterly
corrosive; and watched with envy.

Posing in the garden,
squinting into the sun.

Tu Fu Watches the Spring Festival Across Serpentine Lake

*In 753 Tu Fu, along with a crowd of others, watched
the imperial court—the emperor's mistress, her sisters,
the first minister—publicly celebrate the advent of spring.*

Intricate to celebrate still-delicate
raw spring, peacocks in *passement* of gold

thread, unicorns embroidered palely in silver.
These are not women but a dream of women:—

bandeaux of kingfisher-feather

                              jewelry, pearl

netting that clings to the breathing body

veil what is, because touched earth
is soiled earth, invisible.

As if submission to dream were submission
not only to breeding but to one's own nature,

what is gorgeous is remote now, pure, true.

•

The Mistress of the Cloud-Pepper Apartments
has brought life back to the emperor, who is

old. Therefore charges of gross extravagance, of
pandering incest between her sister Kuo and her cousin

are, in the emperor's grateful eyes, unjust. Her wish
made her cousin first minister. Three springs from this

spring, the arrogance of the new first minister
will arouse such hatred and fury even the frightened

emperor must accede to his execution. As bitterly to
hers. She will be carried on a palanquin of

plain wood to a Buddhist chapel
deep in a wood and strangled.

•

Now the Mistress of the Cloud-Pepper Apartments,—
whose rooms at her insistence are coated with

a pepper-flower paste into which dried pepper-
flowers are pounded because the rooms of the Empress

always are coated with paste into which dried pepper-
flowers are pounded and she is Empress

now in all but name, — is encircled by her
sisters, Duchesses dignified by imperial

favor with the names of states that once had
power, Kuo, Ch'in, Han. Now rhinoceros-horn

chopsticks, bored, long have not descended.
The belled carving knife wastes its labors. Arching

camel humps, still perfect, rise like purple hills
from green-glazed cauldrons. Wave after

wave of imperial eunuchs, balancing fresh
delicacies from the imperial kitchens, gallop up

without stirring dust.

●

With mournful sound that would move demon
gods, flutes and drums now declare to the air

he is arrived. Dawdlingly

he arrives, as if the cloud of

suppliants clinging to him cannot obscure the sun.

Power greater than that of all men except one
knows nothing worth rushing toward

or rushing from. Finally the new first minister
ascends the pavilion. He greets the Duchess of

Kuo with that slight
brutality intimacy induces.

Here at last is power that your
soul can warm its hands against!

Beware: success has made him
incurious, not less dangerous.

(AFTER TU FU, "BALLAD OF LOVELY WOMEN")

The Old Man at the Wheel

Measured against the immeasurable
universe, no word you have spoken

brought light. Brought
light to what, as a child, you thought

too dark to be survived. *By exorcism*
you survived. By submission, then making.

You let all the parts of that thing you would
cut out of you enter your poem because

enacting there all its parts allowed you
the illusion you could cut it from your soul.

Dilemmas of choice given what cannot
change alone roused you to words.

As you grip the things that were young when
you were young, they crumble in your hand.

Now you must drive west, which in November
means driving directly into the sun.

Like Lightning Across an Open Field

This age that has tried to use indeterminacy
to imagine we are free

Days and nights typing and retyping

revisions half in
relish because what you have

made is ill-made

·

Picking up the phone next to your bed
when her voice said he is dead you

stood up on your bed

Like lightning across an open field
I he said

wound the ground

·

His body had risen up to kill him
because beneath him there was no

earth where the soul could stand

●

Renewed health and renewed illness
meant the freedom

or necessity to risk a new life

Bar by bar he built meticulously
a new cage to escape each cage he built

why why why why

It is an illusion you were ever free

The voice of the bird you could not help
but respond to

You Cannot Rest

The trick was to give yourself only to what
could not receive what you had to give,

leaving you as you wished, free.
Still you court the world by enacting yet once

more the ecstatic rituals of enthrallment.
You cannot rest. The great grounding

events in your life (weight lodged past
change, like the sweetest, most fantastical myth

enshrining yet enslaving promise), the great
grounding events that left you so changed

you cannot conceive your face without their
happening, happened when someone

could receive. Just as she once did, he did—past
judgment of pain or cost. Could receive. Did.

Poem Ending With Three Lines From "Home On the Range"

Barred from the pool twenty-three years ago, still I dove
straight in. You loved to swim, but saw no water.

Whenever Ray Charles sings "I Can't Stop Loving You"

I can't stop loving you. Whenever the unstained-by-guilt
cheerful chorus belts out the title, as his voice, sweet

and haggard reminder of what can never be remedied,

answers, correcting the children with "It's useless to say,"
the irreparable enters me again, again me it twists.

The red man was pressed from this part of the West—

'tis unlikely he'll ever return to the banks of Red River, where
seldom, if ever, their flickering campfires burn.

An American in Hollywood

After you were bitten by a wolf and transformed
into a monster who feeds on other human beings

each full moon and who, therefore, in disgust

wants to die, you think *The desire to die is not
feeling suicidal. It abjures mere action. You have*

wanted to die since the moment you were born.

Crazy narratives—that lend what is merely
in you, and therefore soon-to-be-repeated,

the fleeting illusion of logic and cause.

You think *Those alive there, in the glowing rectangle,
lead our true lives! They have not, as we have been*

forced to here, cut off their arms and legs.

There, you dance as well as Fred Astaire,
though here, inexplicably, you cannot.

Sewer. Still black water

above whose mirror
you bend your face. Font.

Seduction

Show him that you see he carries
always, everywhere, an enormous

almost impossible to balance or bear

statue of himself: burden that
flattering him

dwarfs him, like you. Make him

see that you alone decipher within him
the lineaments of the giant. Make him

see that you alone can help him shape

the inchoate works of his hand, till what
the statue is he is. *He watches your helpless*

gaze; your gaze

tells him that the world someday must see.
You are the dye whose color dyes

the mirror: he can never get free.

•

You ask what is this place. He says
kids come to make out here. He has driven

out here to show you lovers' lane.

Because your power in the world exceeds
his, he must make the first move.

His hand on the car seat doesn't move.

●

He is Ralegh attending Elizabeth, still
able to disguise that he does not want her.

In banter and sweet colloquy, he freely,

abundantly shows you that what his
desire is is endless

intercourse with your soul. Everything

he offers, by intricate
omissions, displays what he denies you.

Beneath all, the *no* that you

persuade yourself
can be reversed.

•

You cannot reverse it: as if he is

safe from
engulfment only because he has

placed past reversal

the judgment that each
animal makes facing another.

You are an animal facing another.

•

Still you persuade yourself that it can be
reversed because he teasingly sprinkles

evasive accounts of his erotic history

with tales of dissatisfying but repeated
sex with men. He adds that he

could never fall in love with a man.

Helplessly, he points to the soiled
statue he strains to hold

unstained above him. He cannot.

●

You must write this without the least
trace of complaint. Standing at the edge of

the pool, for him there was no water.

You chose him not despite, but
because of. In the twenty-three years since

breaking with him, his spectre

insists that no one ever replaces anyone.
He is the dye whose color dyes

the mirror: you can never get free.

●

What is it that impels

What is it that impels us at least in
imagination

What is it that impels us at least in

imagination to close with to
interpenetrate flesh that accepts

craves interpenetration from

us with us
What is it What

●

Sweet cow, to heal the world, you must

jump over the moon. All you ask is
immolation, fantastic love resistlessly

drawn out of a withdrawn creature who

must turn himself inside out to give it:
dream coexistent with breathing.

●

Near the end, when the old absorbing

colloquy begins again, both he and you
find yourselves surrounded by ash.

To his meagre circumscribed desire whose

no you knew from the beginning, that you
want to pluck out of your eye forever,

you submit as if in mourning.

To ash, he too submits. In revenge
you chose submission, chose power.

Catullus: Id faciam

What I hate I love. Ask the crucified hand that holds
the nail that now is driven into itself, why.

Song of the Mortar and Pestle

The desire to approach obliteration
preexists each metaphysic justifying it. Watch him
fucked want to get fucked hard. Christianity

allowed the flagellants

light, for even Jesus found release from flesh requires
mortification of the flesh. From the ends of
the earth the song is, *Grind me into dust.*

Valentine

How those now dead used the word *love* bewildered
and disgusted the boy who resolved he

would not reassure the world he felt
love until he understood love

Resolve that too soon crumbled when he found
within his chest

something intolerable for which the word
because no other word was right

must be love
must be love

Love craved and despised and necessary
the Great American Songbook said explained our fate

my bereft grandmother bereft
father bereft mother their wild regret

How those now dead used love to explain
wild regret

With Each Fresh Death the Soul Rediscovers Woe

from the world that called you Piñon not one voice is now not stopped
Piñon little pine nut sweet seed of the pine tree which is evergreen

Soul that discovered itself as it discovered the irreparable

breaking through ice to touch the rushing stream whose skin
breaking allowed darkness to swallow blondhaired Ramona

in 1944 age six high in the cold evergreen Sierras as you

age five luckily were elsewhere but forever after Soul there
failing to pull her for years of nights from the irreparable

Sanjaya at 17

As if fearless what the shutter will unmask
he offers himself to the camera, to
us, sheerly—
vulnerable like Monroe, like Garbo.

Now he is a cock that raises
high above his wagging head
the narrow erected red
flag of arousal—

Of course the ignorant, you say, *hate him.*
In the world's long conversation, long
warfare about essence, each taunting
song, each disarming photograph, a word.

There is a creature, among all others, one,
within whose voice there is a secret voice
which once heard
unlocks the door that unlocks the mountain.

Winter Spring Summer Fall

Like the invisible seasons

Which dye then bury all the eye
sees, but themselves cannot be seen

Out of ceaseless motion in edgeless space

Inside whatever muck makes words in
lines leap into being is the intimation of

Like the invisible seasons

Process, inside chaos you follow the thread
of just one phrase instinct with cycle, archaic

Out of ceaseless motion in edgeless space

Promise that you will see at last the buried
snake that swallows its own tail

Like the invisible seasons

You believe not in words but in words in
lines, which disdaining the right margin

Out of ceaseless motion in edgeless space

Inside time make the snake made out of
time pulse without cease electric in space

Like the invisible seasons

Though the body is its
genesis, a poem is the vision of a process

Out of ceaseless motion in edgeless space

Carved in space, vision your poor eye's single
armor against winter spring summer fall

Ulanova At Forty-Six At Last Dances Before a Camera Giselle

Many ways to dance Giselle, but tonight as you
watch you think that she is what art is, creature

who remembers

her every gesture and senses its relation to the time
just a moment before when she did something

close to it

but then everything was different so what she feels
now is the pathos of the difference. Her body

hopping forward

remembers the pathos of the difference. Each
hop is small, but before each landing she has

stepped through

many ghosts. This and every second is the echo
of a second like it but different when you had

illusions not

only about others but about yourself. Each gesture
cuts through these other earlier moments to exist as

a new gesture

but carries with it all the others, so what you dance
is the circle or bubble you carry that is all this.

●

Inside the many ways to dance Giselle

the single way that will show those who sleep what
tragedy is. What tragedy is is

your work in Act One. Then comes something else.

●

The poem I've never been able to write has a very tentative title:
"Ulanova At Forty-Six At Last Dances Before a Camera Giselle."
A nice story about an innocent who dies because tricked by the
worldly becomes, with Ulanova, tragedy. A poem about being in
normal terms too old to dance something but the world wants to
record it because the world knows that it is precious but you also
know the camera is good at unmasking those who are too old to
create the illusion on which every art in part depends. About burn-
ing an image into the soul of an eighteen-year-old (me) of the
severity and ferocity at the root of classic art, addicted to mimesis.

●

After her entrance, applause. We are watching

a stage production, filmed one act per
night after an earlier public performance.

But without an audience, who is applauding?

The clapping is
artifice, added later. We are watching

the illusion of a stage performance, filmed

by Mr. Paul Czinner using techniques he specially
developed to record the Bolshoi Ballet's first

appearance in the west. Despite the Iron

Curtain, at the height of the Cold War, the Russian
government now has decreed we may see Ulanova.

●

Whether out of disgust or boredom, the young

Duke of Silesia has buried what the world
understands as his identity

here, in a rural dream. Watching her

from the safety of his disguise
he is charmed: he smiles. She is a bird whose

wings beat so swiftly they are invisible.

•

Tragedy begins with a *radical given*—your uncle has murdered
your father and married your mother. Before your birth a
prophecy that you will kill your father and marry your mother
leads your father to decree your murder. The *radical given*—
irremediable, inescapable—lays bare the war that is our birth-
right. *Giselle* begins with the premise of an operetta: a duke is in
love with a peasant girl.

•

Impossible not to reach for, to touch
what you find is beautiful,

but had not known before existed.

•

. . . The princess. *Her brocaded dress, cloth of*
gold. Behind her back and

embarrassingly before everyone, Giselle

cannot resist caressing it. *Her dangling,
glittering necklace.* Out of graciousness or

condescension, the princess

removed it from her neck, then so
everyone could see, placed it

around yours. How pleased you were!

•

. . . Or Albrecht, stranger, clear
spirit, to whom despite your

dread you gave your heart.

•

Impossible—; to your shame.

•

The princess, to whom Albrecht is betrothed, arrives in the village
during a hunt and takes rest in Giselle's home. A young forester,
jealously in love with Giselle, now finds Albrecht's hidden silver
sword and betrays his secret. Albrecht tries to hide his real status,

but the returning princess greets him affectionately, thus proving his true identity. Heartbroken by his duplicity, Giselle goes mad and dies.

•

The Nineteenth Century did not discover but

made ripe the Mad Scene, gorgeous
delirium rehearsing at luxuriant but

momentary length the steps, the undeflectable

stages by which each brilliant light
finds itself extinguished. *She stares*

straight ahead at what her empty hands

still number, still fondle.
Such burning is eager to be extinguished.

•

Before her she can see the hand

that reaches into her
cage

closing over her. *The hand is the future*

devoid of what, to her
horror, she had reached for.

As the future closes over her

the creature inside beating its wings in
panic is dead.

●

You have spent your life writing tragedies for a world that does
not believe in tragedy. What is tragedy? Everyone is born some-
where: into this body, this family, this place. Into the mystery of
your own predilections that change as you become conscious of
what governs choice, but change little. Into, in short, particularity
inseparable from existence. Each particularity, inseparable from
its history, offers and denies. There is a war between each offer you
embrace and what each embrace precludes, what its acceptance
denies you. Most of us blunt and mute this war in order to survive.
In tragedy the war is lived out. The *radical given* cannot be evaded
or erased. No act of intelligence or prowess or cunning or goodwill
can reconcile the patrimony of the earth.

●

Act Two, because this *Giselle* has been
abbreviated by L. Lavrovsky, is a sketch of Act Two.

Worse than being dead yourself

is to imagine him dead.
Many ways to dance Giselle, but in the queer

moonlit halflife of the forest

at night, when Giselle in death
dances with Albrecht to save him, Ulanova

executes the classic postures of ecstasy, of

yearning for
union, as if impersonally —

as if the event were not at last

again to touch him, but pre-ordained,
beyond the will, fixed as the stars are fixed.

●

Here, in darkness, in the queer halflife of

remorse, Myrtha, Queen of the *Wilis*, offers
revenge against those who condemned

you forever to remain unchosen, baffled.

Myrtha, refugee from Ovid famished
into sovereign self-parody by

centuries of refusal and hunger, rules

row upon symmetrical row of pitiless
well-schooled virgins, dressed in white.

Their rigid geometry mocks

ballet as the abode of Romantic
purity, harmonious dream.

●

The conscience-stricken duke visits Giselle's grave and is con-
fronted by the *Wilis*. The Queen condemns him to dance until
he dies. The ghost of Giselle appears and pleads for his life—
without success. Giselle, determined to save him, dances in his
place whenever he falters, allowing him time to recover. The
church bell rings: dawn. The power of the *Wilis* is broken.

●

When Giselle dead defies her dead sisters

Death and the dramatist make visible
the pitiless logic within love's *must*.

Love must silence its victims,—
. . . or become their vessel.

She has become his vessel.

•

At dawn, in triumph incapable of youth's
adamant poise, Giselle reenters the ground.

•

"You see how keen the pointed foot looks in the air, during atti-
tudes, arabesques, and passés, how clearly the leg defines and dif-
ferentiates the different classic shapes. Below the waist Ulanova is
a strict classicist; above the waist she alters the shape of classic mo-
tions now slightly, now quite a lot, to specify a nuance of drama.
Neither element—the lightness below or the weight above—is
weakened for the sake of the other." (Edwin Denby)

•

Ulanova came to Pomona California in

1957 as light projected on a screen

to make me early in college see what art is.

Under Julian, c362 A.D.

[   ] or full feeling return to my legs.

My jealous, arrogant, offended by existence
soul, as the body allowing you breath

erodes under you, you are changed—

the fewer the gestures that can, in the future,
be, the sweeter those left to you to make.

Candidate

on each desk mantel refrigerator door

an array of photographs
little temple of affections

you have ironically but patiently made

•

Those promises that make us confront
our ambition, pathetic ambition:

confront it best when we see what it
promised die. Your dead ex-wife

you put back on the mantel
when your next wife left. With her iron

nasals, Piaf regrets NOTHING: crazed
by the past, the sweet desire to return to

zero. Undisenthralled you
regret what could not have been

otherwise and remain itself.
There, the hotel in whose bar you courted

both your wives is detonated, collapsing;
in its ballroom, you conceded the election.

There's your open mouth
conceding.

A good photograph tells you everything
that's really going on is invisible.

You are embarrassed by so many
dead flowers. They lie shriveled before you.

Coat

You, who never lied, lied
about what you at every moment carried.

The shameful, new, incomprehensible

disease which you whose religion was
candor couldn't bear not to hide.

Now that you have been dead thirteen years

I again see you suddenly lay out my coat
across your bed, caressing it as if touch could

memorize it — no, you're flattening, then

smoothing its edges until under your
hand as I watch it becomes

hieratic, an icon.

What I seized on as promise
was valediction.

To the Republic

I dreamt I saw a caravan of the dead
start out again from Gettysburg.

Close-packed upright in rows on railcar flat-
beds in the sun, they soon will stink.

Victor and vanquished shoved together, dirt
had bleached the blue and gray one color.

Risen again from Gettysburg, as if
the state were shelter crawled to through

blood, risen disconsolate that we
now ruin the great work of time,

they roll in outrage across America.

You betray us is blazoned across each chest.
To each eye as they pass: *You betray us.*

Assaulted by the impotent dead, I say it's
their misfortune and none of my own.

I dreamt I saw a caravan of the dead
move on wheels touching rails without sound.

To each eye as they pass: *You betray us.*

(2005)

461

God's Catastrophe in Our Time

when those who decree decree the immemorial

mere habits of the tribe
law established since the foundations of the world

when the brutalities released by
belief engender in you disgust for God

hear the answering baritone sweetness of Mahler's "Urlicht"

I am from God and shall return
to God for this disfiguring

flesh is not light and
from light I am light

when I had eyes what did I do with sight

Little O

To see the topography of a dilemma

through the illusion of
hearing, hearing the voices

of those who, like you, must live there.

•

We are not belated: we stand in an original
relation to the problems of making

art, just as each artist before us did.

At the threshold
you can see the threshold: —

it is a precipice.

When I was young, I tried not to
generalize; I had seen little. At sixty-six,

you have done whatever you do

many times before. Disgust with mimesis, —
disgust with the banality of naturalistic

representation, words mere surface mirroring

a surface, —
is as necessary as mimesis: as the conventions

the world offers out of which to construct your

mirror fail, to see your face you
intricately, invisibly reinvent them. But

imagining that words must make the visible

a little hard to see, —
or speech that imitates for the ear speech

now is used up, the ground sealed off from us, —

is a sentimentality. Stevens was wrong. Genius
leading the disgusted over a cliff.

Everything made is made out of its

refusals: those who follow make it new
by refusing its refusals.

The French thought Shakespeare

a barbarian, because in their eyes he wrote as if
ignorant of decorum, remaking art to cut through.

Watching the Spring Festival

In my dreams all I need to do is bend
my head, and you well up beneath me

We have been present at a great abundance

displayed beneath glass, sealed beneath
glass as if to make earth envy earth

Until my mouth touched the artful

cunning of glass
I was not poor

We have been present at a great abundance

Warring priests of transformation, each
animated by an ecstatic secret, insist

they will teach me how to smash the glass

We have been present at a great abundance
which is the source of fury

Hymn

Earth, O fecund, thou. Evanescent when grasped, when

Venus drives all creatures crazy with desire
to couple and in coupling fill the earth with presences

like themselves
needful, ghostly.

                  Earth, O fecund, thou. Electric ghosts

people the horizon, beguiling since childhood
this son of the desert about to disappear.

They are no less loved and feared because
evanescent. Earth, O fecund, thou.

If See No End In Is

What none knows is when, not if.
Now that your life nears its end
when you turn back what you see
is ruin. You think, It is a prison. No,
it is a vast resonating chamber in
which each thing you say or do is

new, but the same. *What none knows is
how to change.* Each plateau you reach, if
single, limited, only itself, in-
cludes traces of all the others, so that in the end
limitation frees you, there is no
end, if you once see what is there to see.

You cannot see what is there to see —
not when she whose love you failed is
standing next to you. Then, as if refusing the know-
ledge that life *un*separated from her is death, as if
again scorning your refusals, she turns away. The end
achieved by the unappeased is burial within.

*Familiar spirit, within whose care I grew, within
whose disappointment I twist, may we at last see
by what necessity the double-bind is in the end
the figure for human life, why what we love is
precluded always by something else we love, as if
each no we speak is yes, each yes no.*

The prospect is mixed but elsewhere the forecast is no
better. The eyrie where you perch in
exhaustion has food and is out of the wind, if
cold. You feel old, young, old, young—: you scan the sea
for movement, though the promise of sex or food is
the prospect that bewildered you to this end.

Something in you believes that it is not the end.
When you wake, sixth grade will start. The finite you know
you fear is infinite: even at eleven, what you love is
what you should not love, which endless bullies in-
tuit unerringly. The future will be different: you cannot see
the end. What none knows is when, not if.

Song

At night inside in the light

when history
is systole
diastole

awake I am the moment between.

At night when I fold my limbs up
till they fit
in the tiniest box

I am a multiple of zero.

In the sun
even a tick
feeding on blood

to his sorrow becomes visible.

A bat who grows in love with the sun
becomes sick unless disabused of the illusion
he and the sun are free.

Surreal God

you too a multiple of zero
you who make
all roads lead nowhere

Surreal God

I find nothing
except you
beautiful.

When thus in ecstasy I lie to the god of

necessity he replies the world he has devised is
a labyrinth where travelers at last achieve to their
dismay eternal safety in eternal night.

Columbus is dead

so try as you will
you cannot make me feel
embarrassment

at what I find beautiful.

Collector

As if these vessels by which the voices of
the dead are alive again

were something on which to dream, without

which you cannot dream—
without which you cannot, hoarder, breathe.

Tell yourself what you hoard

commerce or rectitude cannot withdraw.
Your new poem must, you suspect, steal from

The Duchess of Malfi. Tonight, alone, reread it.

•

By what steps can the Slave become
the Master, and is

becoming the master its only release?

It is not release. When your stepfather
went broke, you watched as your mother's

money allowed survival—

It is not release. You watched her pay him
back by multitudinous

daily humiliations. In the back seat of

the car you were terrified as Medea
invented new ways to tell

Jason what he had done to her.

•

You cannot tell that it is there
but it is there, falling.

Once you leave any surface

uncovered for a few hours
you see you are blind.

Your arm is too heavy to wipe

away what falls on a lifetime's
accumulations. The rituals

you love imply that, repeating them,

you store seeds that promise
the end of ritual. Not this. Wipe this

away, tomorrow it is back.

●

The curator, who thinks he made his soul
choosing each object that he found he chose,

wants to burn down the museum.

●

Stacked waist-high along each
increasingly unpassable

corridor, whole lifeworks

wait, abandoned or mysteriously
never even tested by your

promiscuous, ruthless attention.

●

The stratagems by which briefly you
ameliorated, even seemingly

untwisted what still twists within you—

you loved their taste and lay there
on your side

nursing like a puppy.

●

Lee Wiley, singing in your bathroom
about "ghosts in a lonely parade,"

is herself now one—

erased era you loved, whose maturity
was your youth, whose blindnesses

you became you by loathing.

●

Cities at the edge of the largest
holes in the ground

are coastal: the rest, inland.

The old age you fear is Lady
Macbeth wiping away

what your eyes alone can see.

Each of us knows that there is a black
hole within us. No place you hole up is

adequately inland.

•

*The song that the dead sing is at one
moment as vivid, various, multi-voiced*

as the dead were living—

*then violated the next moment, flattened
by the need now to speak in*

such a small space, you.

•

He no longer arrives even
in dreams.

You learned love is addiction

when he to whom you spoke on
the phone every day

dying withdrew his voice —

more than friends, but
less than lovers.

There, arranged in a pile, are his letters.

•

The law is that you
must live

in the house you have built.

The law is absurd: it is
written down nowhere.

You are uncertain what crime

is, though each life writhing to
elude what it has made

feels like punishment.

•

Tell yourself, again, *The rituals
you love imply that, repeating them,*

you store seeds that promise

the end of ritual. You store
seeds. Tell yourself, again,

what you store are seeds.

METAPHYSICAL

DOG

(2013)

ONE

Metaphysical Dog

Belafont, who reproduced what we did
not as an act of supine

imitation, but in defiance —

butt on couch and front legs straddling
space to rest on an ottoman, barking till

his masters clean his teeth with dental floss.

How dare being
give him this body.

Held up to a mirror, he writhed.

Writing "Ellen West"

was exorcism.

●

Exorcism of that thing within Frank that wanted, after his mother's death, to die.

●

Inside him was that thing that he must expel from him to live.

●

He read "The Case of Ellen West" as a senior in college and immediately wanted to write a poem about it but couldn't so he stored it, as he has stored so much that awaits existence.

●

Unlike Ellen he was never anorexic but like Ellen he was obsessed with eating and the arbitrariness of gender and having to have a body.

●

Ellen lived out the war between the mind and the body, lived out in her body each stage of the war, its journey and progress, in which compromise, reconciliation is attempted then rejected then mourned, till she reaches at last, in an ecstasy costing not less than everything, death.

●

He was grateful he was not impelled to live out the war in his body, hiding in compromise, well wadded with art he adored and with stupidity and distraction.

●

The particularity inherent in almost all narrative, though contingent and exhausting, tells the story of the encounter with particularity that flesh as flesh must make.

●

"Ellen West" was written in the year after his mother's death.

●

By the time she died he had so thoroughly betrayed the ground of intimacy on which his life was founded he had no right to live.

●

No use for him to tell himself that he shouldn't feel this because he felt this.

•

He didn't think this but he thought this.

•

After she died his body wanted to die, but his brain, his cunning, didn't.

•

He likes narratives with plots that feel as if no one willed them.

•

His mother in her last year revealed that she wanted him to move back to Bakersfield and teach at Bakersfield College and live down the block.

•

He thought his mother, without knowing that this is what she wanted, wanted him to die.

•

All he had told her in words and more than words for years was that her possessiveness and terror at his independence were wrong, wrong, wrong.

●

He was the only person she wanted to be with but he refused to live down the block and then she died.

●

It must be lifted from the mind

must be lifted and placed elsewhere
must not remain in the mind alone

●

Out of the thousand myriad voices, thousand myriad stories in each human head, when his mother died, there was Ellen West.

●

This is the body that you can draw out of you to expel from you the desire to die.

●

Give it a voice, give each scene of her life a particularity and necessity that in Binswanger's recital are absent.

•

Enter her skin so that you can then make her other and expel her.

•

Survive her.

•

Animal mind, eating the ground of Western thought, the "mind-body" problem.

•

She, who in the last months of her life abandoned writing poems in disgust at the failure of her poems, is a poem.

•

She in death is incarnated on a journey whose voice is the voice of her journey.

•

Arrogance of Plutarch, of Shakespeare and Berlioz, who thought they made what Cleopatra herself could not make.

•

Arrogance of the maker.

•

Werther killed himself and then young men all over Europe imitated him and killed themselves but his author, Goethe, cunning master of praxis, lived.

•

Frank thought when anything is made it is made not by its likeness, not by its twin or mirror, but its opposite.

•

Ellen in his poem asks *Without a body, who can* know *himself at all?*

•

In your pajamas, you moved down the stairs just to the point where the adults couldn't yet see you, to hear more clearly the din, the sweet cacophony of adults partying.

•

Phonograph voices among them, phonograph voices, their mag-
pie beauty.

•

Sweet din.

•

Magpie beauty.

•

One more poem, one more book in which you figure out how to
make something out of not knowing enough.

Like

Woe is blunted not erased
by *like*. Your hands were too full, then

empty. At the grave's

lip, secretly you imagine then
refuse to imagine

a spectre

so like what you watched die, the unique
soul you loved endures a second death.

The dead hate *like*, bitter

when the living with too-small
grief replace them. You dread

loving again, exhausted by the hungers

ineradicable in his presence. *You resist*
strangers until a stranger makes the old hungers

brutally wake. We live by symbolic

substitution. At the grave's lip, what is
but is not is what

returns you to what is not.

TWO

HUNGER
FOR THE
ABSOLUTE

Those Nights

(FOR M.P.)

Those nights when despite his exhaustion or indifference
you persisted, then finally it

caught, so that at last he too

wanted it, suddenly was desperate to reach it,
you felt his muscles want it

more than anything, as if through this chaos, this

wilderness he again knew the one thing he must reach
though later, after

he found it, his resentment implied he had been forced.

•

Those nights ended because what was
missing could never be by
the will supplied. We who could get
somewhere through
words through
sex could not. I was, you said, your
shrink: that's how
I held you. I failed as my own.

●

Now you surely are dead. I've searched
the databases: you everywhere
elude us. Long ago without your
reaching to tell me, surely
the plague killed you. Each thing in your life
you found so
incommensurate to the spirit
I imagine that becoming
untraceable makes you smile.

Name the Bed

Half-light just after dawn. As you turned back
in the doorway, you to whom the ordinary

sensuous world seldom speaks

expected to see in the thrown-off
rumpled bedclothes nothing.

●

Scream stretched across it.

●

Someone wanted more from that bed
than was found there.

●

Name the bed that's not true of.

●

Bed where your twin
died. Eraser bed.

Queer

Lie to yourself about this and you will
forever lie about everything.

Everybody already knows everything

so you can
lie to them. That's what they want.

But lie to yourself, what you will

lose is yourself. Then you
turn into them.

●

For each gay kid whose adolescence

was America in the forties or fifties
the primary, the crucial

scenario

forever is coming out—
or not. Or not. Or not. Or not. Or not.

●

Involuted velleities of self-erasure.

•

Quickly after my parents
died, I came out. Foundational narrative

designed to confer existence.

If I had managed to come out to my
mother, she would have blamed not

me, but herself.

*The door through which you were shoved out
into the light*

was self-loathing and terror.

•

Thank you, terror!

You learned early that adults' genteel
fantasies about human life

were not, for you, life. You think sex

is a knife
driven into you to teach you that.

History

For two years, my father chose to live at

The Bakersfield Inn, which called itself
the largest motel in the world.

There, surrounded by metal furniture

painted to look like wood, I told him that I
wanted to be a priest, a Trappist.

He asked how I could live without pussy.

He asked this earnestly. This confession
of what he perceived as need

was generous. I could not tell him.

•

Sex shouldn't be part of marriage.

Your father and I,—
. . . sex shouldn't be part of marriage.

•

That she loved and continued to love him
alone: and he, her: even after marrying others—

then they got old and stopped talking this way.

●

Ecstasy in your surrender to adolescent

God-hunger, ecstasy
promised by obliterated sex, ecstasy

in which you are free because bound—

in which you call the God who made
what must be obliterated in you love.

●

In a labyrinth of blankets in the garage

at seven
with a neighbor boy

you learned abasement

learned amazed that what must be
obliterated in you is the twisted

obverse of what underlies everything.

•

Chaos of love, chaos of sex that
marriage did not solve or

mask, God did not solve or mask.

•

Grant and Hepburn in *Bringing Up Baby,*

in which Grant finally realizes being
with her is more fun than anything.

•

What they left behind

they left behind
broken. The fiction

even they accepted, even they believed

was that once
it was whole.

Once it was whole

left all who swallowed it,
however skeptical, forever hungry.

•

The generation that followed, just like their
famished parents, fell in love with the fiction.

They smeared shit all over

their inheritance because it was broken,
because they fell in love with it.

But I had found my work.

Hunger for the Absolute

Earth you know is round but seems flat.

You can't trust
your senses.

You thought you had seen every variety of creature
but not

this creature.

·

When I met him, I knew I had

weaned myself from God, not
hunger for the absolute. O unquenched

mouth, tonguing what is and must
remain inapprehensible—

saying *You are not finite. You are not finite.*

Defrocked

Christ the bridegroom, the briefly
almost-satiated soul forever then

the bride —

the true language of ecstasy
is the forbidden

language of the mystics:

I am true love that false was never.

      I would be pierced
And I would pierce

      I would eat
And I would be eaten

I am peace that is nowhere in time.

Naked their
encounter with the absolute, —

pilgrimage to a cross in the void.

A journey you still must travel, for
which you have no language

since you no longer believe it exists.

•

When what we understand about
what we are

changes, whole
parts of us fall mute.

•

We have attached sensors to your most intimate

body parts, so that we may measure
what you think, not what you think you think.
The image now on the screen
will circumvent your superego and directly stimulate your

vagina or dick

or fail to. Writing has existed for centuries to tell us
what you think you think. Liar,
we are interested in what lies
beneath that. This won't hurt.

•

Even in lawless dreams, something
each night in me again

denies me

the false coin, false
creature I crave to embrace—

for those milliseconds, not

false. Not false. Even if false,
the waters of paradise

are there, in the mind, the sleeping

mind. *Why this puritan each
night inside me that again denies me.*

•

Chimeras glitter: fierce energy you
envy.

Chimeras ignorant they're chimeras
beckon.

As you reach into their crotch, they foretell
your fate.

With a sudden rush of milk you taste
what has

no end.

•

We long for the Absolute, Royce
said. Voices you once

heard that you can never *not* hear again,—

. . . spoiled priest, liar, if you want something
enough, sometimes you think it's there.

He is Ava Gardner

He is Ava Gardner at the height of her beauty
in *Pandora and the Flying Dutchman*.

I had allowed him to become, for me, necessity.
I was not ever for him necessity.

An adornment, yes. A grace-note. Not
necessity.

Everyone, the men at least, are crazy about
Pandora. She is smart,

self-deprecating, funny. She who has seen,
seemingly, everything about love, and says

she has no idea what love is—
who knows the world finds her beautiful, so that

she must test every man and slightly disgusted
find him wanting—clearly she has not, in this

crowd of men eager to please her, to flatter
and bring her drinks, found someone

who is, for her, necessity. Watching
Pandora and the Flying Dutchman, you feel sympathy

for the beautiful
who cannot find anyone who is for them necessity.

•

He is Ava Gardner
at the height of her beauty.

Fucked up, you knew you'd never fall for someone
not fucked up.

You watch her test each suitor. She sings about
love to an old friend, drunk, a poet.

He asks her to marry him. After she again
refuses, you see him slip something into his drink—

then he dies, poisoned. She says he has tried that
too many times, now she feels nothing.

Promising nothing, she asks the famous
race-car driver, who also wants to marry her,

to shove the car he has worked on for months
over the cliff, into the sea. He

does. In the first flush of
pleasure, she agrees to marry him. The next day

he has the car's
carcass, pouring water, dragged up from the sea.

You are the learned, amused professor surrounded
by his collections, who carefully pieces together

fragments of Greek pots. You know it is foolish
to become another suitor. *Hors de*

combat, soon you are the only one she trusts.
You become, at moments, her confessor.

●

Then she meets the Dutchman.
He offers little, asks nothing.

When she withdraws her
attention, he isn't spooked.

Because, when she meets him, he is
painting the portrait of someone who has

her face, with petulance
she scrapes off the face.

He charmingly makes her head a blank
ovoid, and says that's better.

She thinks that she is the knife
that, cutting him, will heal him.

●

You know she is right. You have discovered
he is the fabled Dutchman—who for

centuries has sailed the world's seas
unable to die, unable to die though

he wants to die. You know what it is to
want to die. His reasons

are a little contrived, a mechanism of the plot:
reasons that Pandora, at the end, discovers:

he murdered, centuries earlier, through
jealousy and paranoia, his wife: now

unless he can find a woman
willing to die

out of love for him, sail out with him
and drown, he cannot ever

find rest. This logic
makes sense to her: she who does not

believe in love
will perform an act proving its existence.

●

She wants, of course, to throw her life away.
The Dutchman will always arrive

because that's what she wants.
Those of us who look on, who want

the proximate and partial to continue,
loathe the hunger for the absolute.

●

All your life you have watched as two creatures
think they have found in each other

necessity. Watched as the shell
then closes, for a time, around them.

You envy them, as you gather with
the rest of the village, staring out to sea.

When she swims out to his boat, to give
herself, both succeed at last in drowning.

●

Couples stay together when each of the two
remains a necessity for the other. Which you

cannot know, until they
cease to be. Tautology

that is the sum of what you know.
He is a master, he has lived by

becoming the master
of the alchemy that makes, as you

stare into some one
person's eyes, makes you adore him.

Eyes that say that despite the enormous
landscapes that divide you

you are brothers, he too is trapped in
all that divides soul from soul. Then

suddenly he is fluttering his finger ends
between yours. He rises

from the table, explains he had no
sleep last night, and leaves.

•

You couldn't worm your way into
becoming, for him, necessity.

When did he grow bored with seduction and
confessors, and find the Dutchman? —

For months there has been nothing
but silence. When you sent him a pot only

you could have with care pieced together
from the catastrophe of history, more

silence. *The enterprise is abandoned.*

●

Something there is in me that makes me
think I need this thing. That gives this thing

the illusion of necessity.

As enthralled to flesh
as I, he could not see beneath this old

face I now wear, this ruinous, ugly
body, that I

I am the Dutchman.

But nobody knows, when living, where
necessity lies. Maybe later, if history

is lucky, the urn
will not refuse to be pieced together.

This is neither good nor bad.
It is what is.

Mourn

Why so hard
to give up

what often
was ever

even then
hardly there.

But the safe
world my will

constructed
before him

this soul could
not find breath

in. He brought
electric

promise-crammed
sudden air.

Then withdrew
lazily

as if to
teach you how

you must live
short of breath.

Still now crave
sudden air.

The enterprise is abandoned.

I'm not a fool, I knew from the beginning
what couldn't happen. What couldn't happen

didn't. *The enterprise is abandoned.*

But half our life is
dreams, delirium, everything that underlies

that feeds

that keeps alive the illusion of sanity, semi-
sanity, we allow

others to see. The half of me that feeds the rest

is in mourning. Mourns. Each time we must
mourn, we fear this is the final mourning, this time

mourning never will lift. A friend said when a lover

dies, it takes
two years. Then it lifts.

Inside those two years, you punish

not only the world,
but yourself.

At seventy-two, the future is what I mourn.

Since college I've never forgotten Masha
in *The Seagull* saying *I am in mourning for my life.*

She wears only black, she treats others with

fierce solicitude
and sudden punishment.

The enterprise is abandoned. And not.

Janáček at Seventy

It was merely a locket but it was
a locket only

I could have made —

Once she is told that it was made
for her, recognizes it as a locket

her little agile famous-in-his-little-world

Vulcan
himself

made only for her, she must

reach for it, must
place it around her neck.

Soon the warmth of her flesh

must warm what I have made.
Her husband will know who made it

so she will wear it

only when
alone, but wear it she will.

Threnody on the Death of Harriet Smithson

She was barely twenty, she was called
Miss Smithson, but through her

Juliet, Desdemona

found superb utterance. A new
truth, Shakespeare's old truth

bewitched us, unheard

until she made us hear it—she
heralded a revolution

Madame Dorval, Lemaître, Malibran,

yes, Victor Hugo
and Berlioz

then taught us we had always known.

Now, at fifty-four, she is dead,—
. . . bitter that fame long ago abandoned her.

I think her fate our fate, the planet's fate.

•

These fleeting creatures, that flit by
giving themselves to us

and the air

unable to etch there
anything permanent

Addicted to the ecstasies of

carving again from darkness
a shape, an illusion of light

They say, *I wash my hands of the gods*

this has existed
whether the whirling planet tomorrow

survive, whether recording angels exist

•

On this stage at this
moment *this* has existed

unerasable because already erased

Everything finally, of course, is
metaphysical

this has existed

THREE

HISTORY IS
A SERIES
OF FAILED
REVELATIONS

Dream of the Book

That great hopefulness that lies in
imagining you are an unreadable, not

blank slate, but something even you cannot

read because words will rise from its
depths only when you at last

manage to expose it to air, —

the pathology of the provinces. *You need
air.*

•

Then you find air. Somehow somewhere

as if whatever feeds expectation were
wounded, gutted by the bewildering self-

buried thousand impersonations

by which you know you
made and remade

yourself, —

one day, staring at the mountain,
you ceased to ask

Open Sesame

merely requiring that narrative reveal
something structural about the world.

●

Reading history

you learn that those who cannot read
history are condemned to repeat it

etcetera

just like those who
can, or think they can.

Substitute the psyche for history   substitute myth for

the psyche   economics
for myth   substitute politics, culture, history etc.

●

As if there were a book

As if there were a book inside which you can
breathe

Where, at every turn, you see at last the lineaments

Where the end of the earth's long dream of
virtue is *not*, as you have

again and again found it here, the will

gazing out at the dilemmas
proceeding from its own nature

unbroken but in stasis

●

Seduced not by a book but by the idea
of a book

like the *Summa* in five fat volumes, that your priest

in high school explained Thomas Aquinas
almost finished, except that there were,

maddeningly, "just a few things he didn't

have time, before dying, quite
to figure out"

•

That history is a series of failed revelations

you're sure you hear folded, hidden
within the all-but-explicit

bitter

taste-like-dirt inside Dinah Washington's
voice singing *This bitter earth*

•

A few months before Thomas'

death, as he talked with Jesus
Jesus asked him

what reward he wanted for his

virtue—
to which Thomas replied, *You, Lord,*

only You—

which is why, as if this vision
unfit him for his life, he told the priest

prodding him to take up once again

writing his book, *Reginald, I cannot:*
everything I have written I now see is straw.

•

Though the Book whose text articulates

the text of
creation

is an arrogance, you think, flung by priests

at all that is
fecund, that has not yet found being

Though priests, addicted to

unanswerable but necessary questions,
also everywhere are addicted to cruel answers

you wake happy

when you dream
you have seen the book, the Book exists

•

You sail protested, contested
seas, the something within you that

chooses your masters

itself not chosen. Inheritor inheriting
inheritors, you must earn what you inherit.

Inauguration Day

(JANUARY 20, 2009)

Today, despite what is dead

staring out across America I see since
Lincoln gunmen
nursing fantasies of purity betrayed,
dreaming to restore
the glories of their blood and state

despite what is dead but lodged within us, hope

under the lustrous flooding moon
the White House is still
Whitman's White House, its
gorgeous front
full of reality, full of illusion

hope made wise by dread begins again

Race

(FOR LEON WOOD, JR.)

America is ours
to ruin but
not ours to dream.

The unstained but
terrifying land
Europe imagined

soon the whole
stained
planet dreamed.

●

My grandmother, as a teenager,
had the guts to leave

Spain, and never see her parents again—

arriving in America
to her shame

she could not read. O you taught by

deprivation
that your soul is flawed:—

to her shame she could not read.

·

Olive-skinned, bewildcringly
dark, in this California surrounded

everywhere by the brown-skinned

dirt-poor progeny of those her ancestors
conquered and enslaved, she insisted we are

Spanish. Not Mexican. Spanish-Basque.

·

Disconsolate to learn her
seven-year-old grandson

spent the afternoon visiting the house—

had entered, had
eaten at the house—

of his new black friend, her fury

the coward grandson sixty-five years
later cannot from his nerves erase.

•

Or the rage with which she stopped her

daughter from marrying a Lebanese
doctor whose skin was

too dark. Actual Spain

was poverty and humiliation so
deep she refused to discuss it—

or, later, richer, to return.

But the Spanish her only
daughter, my mother, divorced, light-

skinned, spoke

was pure
Castilian. On her walls, the dead world

she loathed and obeyed

kept vigil
from large oval dark oak frames.

•

The terrifying land the whole stained
planet dreamed unstained

Europe first imagined. To me, as a child,
Europe was my grandmother—

clinging to what had
cost her everything, she thought

the mutilations exacted by
discriminations of color

rooted in the stars. We brought
here what we had.

Glutton

Ropes of my dead
grandmother's unreproducible

sausage, curing for weeks

on the front porch. My mother,
thoroughly

Americanized, found them

vaguely shameful.
Now though I

taste and taste

I can't find that
taste I so loved as a kid.

Each thing generates the Idea

of itself, the perfect thing that it
is, of course, not—

once, a pear so breathtakingly

succulent I couldn't
breathe. I take back that

"of course."

It's got to be out there again, —
. . . *I have tasted it.*

Whitman

Once, crossing the Alps by car at night, the great glacier suddenly there
    in the moonlight next to the car, in the silence

alone with it.

        •

I heard Robert Viscusi read only once, on a rainy night in Manhattan.

At the end of a long evening, he read the final lines of the first poem
    in the first *Leaves of Grass*, before the poems had titles.

He read with a still, unmelodramatic directness and simplicity that
    made the lines seem as if distilled from the throat of the generous
    gods.

Early Whitman's eerie
equilibrium staring as if adequately at war's carnage, love's carnage,—

        •

. . . suspended, I listen.

        •

This is the departing
sun, distributing its gifts to the earth as it disengages from earth

without grief.

Elation as the hand disengages from its consequence, as the sovereign soul
charmed by its evanescence

toys with and mocks the expectations of worlds.

As you listen, you think this inaccessible
exultation indifferent to catastrophe's etiology or end

is wisdom.

•

A poem read aloud is by its nature a vision of its nature.

Vision you cannot now reenter, from which when you sound the words
     within later unaided and alone, you are expelled.

2. *Soundings*

Soundings of the world, testings
later forgotten but within whose

corpses you then burrowed, feeding: wounds

that taught the inverse of what adults
asserted, even thought they believed: taught

you do not have to hold on tight

to what you love, its nature
is not ever to release you: each testing, each

sounding of the world

one more transparent drop
fallen over your eye and hardening

there, to make you what you secretly

think by trial you have become: perfect
eyeball, observer

without a master. (Untranscendental

disgusted-with-lies
homemade American boy's eyeball.)

•

Each creature must

himself, you were sure, *grind the lens*
through which he perceives the world.

•

Illusion of mastery the boy could not

sustain. Now you have no image, no
recollection of incidents, people,

humiliations, that showed you how

small, absurd you were—
but as if, in all things human, hegemony

breeds loathing

soon all you can see is that the ravenous,
dependent, rage-ridden

brain you inhabit

is not a lens, not a prism you have
flawlessly honed that transmits

light, but this suffocating

bubble that encases you, partial, mortal,
stained with the creature that created it.

•

You are the creature that created it.

You You You you cried, reaching
for a knife

to cut through the bubble

smelling of you. Why did soiled
you, before you even knew what sex was, want

to put his thing in your mouth?

The corpses on which you had so long
fed, turned their faces toward you—;

priests, they said, you must invite
priests to surround you.

●

The question became not
whether a master, but which.

You schooled and reschooled

yourself to bind with
briars your joys and desires.

●

This. Before a series of glamorous or

pure, compellingly severe
chimeras that mastered

the chaos I perceived within and without

all my life I have
implored: —

this. *REMAKE ME* in the image of *THIS.*

   3.

your gaze, Walt Whitman, through its
mastery of paper

paper on which you invented the illusion of your voice

the intricacies of whose candor and ambition
disarm me

into imagining this is your voice

fueled by the ruthless gaze that
unshackled the chains shackling

queer me in adolescence

(unshackled me maybe for three days
during which I tried to twist out of

knowing what you made me see I knew

and could not bear that I knew

immured in an America that betrayed
the America you taught still must exist)

Ginsberg called you lonely old

courage teacher

but something in young electric you
was before the end

broken

wary alerted listening buck
that seeing all

cannot see or imagine

itself broken
the melancholy spectacle

through your mastery of paper

as you entirely predicted
transformed into the gaze of others

•

The event, or many mini-events, only implicitly recorded in a poem.

After his father's death but before dressing the mutilated bodies of sol-
diers, as he walked the shore-line touching debris, flotsam, pierced
by his own evanescence everywhere assaulting him, by "the old
thought of likenesses,"

his own sweet sole self like debris smashed beneath his feet at the sea's
edge,

as he walked there, the old exultant gaze, like an animal's poise, was
gone.

What is left then but to revise and enlarge your poem till the end of
time, the eerie early equilibrium smashed, the old confidence like
a stream that was always there now gone, like the dust you can't
cease staring at clinging to your shoes?

But impossible to face becoming detritus, impossible to face it naked,
without armor, without ideas about Idea, America, song about
Song,

impossible to smell the breath of death without visions, broken,
makeshift, aiming at an eloquence that so insinuates, so dyes each
vision with the presence, the voice of the singer,

we who have seen what we see through his sight are his progeny,

impossible to face death without progeny as spar on which to cling.

Robert Viscusi, the bullet you aimed at *Leaves of Grass* bounced
off its spine and landed, hot, intact, where I now still sit.

FOUR

Three Tattoos

ONE   *Maria Forever*

TWO   labyrinthine intricate
coiling pent dragon

THREE   B R A D

·

gaudy skin prophesying
the fate of the heart

reminder that if you once

cross me
I can destroy you

indelible capital letters

written in flesh to remind
flesh what flesh has forgotten

·

It must be lifted from the mind

must be lifted and placed elsewhere
must not remain in the mind alone

As You Crave Soul

but find flesh
till flesh

almost seems sufficient

when the as-yet-unwritten
poem within you

demands existence

all you can offer it are words. Words
are flesh. Words

are flesh

craving to become idea, idea
dreaming it has found, this time, a body

obdurate as stone.

To carve the body of the world
and out of flesh make

flesh obdurate as stone.

Looking down into the casket-crib
of your love, embittered by

soul you crave to become stone.

You mourn not
what is not, but what never could have been.

What could not ever find a body

because what you wanted, he
wanted but did not want.

Ordinary divided unsimple heart.

What you dream is that, by eating
the flesh of words, what you write

makes mind and body

one. When, after a reading, you are asked
to describe your aesthetics,

you reply, *An aesthetics of embodiment.*

Things Falling From Great Heights

Spasm of vision you crave like a secular pentecost

The subject of this poem
is how much the spaces that you now move in

cost

the spaces that you were
given

were born to and like an animal used but then ran from

ran from but then thought you had
transformed

enough to accede to

the choices you made to inhabit the spaces where you
when prompted repeat the story of how you arrived

they cost your life

O ruin O haunted

O ruin O haunted
restless remnant of

two bodies, two

histories
you felt the unceasing

force of

but never understood, —
terrified that without an

x-ray, a topography of

their souls
you must repeat their lives.

●

You did not repeat their lives.

You lodged your faith
in Art—

which gives us

pattern, process
with the flesh

still stuck to it.

With flesh, you
told yourself, pattern

is truer, subtler, less

given to the illusion
seeing frees you from it.

●

Or, you did repeat their lives,—

. . . repeated them by
inverting them.

How you hurtled yourself against, how

cunningly you
failed to elude love.

●

Love
is the manna

that falling

makes you
see

the desert

surrounding you
is a desert.

Makes you think dirt is not where you were born.

Plea and Chastisement

When the exact intonation with which
at the sink she said

"Honey"

at last can sound in no one's head
she will become merely the angry

poems written by an angry son

●

"Honey"

●

which is a cry not about something she must
wash or my latest frightening improvidence

but another wound made by my failure of love

which must flatten the world unless I
forgive her for what in an indecipherable

past she fears she *somehow* did to cause this

•

At five
thrillingly I won the Oedipal struggle

first against my father then stepfather

In our alliance against the world
we were more like each other

than anyone else

till adolescence and the world
showed me this was prison

•

Out of immense appetite we make

immense promiscs
the future dimensions of which

we cannot see

then see
when it seems death to keep them

•

I can still hear her
"Honey"

plea and chastisement

•

long since become the pillars of the earth
the price exacted

at the door to the dimensional world

Martha Yarnoz Bidart Hall

Though she whom you had so let
in, the desire for survival will not

allow you ever to admit
another so deeply in again

Though she, *in*, went crazy
vengeful-crazy

so that, as in Dante, there she ate your heart

Though her house that she despised but
spent her life constructing

still cannot, thirty-nine years after
her death, by your ratiocination or rage

be uncon-
structed

you think, *We had an encounter on the earth*

each of us
hungry beyond belief

As long as you are alive
she is alive

You are the leaping
dog

capricious on the grass, lunging
at something only it can see.

Late Fairbanks

As in his early films, still the old
abandon, a mischievous, blithe ardor.

Through unending repetition, it became
part of his muscles.

To leap, push
against earth

then
spring.

But the ground under him has changed.
He doesn't remember when it happened.

When he wasn't looking
the earth turned to mush.

Against Rage

He had not been denied the world. Terrible
scenes that he clung to because they taught him

the world will at last be buried with him.
As well as the exhilarations. Now,

he thinks each new one will be the last one.
The last new page. The last sex. *Each human*

being's story, he tells nobody, *is a boat*
cutting through the night. As starless blackness

approaches, the soul reverses itself, in
the eerie acceptance of finitude.

For the AIDS Dead

The plague you have thus far survived. They didn't.
Nothing that they did in bed that you didn't.

Writing a poem, I cleave to "you." You
means I, one, you, as well as the you

inside you constantly talk to. Without
justice or logic, without

sense, you survived. They didn't.
Nothing that they did in bed that you didn't.

Tyrant

In this journey through flesh
not just in flesh or with flesh

but through it

you drive forward seeing
in the rearview mirror

seeing only

there
always growing smaller

what you drive toward

What you drive toward
is what you once made with flesh

Out of stone caulked with blood

mortared
with blood and flesh

you made a house

bright now in the rearview mirror
white in the coarse sun's coarse light

No more men died making it

than any other ruthless
monument living men admire

Now as your body betrays you

what you made with flesh
is what you must drive toward

what you must before

you die reassure
teach yourself you made

The house mortared with flesh

as if defying the hand of its
maker

when you pull up to it at last

dissolves as it has always
dissolved

In this journey through flesh

not just in flesh or with flesh
but through flesh

Mouth

It was as if, starving, his stomach
rebelled at food, *as quickly as he ate*
it passed right through him, his body
refused what his body needed. Recipe
for death. *But,*
he said, *what others think is food isn't food.*
It passed right through him, he shoved
meat into his mouth but still his
body retained nothing. Absorbed
nothing. He grows
thinner. He thinks he cannot live on
nothing. He has the persistent
sense that whatever object he seeks
is not what he seeks, —
. . . now he repeats the litany of his choices.
Love, which always to his surprise
exhilarated even as it tormented
and absorbed him. Unendingly under
everything, art—; trying to make
a work of art he can continue to inhabit.
The choices he made he said he made
almost without choosing.
The best times, I must confess, are when
one cannot help oneself.
Has his pride at his intricate
inventions come to nothing?
Nothing he can now name or touch is food.

Sex was the bed where you learned to be
naked and not naked at the same time.
Bed
where you learned to move the unsustainable
weight inside, then too often
lost the key to it.
Faces too close, that despite themselves
promise, then out of panic disappoint.
Not just out of panic; only in his mind
is he freely both *here* and *not here*. The imperious
or imagined needs of those you
love or think you love
demand you forget that when you smell your
flesh you smell
unfulfilment.
We are creatures, he thinks, caught in an obscure,
ruthless economy,—
. . . his hunger
grows as whatever his mouth fastens upon
fails to feed him. Recipe
for death. But he's sure he'll learn something
once he sees
La Notte again. He's placed *Duino Elegies*
next to his bed. He craves the cold
catechism Joyce mastered writing "Ithaca."
Now he twists within the box
he cannot exit or rise above.
He thinks he must die
when what will not allow him to retain food
makes him see his body has disappeared.

Rio

I am here to fix the door.

Use has almost destroyed it. Disuse
would have had the same effect.

No, you're not confused, you didn't
call. If you call you still have hope.

Now you think you have
lived past the necessity for doors.

Carmen Miranda
is on the TV, inviting you to Rio.

Go to sleep while I fix the door.

Presage

Here, at the rim of what has not yet
been, the monotonous

I want to die sung

over and over by your
soul to your soul

just beneath sound

which you once again fail
not to hear, cannot erase or obliterate

returns you to the mirror of itself: —

Mumps, Meningitis, Encephalitis
all at once, together, at

age eight or nine —

•

(later, for months, you dragged your left
leg as you walked, that's what everyone

told you because you hadn't noticed, you

were undersea, the entire
perceptual world

undersea, death your new

familiar, like the bright slime-
green bile you watched for days

inexorably pumped from your stomach)

•

or, later, at thirteen, TYPHOID,
when the doctors said the next two days

will decide if you live, or die —;

you tried, very calmly, to ask yourself
whether you did actually want to live,

the answer, you knew, not clear —

then you heard
something say

I want to live, despite the metaphysical

awfulness of this incontinent
body shitting uncontrollably into a toilet in

time, this place, blind self, hobbled, hobbling animal, —

•

You are undersea. These are not entwined
ropes, but thick twisted slime-green

cables. Laid out before you is the fabled
Gordian knot, which you must cut.

Which you must cut not
to rule the earth, but escape it.

All you must do is sever them. Your blade
breaks, as the ties that bind thicken, tighten.

Elegy for Earth

Because earth's inmates travel in flesh

and hide from flesh

and adore flesh

you hunger for flesh that does not die

But hunger for the absolute
breeds hatred of the absolute

Those who are the vessels of revelation

or who think that they are

ravage

us with the promise of rescue

•

My mother outside in the air
waving, shriveled, as if she knew

this is the last time—

watching as I climbed the stairs
and the plane swallowed me. She and I

could no more change what we hurtled toward

than we could change the weather. Finding my
seat, unseen I stared back as she receded.

•

They drop into holes in the earth, everything

you loved, loved and
hated, as you will drop—

and the moment when all was possible

gone. You are still
above earth, the moment when all

and nothing is possible

long gone. Terrified of the sea, we
cling to the hull.

•

In adolescence, you thought your work
ancient work: to decipher at last

human beings' relation to God. Decipher

love. To make what was once whole
whole again: or to see

why it never should have been thought whole.

●

Earth was a tiny labyrinthine ball orbiting

another bigger ball
so bright

you can go blind staring at it

when the source of warmth and light
withdraws

then terrible winter

when burning and relentless
it draws too close

the narcotically gorgeous

fecund earth
withers

as if the sun

as if the sun
taught us

what we will ever know of the source

now too
far

then too close

     •

Blood

island
where you for a time lived

FIVE

Of His Bones Are Coral Made

He still trolled books, films, gossip, his own
past, searching not just for

ideas that dissect the mountain that

in his early old age he is almost convinced
cannot be dissected:

he searched for stories:

stories the pattern of whose
knot dimly traces the pattern of his own:

what is intolerable in

the world, which is to say
intolerable in himself, ingested, digested:

the stories that

haunt each of us, for each of us
rip open the mountain.

•

the creature smothered in death clothes

dragging into the forest
bodies he killed to make meaning

the woman who found that she

to her bewilderment and horror
had a body

●

As if certain algae

that keep islands of skeletons
alive, that make living rock from

trash, from carcasses left behind by others,

as if algae
were to produce out of

themselves and what they most fear

the detritus over whose
kingdom they preside: the burning

fountain is the imagination

within us that ingests and by its
devouring generates

what is most antithetical to itself:

it returns the intolerable as
brilliant dream, visible, opaque,

teasing analysis:

makes from what you find hardest to
swallow, most indigestible, your food.

Poem Ending With a Sentence
by Heath Ledger

Each grinding flattened American vowel smashed to
centerlessness, his glee that whatever long ago mutilated his

mouth, he has mastered to mutilate

you: the Joker's voice, so unlike
the bruised, withheld, wounded voice of Ennis Del Mar.

Once I have the voice

that's
the line

and at

the end
of the line

is a hook

and attached
to that

is the soul.

Dream Reveals in Neon the Great Addictions

LOVE, *with its simulacrum, sex.*

The words, like a bonfire encased
in glass, glowed on the horizon.

POWER, *with its simulacrum, money.*

FAME, *with its simulacrum, celebrity.*

GOD, *survived
by what survives belief, the desire to be*

a Saint.

*Seed of your obsessions, these are
the addictions that tempt your soul.*

Then, seeing the word ART, I woke.

•

Refused love, power, fame, sainthood, your
tactic, like that of modest

Caesar, is to feign indifference and refusal.
You are addicted to what you cannot possess.

You cannot tell if
addictions, secret, narcotic,

damage or enlarge
mind, through which you seize the world.

Ganymede

On this earth where no secure foothold is,
deathbound.

You're deathbound. You can't stop moving when you're
at rest.

Transfixed by your destination, by what
you fear

you want. *Unlike each bright scene, bright thing, each
nervous*

*dumb sweet creature whose death you mourn, you will
not die.*

Chimera to whose voice even Jesus
succumbed.

How you loathed crawling on the earth seeing
nothing.

When the god pulled you up into the air,
taking

you showed you you wanted to be taken.

On This Earth Where No Secure Foothold Is

Wanting to be a movie star like Dean Stockwell or Gigi Perreau, answering an ad at ten or eleven you made your mother drive you to Hollywood and had expensive Hollywood pictures taken.

•

Hollywood wasn't buying.

•

Everyone is buying but not everyone wants to buy you.

•

You see the kids watching, brooding.

•

Religion, politics, love, work, sex—each enthrallment, each enthusiasm presenting itself as pleasure or necessity, is recruitment.

•

Each kid is at the edge of a sea.

•

At each kid's feet multitudinous voices say *I will buy you if you buy me.*

•

Who do you want to be bought by?

•

The child learns this is the question almost immediately.

•

Mother?

•

Father?

•

Both mother and father tried to enlist you but soon you learned that you couldn't enlist on both sides at the same time.

•

They lied that you could but they were at war and soon you learned you couldn't.

•

How glamorous they were!

●

As they aged they mourned that to buyers they had become invisible.

●

Both of them in the end saw beneath them only abyss.

●

You are at the edge of a sea.

●

You want to buy but you know not everyone wants to buy you.

●

Each enthrallment is recruitment.

●

Your body will be added to the bodies that piled-up make the structures of the world.

●

Your body will be erased, swallowed.

●

Who do you want to be swallowed by?

●

It's almost the same question as To be or not to be.

●

Figuring out who they want to be bought by is what all the kids with brooding looks on their face are brooding about.

●

Your weapon is your mind.

For an Unwritten Opera

Once you had a secret love: seeing
even his photo, a window is flung open
high in the airless edifice that is you.

Though everything looks as if it is continuing
just as before, it is not, it is continuing
in a new way (sweet lingo O'Hara and Ashbery

teach). That's not how you naturally speak:
you tell yourself, first, that he is not the air
you need; second, that you loathe air.

As a boy you despised the world for replacing
God with another addiction, love.
Despised yourself. Was there no third thing?

But every blue moon the skeptical, the adamantly
disabused find themselves, like you,
returned to life by a secret: like him, in you.

Now you understand Janáček at
seventy, in love with a much younger
married woman, chastely writing her.

As in Mozart song remains no matter how
ordinary, how flawed the personae. For us poor
mortals: private accommodations. Magpie beauty.

THIRST

(New Poems, 2016)

PART ONE

Old and Young

If you have looked at someone in
a mirror
looking at you in the mirror

your eyes meeting
there
not face to face

•

backstage as you
prepare
for a performance

•

you look into the long horizontal
mirror
that backs the long theatrical

make-up table that runs along one
wall of the high dressing-room aerie
from which you must descend to the stage

•

there in the mirror you see
his eyes
looking into your eyes in the mirror

where you
plural
amused begin to talk

suddenly inspired not
to look at each other
directly but held by this third

thing as his eyes
allow your eyes to
follow his eyes in the mirror

you ask if anyone has ever
made a movie
in which two people talk not

directly to each other but during
the entire
static but dynamic

film as they go about their lives
their eyes are
locked staring at each other in a mirror

that they together hold a few feet
above them
or beside them

knowing if they look away
they will lose
what they now possess

trapped but freed
neither knowing
why this is better

why this
as long as no one enters
is release

because you are
twice
his age

THIS IS THE PLACE IN
NATURE
WE CAN MEET

space which
every other
space merely approximates

you ask again if
anybody made a movie
about this

•

others
enter loudly and when you
plural each look away you plural soon go on

Half-light

That crazy drunken night I
maneuvered you out into a field outside of

Coachella—I'd never seen a sky
so full of stars, as if the dirt of our lives

still were sprinkled with glistening
white shells from the ancient seabed

beneath us that receded long ago.
Parallel. We lay in parallel furrows.

—That suffocated, fearful
look on your face.

Jim, yesterday I heard your wife on the phone
tell me you died almost nine months ago.

Jim, now we cannot ever. Bitter
that we cannot ever have

the conversation that in
nature and alive we never had. Now not ever.

We have not spoken in years. I thought
perhaps at ninety or a hundred, two

broken-down old men, we wouldn't
give a damn, and find speech.

When I tell you that all the years we were
undergraduates I was madly in love with you

you say you
knew. I say I knew you

knew. You say
There was no place in nature we could meet.

You say this as if you need me to
admit something. *No place*

in nature, given our natures. Or is this
warning? I say what is happening now is

happening only because one of us is
dead. You laugh and say, Or both of us!

Our words
will be weirdly jolly.

That light I now envy
exists only on this page.

Across Infinities Without Sentience

2014. 1994. Twenty years.

When this world appearing in a mind is
blotted out, ear and eye

across infinities without sentience

seek the dead. The dead
hide in the past. In what they made.

When you called him each day

he each day
answered. Protected by distance

(Cambridge to New York)

he each day
eagerly answered. Except during summers

with Kenward in Vermont, when he was not

allowed to answer. Or so he said. The distress
with which he said this made you believe him.

Across infinities without sentience

ear and eye
seek the dead.

When you can no longer each day call

him and hear him dead now twenty
years each day answer as once he sweetly did

we are queers of the universe.

End of a Friendship

The United States (*salvation of both our*
families) was built (*stomach-*
churning to admit it) was built across a continent

on genocide. An abattoir. Mere

prudence, enlightened self-interest, cannot
account for why the head of

Metacomet

whom the colonists called King Philip, at the end of
King Philip's War, his corpse drawn and quartered, his
wife and youngest son sold into slavery in the West Indies,

why his head in Plymouth was exhibited on a pole

for twenty
years.

I know this not because I know what is
not taught in American
history, but because I've read Robert Lowell's poems.

America the salvation of both our families. History an obscenity

those who inherit the depeopled
and repeopled

land try to forget. *Genocide*. Long abattoir. But those

who perform amputations
convince themselves amputation is

necessary—; an emblem
against the horizon for which the empty horizon begs.

⋅

Fun: the immense pleasure of watching, goading
someone into becoming
himself on paper: so many of your best early poems

offended what others thought made good
art: the immensity that *The New Yorker* would print
only if you agreed to cut the one thing that offended

invisible decorums of impersonality, the provocation
that made it remarkable and yours and which you of
course refused to cut: what

fun: *my work not just to watch, but to goad*: a privilege.

⋅

Now we are going to die in estrangement. This
once seemed, still

seems, intolerable; not to be believed.

•

Yesterday, which lasted more or less
forty years, we walked along the bottom of the sea absorbed

picking up tin cans, tossing them back and forth, laughing

at what others rightly had discarded, astonished at the few
we both recognized as

gold. They were

gold. We kept them to show the world
what gold was.

We disagreed
seldom. Then,

somehow, our capacity to find what others were blind to
diminished, shriveled, all but stopped.

We were alone with each other at the bottom of the sea.

•

The reasons for the wound existed long before
the wound.

The reasons (jealousy, humiliation) exist between
any two writers.

For over forty years we willed to keep the space
we shared

the space in which we thought and breathed

free, safe from the inevitable
inherent

enmity of equals.

I cannot name
when that stopped.

Nor can I, to my
torment, name

why that stopped.

•

Why did that stop?

•

Now I must construct the song of
disenthrallment—

I was, I think I now can see, ripe for disenthrallment.

The exhaustion of making invisible
those tiny acts in thought and in deed

which, if revealed, the other
takes as disloyal. After decades I became

giddy, reckless, avid
to change the terms of what seemed

submission, enslavement—; as well as full of

dread, this long-
anticipated, necessary mourning.

        •

It is not cruelty, those who amputate
insist, *It is amputation.*

Because wound
begets silence
begets rage

each of us secretly (hidden, each in his
way) raises

high on its stake the head of Metacomet.

●

My father's head
hung outside my mother's window
for years when I was a kid.

She pretended that it wasn't there; but hers
also did outside his.

All over town the heads sing the same thing:

This severed head
that pollutes the air
that dominates the horizon

betrayed the intimacy lavished upon it.

●

I was invited to your house. You
invited me into your living room. In the old days,

a small thing. I saw how long it has been forbidden

when it was no longer. You invited
me to sit down among the chairs, the couch, the coffee table.

I saw this was forbidden when it was no longer. You invited

me to sit down among the chairs, the couch, the coffee table.
I said to myself I must be dreaming. I was.

●

You say, *There seems to be a floor
beneath one's feet, but there is not.*

Why must you write this poem?

●

Memory is punishment.

●

Meat is flesh, but doesn't say
flesh when teeth bite into it.

Sum

All around you of course will die but when the fingers of
your left hand no longer can button

tiny and not so tiny buttons

you know you will die quicker.
Anguish more verb than noun hides their incompetence.

•

ANGUISH, *duplicitous, hidden, can, for*
a time, deny what promises never to return.

•

The elegant ocean
inside, frictionless, that moved as quickly as the eye once moved,

now when your anguished eye shifts
tips deadweight with inertia, almost splashing over.

•

Each morning you wake to long slow piteous
swoops of sound, half-loon, half-dog.

He is wandering in the yard.

The dog at eighteen who at sixteen began protesting each dawn.

Thirst

The miraculous warmth that arose so implausibly from rock had, within it, thirst.

•

Thirst made by a glimpse that is, each time, brief.

•

As if, each time, that is all you are allowed.

•

The way back to it never exactly the same.

•

Once you have been there, always the promise of it.

•

Promise made to beguile and haunt, you think, residue of an injunction that is ancient.

•

Not only ancient, but indifferent?

•

Half the time when you pursue it you fear that this time, out of distraction or exhaustion or repetition, this time it cannot be reached.

•

I hope you're guessing Orgasm, or Love, or Hunger for the Absolute, or even The Sublime —

•

History littered with testimonies that God gives his followers a shot of God; then withdraws.

•

The pattern, the process each time the same.

•

There, —

•

. . . then, not there (withdrawn).

•

Each time you think that you can predict how to get there the next time, soon you cannot.

•

The singer's voice, the fabled night the microphone captured her at the height of her powers—

•

You have been the locus of ecstasy.

•

You have been a mile above the storm, looking down at it; and, at the same time, full of almost-insight, obliterated at its center.

•

Creature coterminous with thirst.

PART TWO

Disappearing during sleep

[FOR ROBERT LOWELL]

seems release, merciful
ideal not to have to greet (perhaps) oblivion

with panic, remorse, or self-laceration; —
but what I hear is your voice

say that unconscious death
thrust at you asleep in the back seat of a taxi

was never the ideal your work spoke, —

. . . dying again for the first
time, as if relieved you say *It is, at*

last, happening.

The Fourth Hour of the Night

I.

Out of scarcity, —
. . . being.

Because, when you were nine, your father

was murdered,
betrayed.

Because the traveler was betrayed by those with

whom he had the right to seek
refuge, the Tatars.

Because the universe then allowed a creature

stronger, taller, more
ruthless than you

to fasten around your neck a thick wooden wheel

impossible
to throw off.

Because at nine your cunning was not equal

to iron-fastened
immense wood.

Because, stripped of what was his from birth, the slave

at ten
outwitted

the universe, tore the wheel from his neck: —

because your neck
carries it still, *Scarcity is the mother of being.*

•

Hour in which betrayal and slavery
are the great teachers.

Hour in which acquisition

looks like, and for
a moment is, safety.

Hour in which the earth, looking into

a mirror, names what it sees
by the history of weapons.

Hour from which I cannot wake.

II.

Ch'ang-ch'un was determined that he would not
prostrate himself before

the conqueror of the world

though Alexander the Great, drunk, had executed
Aristotle's nephew when he refused

to grovel before his uncle's pupil.

●

Ch'ang-ch'un bowed his head with clasped
hands. The Great Khan was gracious.

Though Ch'ang-ch'un, much younger,
had refused invitations from the King of Gold

and even the emperor of Hang-chou, now,
in his old age, he discovered he was

tired of waiting for apotheosis.

At last invited to court by the terrifying
conqueror of the world, he said *Yes*.

●

He traveled for a year and a half
following the route the Great Khan

himself had taken. He passed valley after valley

that, years later, still were filled
with ungathered, whitening bones.

•

He bowed his head with clasped hands.

The most powerful man on earth
then asked him to teach him the secret

of the Taoist masters—

the elixir
that allows men to cheat death.

Temujin was in pain. Temujin

for fifty years lived as if immortal—
though surrounded, all his life, by death.

Now he had fallen from a horse. The injury

had not entirely, after much
time, healed. He brooded about death, his

death. Now he must conquer the ancient

secret
that would bend

heaven to his need.

He asked Ch'ang-ch'un for the fabled
elixir.

III.

The world. He was born at the great world's
poor far edge. In order to see the rich

debris that must lie at the bottom of the sea,

he sucked and sucked
till he swallowed the ocean.

●

Buddhists, Taoists, Muslims, Nestorians —
he summoned

each. Each eloquent spokesman

praised abnegations, offered transformation, even
ecstasies—; just renounce

sex, or food, or love.

●

Eating power, he fucked a new woman every night.
Best, he said, was the wife or daughter or mother of

an enemy.

●

He watched his friend Bo'orchu hunt
each day as if hunting were the purpose of life, work

sufficient for a man. As a boy he discovered his

work
when he had a wooden wheel around his neck:

to escape the wheel.

Every single thing tastes like, reeks with
the power that put it there. Weapons

keep in place
who gets rewarded how much for what. *The world*

•

is good at telling itself this is a lie. The world.

IV.

Each unit made up of

ten: ten soldiers
whose leader reports to a unit of one

hundred soldiers, whose leader reports to a unit of one
thousand soldiers, whose leader reports to a unit of

ten thousand.

With iron logic he had raised the great structure

from the flat
internecine earth

(*—abyss where absolute, necessary*

power
is fettered, bewildered by something working within us,

MUD IN THE VEINS, *to paralyze*

decision—; as well as by that necessary
sweet daring

that leaps across the abyss to risk all, to correct and cripple

power,—
. . . but then finds, in despair, it must try to master it).

V.

Though Temujin's father, alive, was
khan

the remnant of his family was, at his
poisoning, driven from the circle of the wagons.

Temujin
had shining eyes, but at nine no force.

They survived by eating roots, berries, stray
rodents, birds the boys'

cunning pulled from the air.

•

Temujin's father out of his mother
had two sons. His poisoned

father, out of his second wife, also had two sons.

•

One day, with a freshly sharpened juniper
arrow, he brought down a lark, and his

half-brother, Bekter, nearly his age,
reaching the bird first, refused to give it up.

Temujin ran to his mother, who told him he must
accept this, that four boys with two

defenseless women alone must
cease fighting.

With his bow and arrow, the next day Temujin
murdered his half-brother.

•

His half-brother at each moment relentlessly
disputed and clearly forever would

dispute everything Temujin possessed.

●

When he confessed to his mother she shrieked
only his shadow

ever again could bear to be with him.
He didn't believe her. She lived

blinded by panic. He looked
around him. Human beings

live by killing other living beings.

●

His father's rival, who told his father that Temujin
had shining
eyes, when his father died

decided he now could make Temujin a slave.

Temujin rammed
the wheel down on the idiot guard's
skull.

Sorqan-shira and his sons found him
drowning among
reeds at the edge of the river.

Frenzied, risking their
lives, Sorqan-shira and his sons
work to cut away the wheel from his body.

●

The arrow flew
as if of itself.

Temujin's half-brother turned and saw

Temujin's unerring aim
aimed at

his chest.

Before the arrow
was released

his half-brother did not beg to live.

His half-brother's
gaze was filled with

everything that would happen would happen.

●

In the delirium of Temujin's adult
dreams, the knife he stole
escaping

is useless
in unlocking
the wheel.

•

How each child finds that it must deal with
the intolerable

becomes its fate.

•

WORLD

with this A R R O W

I thee wed.

VI.

Even the conqueror of the world
is powerless against the dead.

The most intricate plan his friend Jamuqa
ever accomplished

was to make Temujin execute him.

•

They met as boys.

By the frozen waters of the Onon, Temujin
gave Jamuqa the knucklebone of a deer.

Jamuqa gave Temujin the knucklebone of a deer.

They could see their breaths. They mingled
breaths. They swore they were *anda*,

brothers. They sharpened arrows—juniper, cypress.

•

When they met again, many years
later, Temujin's

wife, Borte, had been seized by another tribe.

Fearless, lithe, full of ardor, Jamuqa

commanded a whole tribe. He
pledged his friend twenty thousand men.

Temujin also by this time was chief, but of

many fewer. The two friends and two armies
found and freed Borte after nine months.

The *anda* celebrated by the waters of the Onon.

·

They were too drunk, too happy. Jamuqa
pulled a blanket over himself and Temujin.

They lay all night under the same blanket.

·

For either to have expressed desire, to have
reached, would have been to offer the object of desire

power. It could not be done.

·

Jamuqa forever wants them to
do it to them

together, in tandem, two couples next to
each other—; so Temujin can and must

look over and see Jamuqa's insouciant

bravado as he dismounts, hear Jamuqa's
girl cry out first, more jaggedly.

●

When the chiefs gather to choose, for
the first time in decades, a Great Khan

to Jamuqa's surprise

Temujin is chosen. Someone points out
his family is royal—; Jamuqa

is merely descended from a favorite concubine.

●

At feasts, Jamuqa thinks supplicants
shuffle him aside to reach Temujin.

As the world more and more defers to Temujin

Jamuqa becomes, in his own eyes, a ghost.
He is the memory of Jamuqa.

●

In the new army under Temujin, aristocracy has
few privileges. A friend who has fought under

Jamuqa for years must, to rise, compete

against peasants. Panache, the sweet disdain for
mere consequences, gain, victory, is lost.

•

Many, like the tribe that tried to enslave him, will
never accept Temujin.

Whenever a new group rebels, Temujin finds
Jamuqa is in their company.

•

Men don't want to serve under Jamuqa—

because his friend would not fight against
the Great Khan, he cut off the friend's

head, and hung it from his horse's tail.

•

Jamuqa joined the Nayman army;
Jamuqa deserted the Nayman army.

•

An outcast with five
last remaining followers, Jamuqa

in the high snowy Tangu mountains
at the very limit of his native country

as he eats a wild ram he has killed and roasted

is taken prisoner by his companions
and delivered to Temujin.

VII.

Your father seized your mother as a girl
just after her

marriage to someone from her own tribe. This was
common practice. Just after

your marriage, the same tribe

seized your wife, and gave her to the brother of the chief.
All proceeded from desire—from deferred

justice, the chancre of unclosed

injury. This bred
enmity through generation after generation, blood

feuds, tribe against tribe against tribe.

As the Great Khan, Temujin outlawed such
seizures. He did *What was there to be done.*

•

The axes of your work, work that
throughout the illusory chaos of your life

absorbed your essential

mind, were there always—*What was
there to be done.* You saw many men

refuse, or try to refuse

what needed to be done. Whether they could not
find it, or were, finding it, disgusted, they

without it wandered, like Jamuqa.

•

When Temujin entered the dark room the prisoner
was naked.

His genitals hung pendant, bulbous—

as if swollen
from rubbing.

He still is a creature that is beautiful, but all dirty.

●

Jamuqa said, *What you must do is kill me.*

I will never accede to your power.

Alive, I will rally your enemies.

Dead, I will, in their eyes, just be one more fool.

Temujin replied that he
could not. They had been, since boyhood,

anda. Without him, would he have recovered
Borte?

Jamuqa replied that he did not want his skin

broken during
execution. He repeated, twice,

I will never accede to your power.

Temujin refused. Jamuqa was
sick in the head. Healthy men don't want to die.

●

Jamuqa escaped. Two men who Temujin valued
died bringing him back.

Then he escaped again. When he was

returned again, Temujin
hesitated for months.

Then he granted his wish.

●

He insisted the skin not be broken.
When he saw the body, the head was severed,
as if someone for some reason had been
furious.

●

Temujin was furious with him for letting
pride, some

sickness of the mind, poison

feeling,—
. . . they had been, since boyhood, *anda*.

●

Even the conqueror of the world
is powerless against the dead.

He saw, smelt

the carcass of
Jamuqa,—

. . . who had known that Temujin was too
smart not to be, by his

death, forever tormented.

●

*He watched you take from him what he thought was
his—the world of indolent chaos*

inhabited by the beautiful

and lucky—
fuck anything that walks, if that is whatever inside you

demands. In the end the something

that was broken in him was mute.
He insisted that it did not exist.

VIII.

There was an immense silence between Temujin and Borte.

 •

In the beginning, sweetness, because there had been no need to talk.

 •

Temujin's father had taken him at nine on a journey to find Temujin
 a bride.

 •

She was ten, and beautiful.

 •

His father and her father were old allies, and it was agreed.

 •

On the way home the Tatars poisoned his father.

•

Temujin was sixteen when they were at last married.

•

Within days, Borte was abducted.

•

Borte was abducted because, when their camp was attacked, there was only one free horse.

•

Temujin thrust the horse at his mother, not his wife.

•

This was as it should be.

•

Borte knew this, accepted this.

•

When she returned from those who had seized her, she returned about to give birth.

•

Temujin did not ask what humiliations she had endured.

•

Whose child was it?

•

It could have been Temujin's or the creature's who took her.

•

Temujin declared the child, a son, his.

•

He needed to be perceived, among his own people, as someone of impeccable justice.

•

Someone whose rectitude is above vanity.

•

They had three more sons.

•

He needed legitimate sons.

•

Borte raised, as well, orphans that Temujin's soldiers plucked from burning villages that they themselves had burned.

•

Those thus saved proved to be among the fiercest, the most loyal of his soldiers.

•

After Borte returned, the armies of Temujin and Jamuqa camped together for a year and a half.

•

Borte and Temujin's mother found the closeness between the two men humiliating, an insult, an embarrassment.

•

Borte and Temujin's mother told Temujin that as long as he was tied to this debauched, fickle friendship, the other chiefs never would choose Temujin as the Great Khan.

•

It was the first month of spring.

●

The two armies had to move off to fresh grazing.

●

Temujin, furious, listened to the two women as if he were a statue.

●

He heard Jamuqa say that camp pitched on the slopes of the moun-
tain gave the herders of horses what they wanted, but camp
pitched on the banks of the river was better for the herders of
sheep.

●

The women said that when night fell and Jamuqa's wagon stopped
to pitch camp Temujin's wagon should continue.

●

Temujin's wagon as Jamuqa's wagon stopped to pitch camp on a
mountainside continued.

●

As the night passed the clans realized what was happening, and, frightened, debated to stop with Jamuqa or stop with Temujin.

•

Schisms within a tribe, even sometimes within a clan.

•

One shaman dreamt that a cow white as snow struck at Jamuqa's wagon until it broke one of its horns, bellowing that Jamuqa had to give back its lost horn, striking the ground with its hoof.

•

The shaman dreamt that a white bull followed Temujin's wagon bellowing that Heaven and Earth have decided the empire should be Temujin's.

•

When Temujin heard this he promised the shaman thirty concubines.

•

As day broke and Temujin at last stopped, count could be taken of which clans followed Temujin and which stopped with Jamuqa.

•

Temujin camped near the sources of the Onon.

•

The clans who had chosen Temujin in the disorder and uncertainty
of the night now were joined by others.

•

They had weighed the situation.

•

Temujin was famous for the care and probity of his decisions.

•

The princes of the royal blood joined Temujin.

•

Many days passed before Temujin looked directly at Borte when
they spoke.

•

She was the vehicle of necessity.

●

Of what had to be.

●

He would not forgive her.

●

In time, he lost interest in forgiving her.

●

When he returned from his last long campaign which lasted eight unbroken years, he was grateful she did not ask about each night's new woman.

●

In time, near the sources of the Onon the princes of the royal blood elected Temujin Great Khan.

●

Fame clung to the story of how he saved the beautiful Borte.

•

The irony was not lost on Borte that as Mother of Orphans she
    was married to the force that made them orphans.

IX.

Only at the age of thirty-nine Temujin
at last was master of all Mongolia.

The emissaries of the Kings of Gold

had played tribe against tribe
all his life, to castrate them.

To achieve unity, to achieve the empire
essential to maintain unity

half the tribes had to be massacred.

•

The Tatars killed his father, then after
subduing them, followed by their unending

involuted betrayals and rebellions,

Temujin without
sorrow exterminated them.

Every male standing higher than a wagon axle

was killed;
the rest enslaved.

•

Extermination
is not a question of vengeance. It is a question of

safety. Of not allowing what happened to happen.

•

Under Temujin, the Mongols crossed the Great Wall
that the Kingdom of Gold over centuries

built to contain them.

Before them, the lush, cultivated great plain

stretched five hundred miles,—
. . . from Beijing to Nanjing.

•

Between the Mongols and the Kings of Gold
lay a trench of

blood, inexpiable wrongs.

Fifty years earlier, betraying Tatars handed off
the Mongol khan Ambaqay

to Beijing's
King of Gold,—

. . . who impaled him on a wooden ass.

●

Temujin drummed into his troops past atrocities.

After they took Huai-lai, the ground for some ten miles
around for years was still strewn with human bones.

●

The full fury of the Mongols was reserved
for the great cities of Islam.

Their Sultan had twice murdered Temujin's emissaries—

what rose in Temujin was the rage to annihilate
not just the civilization that

insulted him, but what made it possible. . . .

In the end, there was little left for his tax collectors
in the future to tax.

This was a world everywhere on the edge of desert—

the Mongols in fury dismantled the intricate
networks that preserved and gathered and channeled

water. Without dams, without the multitudinous

screens of trees that were the handiwork of centuries,
for Samarkand, for the cities of Scheherazade,

not just defeat, but dismemberment.

●

Nightmare from which not even the rich awoke.

●

. . . . Stonework

of hive-like
intrication, its hard
face airy as lace,

indifferent hooves erased to sand.

X.

Ch'ang-ch'un thought if he answered honestly
he would be executed.

He asked Temujin
to tell him Temujin's story.

The Great Khan, to his own surprise, wasn't
offended. He liked the earnest old man.

Seized, suddenly absorbed, with relish
he began to tell the old man his

story, omitting nothing he imagined essential.

The Taoist master at last answered that there exists
no elixir for eternal life.

He told him that the largest square
has no corners.

He told him that they go east and west at
the will of the wind, so that in the end

they know not if the wind carries them
or they the wind.

But as Temujin listened to his own voice tell
his story, the lineaments of his story, this

is what he heard: —

Because you could not master whatever
enmeshed you

you became its slave —

You learned this bitterly, early.
In order not to become its slave

you had to become its master.

You became
its master.

Even as master, of course, you remain its slave.

●

A S H. What yesterday was the lock-step
logic of his every

position, purity in which he took just
pride, cunning

solutions to what the universe thrust at him

appeared to him now ash, not
his, or, if

his, not his.

●

Too often now he woke with his mouth
gasping above water, the great wooden

wheel around his neck now

buoy, now too
heavy to lift.

Jamuqa's face, mutilated —

Jamuqa, with whom
he lay under the same blanket.

The familiar universe began to assume its shape.

Inherent
enmity of equals. Each master

not a master. A fraud. A master slave.

●

His own voice said it.

•

Old, he included
himself in his scorn for those who

young want the opposite of this earth

then settle for
more of it.

•

The life he had not
led, could not even now lead

was a burning-glass

between himself
and the sun.

•

Temujin saw that the Taoist master
was terrified.

The old man, facing
the verge, had leapt into the sea —

he had given the conqueror of the world
simply what he had already.

He liked the old man. After dallying
for months discussing

the dead surrounding them
he allowed him to return to his own country.

•

Master
slave, you who have survived thus far

the lottery of who will live, and who will die—
contemplate Genghis Khan, great,

ocean
khan, born Temujin, master slave.

XI.

The death of his grandson Mutugen
seemed to Temujin

harbinger of his own death. This boy

raised in a desert dust-storm
was innocent of dust.

He who made one imagine something
undeformed could emerge from deformity

died by an arrow.

That he should die — .

That he should die assaulting a Muslim citadel
meant that Temujin himself, bareheaded,

took part in the final attack that destroyed it,

that every living thing therein, man and beast,
the child slain in its mother's womb,

must die — ; that no loot, no booty

should be taken, but everything inexorably
erased; a place thereafter forever accursed.

●

When Temujin heard of his grandson's death,
he learned it before the boy's own father.

He called all his sons to share a meal, and at it

announced that he was angry
his sons no longer obeyed him.

Jaghatay, Mutugen's father, protested.

Then Temujin told Jaghatay that the boy
was dead.

Gazing fixedly, Temujin with a choked

voice forbade
Jaghatay GRIEF.

Forbade him not just the signs of grief, but GRIEF itself.

He kept them at table for hours. At the end
Jaghatay, when Temujin left the room, wept.

•

He now knew how he wanted to be buried.

He wanted the course of the Onon temporarily
diverted—; there, at its muddy center,

burial in a sealed chamber.

Then the river
sent back over it.

Any travelers encountering by chance

the funeral cortege
were to be executed.

XII.

Imagination
clings to
apotheosis,—

. . . those who inherit

the powerful
dead imagine
them and cling.

HERO to his people,—

. . . curse (except in
imagination)
to everyone else.

The dream I dreamed

was not denied me.
It was not, in
the mind, denied me.

●

This is the end of the fourth hour of the night.

Radical Jesus

Judge not.

Restrain, incarcerate
the knife that can and would cut you.

But judge

not. Some dream law their sure guide.
But law is

a labyrinth,

each law at war with another law, animated
by an imperative you recognize.

Your soul

must thread its way through warring
imperatives you recognize. You are standing

in ash

without guide in a labyrinth. The ash
that is falling implacably is from fires

you lit.

Jesus (*enemy of the State, ground upon which no State has been built*)

Jesus says

only those who have been justly
condemned to die can act as judge.

Visions at 74

The planet turns there without you, beautiful.
Exiled by death you cannot
touch it. Weird joy to watch postulates

lived out and discarded, something crowded
inside us always craving to become something
glistening outside us, the relentless planet

showing itself the logic of what is
buried inside it. To love existence
is to love what is indifferent to you

you think, as you watch it turn there, beautiful.
World that can know itself only by
world, soon it must colonize and infect the stars.

You are an hypothesis made of flesh.
What you will teach the stars is constant
rage at the constant prospect of not-being.

●

Sometimes when I wake it's because I hear
a knock. *Knock,*
Knock. Two
knocks, quite clear.

I wake and listen. It's nothing.

Note on the Text

In 1990, *In the Western Night* collected my first three volumes in reverse chronological order, prefaced and followed by new poems. The idea was that the reader would journey backward from new work to where it all began, a first book about family and the world where I grew up. The volume ended with "The First Hour of the Night," intended as the beginning of a sequence.

The books that followed are collected here in the order of publication, as hour of the night has followed hour of the night.

•

Passages in three long poems from *In the Western Night* have been changed. (The three are "The War of Vaslav Nijinsky," "Confessional," and "The First Hour of the Night.") None of the words are different. But in terms of punctuation and "set-up," they seemed to me too often spoken *à haute voix*, as if declaimed to the last row of the balcony. I have always heard the voice in them more intimately. They increasingly to my eye lacked this intimacy. I have tried to modulate the voices, by shifting punctuation, spacing, pacing.

"The First Hour of the Night," especially, has a new body. When I wrote this poem I now think I had no idea how to set it up, how it should exist in space.

Inevitably some readers will prefer the first versions. Some readers prefer the first version of "The Rime of the Ancient Mariner"; I don't, decisively.

•

The aim, throughout, has been not chronology, but a kind of topography of the life we share—in chaos, an inevitable physiognomy.

Notes

In the Western Night

"To the Dead" (p. 5): The final three lines are stolen, ultimately, from Antoine de Saint-Exupéry's *Night Flight*. I first encountered this vision of the nature of love in Rudy Kikel's sequence "Local Visions" (1975), where it is attributed to Auden.

"In the Western Night: 3. Two Men" (p. 13): These lines are indebted to an unpublished lecture by V. A. Kolve, "Fools In and Out of Motley" (Wellesley College, 1979).

"The War of Vaslav Nijinsky" (p. 23): Readers not familiar with Nijinsky's life may find some biographical background useful. Nijinsky came to the West as the principal male dancer of the Ballets Russes—which was directed by the man who had created it, Serge Diaghilev. He lived with Diaghilev for several years. With Diaghilev's encouragement, he became a choreographer: he did the first productions of, among others, "L'Après-midi d'un Faune" (1912), "Le Sacre du Printemps" (1913). Revolutionary, Modernist, his choreography remained as controversial as his dancing was admired. On the company's first trip to South America—Diaghilev, who hated sea travel, was absent—Nijinsky met and married a young woman traveling with the troupe, Romola de Pulzky. The break with Diaghilev precipitated by this was never healed.

Prose passages in the poem are based on Romola Nijinsky's biography, *Nijinsky* (Simon & Schuster, 1934), and sentences by Richard Buckle, Serge Lifar, Maurice Sandoz.

"Genesis 1–2:4" (p. 94): In the first vision, first version of creation in the Hebrew Bible, God creates by dividing, separating what is without form—and therefore is waste—into a landscape built of oppositions, that then all living creatures are told to fill. But the mechanism thus created must be, on the sixth day, checked—the first *Thou shalt not*. In the Hebrew Bible, the injunction against eating other living creatures remains in force until after Noah's flood.

"The Book of the Body" (p. 129): Lines 12–15: Vergil, *Eclogue V*, 56–57.

"Ellen West" (p. 132): This poem is based on Ludwig Binswanger's "Der Fall Ellen West," translated by Werner M. Mendel and Joseph Lyons (*Existence*; Basic Books, 1958). Binswanger names his patient "Ellen West."

"Book of Life" (p. 174): The Snake parable is from John McPhee's *Oranges* (1966). This is the first poem I wrote about my family. The four-line refrain now makes me wince—such confidence about what the alternatives are, such speed in judgment. Hard to encounter in writing one's old self. I feel some version of this throughout this book, but most acutely in *Golden State* (1973). *Such confidence about what the alternatives are.* [2016]

"After Catullus" (p. 199): Catullus, *Carmen LVI* ("*O rem ridiculam, Cato, et iocosam*").

"The First Hour of the Night" (p. 215): The source for the "dream of the history of philosophy," and the major source for the poem as a whole, is Wilhelm Dilthey's "The Dream," translated by William Kluback (*The Philosophy of History in Our Time*; Doubleday/Anchor Books, 1959). The final dream is based on a dream reported by E. L. Grant Watson in a letter to Jung (C. G. Jung, *Letters*, vol. 2, p. 146, note 1; Princeton University Press, 1975).

Desire

I have treated sources as instances of the "pre-existing forms" mentioned in the first sentence of "Borges and I," and done this so freely that it needs acknowledgment. "As the Eye to the Sun" uses as building blocks phrases, sometimes reversed, from George Long's Marcus Aurelius. "Adolescence" is a "found" poem, carved out of anonymously-published prose. "The Return" steals from Michael Grant's translation of *The Annals of Tacitus*, as well as versions by John Jackson, Alfred John Church, and William Jackson Brodribb. David Cairns's *The Memoirs of Hector Berlioz* lies behind the first part of "The Second Hour of the Night"; *A Manichaean Psalm-Book*, translated by C.R.C. Allberry, suggested the "taste" litany; the poem throughout is indebted to Stephen MacKenna's translation of Plotinus.

Star Dust

I. MUSIC LIKE DIRT

K.218 is Mozart's Fourth Violin Concerto. The phrase *music like dirt* is a refrain in Desmond Dekker's song "Intensified." I have never met Mr. Dekker; he is not the "you" of "Music Like Dirt." Think of "Advice to the Players" as a manifesto written by someone who does not believe in manifestos. Think of "Injunction" as the injunction heard by an artist faced with the forever warring elements of the world that proceed from the forever unreconciled elements of our nature. "Lament for the Makers" is the title of a poem by the Scots writer William Dunbar (1460?–1520?).

I hoped to make a sequence in which the human need to make is seen as not only central but inescapable. I wanted not a tract, but a tapestry in which making is seen in the context of the other processes—sexuality, mortality—inseparable from it.

I I

"Curse" (p. 361): The "you" addressed here brought down the World Trade Center towers; when I wrote the poem I didn't imagine that it could be read in any other way, though it has been. The poem springs from the ancient moral idea (the idea of Dante's *Divine Comedy*) that what is suffered for an act should correspond to the nature of the act. Shelley in his *Defense of Poetry* says that "the great secret of morals is love"—and by love he means not affection or erotic feeling, but sympathetic identification, identification with others. The "secret," hidden ground of how to act morally is entering the skin of another, imagination of what is experienced as the result of your act. Identification is here called down as punishment, the great secret of morals reduced to a curse.

"Hadrian's Deathbed" (p. 369): Hadrian, "Animula vagula blandula."

"Song" (p. 370): "It takes talent to live at night, and that was the one ability I never doubted I had" (Ava Gardner, *Ava: My Story*, 1990). "It's not raining inside tonight" (Johnny Standley, "It's In the Book," 1952).

"The Third Hour of the Night" (p. 373): In part II, my largest debts are to John Addington Symonds's translation *The Life of Benvenuto Cellini, Written by Himself* (1887); and to Michael W. Cole's *Cellini and the Principles of Sculpture* (2002). Part III, section one, is based on W. Lloyd Warner's *A Black Civilization* (1958), pages 198–200; reprinted under the title "Black Magic: An Australian Sorcerer (Arnhem Land)" in Mircea Eliade's *From Primitives to Zen: A Thematic Sourcebook of the History of Religions* (1977), 443–45.

Watching the Spring Festival

"Marilyn Monroe" (p. 423): Throughout, "she" is Monroe's mother. She was a film-cutter in a Hollywood studio, a professional. Born after her mother's second—and last—marriage ended, Monroe was never certain who her father was.

"Tu Fu Watches the Spring Festival Across Serpentine Lake" (p. 424): In conception and many phrases, this version of Tu Fu's "Li-ren" is indebted to David Hawkes's *A Little Primer of Tu Fu* (1967).

"Little O" (p. 463): I mean for my title to echo Shakespeare's phrase for the Globe Theatre in *Henry V*, "this wooden O." The argument here is with Stevens's "The Creations of Sound," his argument with Eliot.

"Collector" (p. 473): Lee Wiley's career, insofar as it flourished at all, thrived in the thirties, forties, and fifties. This era—from screwball comedies to film noir, from Ella Fitzgerald and Duke Ellington to the Great American Songbook—remains the period that, for solace and pleasure, I most often return to. But it was also a suffocating box: what a relief to discover Antonioni and Satyajit Ray, Lowell, and Ginsberg. They were part of a movement that, to my mind, was not Post-Modernist but Neo-Modernist, a movement that was not a repudiation of Modernism's seriousness and ambition, but a reinvention—a continuing attempt to discover what Modernism left out.

Metaphysical Dog

"Writing 'Ellen West'" (p. 486): "The Case of Ellen West" by Ludwig Binswanger is included in *Existence*, edited by Rollo May, Ernest Angel, and Henri F. Ellenberger, translated by Werner M. Mendel and Joseph Lyons (Basic Books, 1958). The poem "Ellen West" begins on p. 132.

The gestures poems make are the same as the gestures of ritual injunction—curse; exorcism; prayer; underlying everything perhaps, the attempt to make someone or something live again. Both poet and shaman make a model that stands for the whole. Substitution, symbolic substitution. The mind conceives that something lived, or might live. Implicit is the demand to understand. The memorial that is ward and warning. Without these ancient springs poems are merely more words.

"Defrocked" (p. 507): In the first section, the anonymous lyrics are quoted from Evelyn Underhill's *Mysticism*, chapter VI, section 1, except for "*pilgrimage to a cross in the void*," from Ginsberg's *Howl*, part III.

"Threnody on the Death of Harriet Smithson" (p. 524): This is a kind of fantasia based on an essay by Jules Janin (*The Memoirs of Hector Berlioz*, translated by David Cairns). Smithson was an actress, and became the wife of Berlioz.

"Dream of the Book" (p. 529): The passage ending with "unbroken but in stasis" uses a sentence from Lionel Trilling's essay "Art and Fortune" (*The Liberal Imagination*, 1950). The sentence is quoted in full in the interview with Mark Halliday (see p. 681).

"Whitman" (p. 542): "The old thought of likenesses" is from "As I Ebb'd with the Ocean of Life," first published in 1860; the version of *Leaves of*

Grass discussed at the beginning of my poem appeared five years earlier, in 1855. Whitman revised and enlarged *Leaves of Grass* for the rest of his life.

"Martha Yarnoz Bidart Hall" (p. 563): "As in Dante, there she ate your heart" refers to the first sonnet in *La Vita Nuova*. There is a very free version in *Desire* (1997) titled "Love Incarnate" (p. 269 of this book).

"Mouth" (p. 570): The two lines beginning *"The best times"* are based on words by Otto Klemperer, *Klemperer on Music* (Toccata Press, 1986), p. 21. *La Notte* is the film by Michelangelo Antonioni. "Ithaca" is the next-to-last chapter of *Ulysses*.

"Presage" (p. 573): The prophecy about the Gordian knot was that the person who succeeded in untying it would rule Asia. Alexander the Great, newly arrived in Asia, did not untie it but cut through it.

"Of His Bones Are Coral Made" (p. 583): This statement appeared with the poem in *Best American Poetry 2012*:

> I've written little prose about poetry, but can't seem to stop writing poems about poetics. Narrative is the Elephant in the Room when most people discuss poetry. Narrative was never a crucial element in the poetics surrounding the birth of Modernism, though the great works of Modernism, from *The Waste Land* to the *Cantos* to "Home Burial," *Paterson* and beyond, are built on a brilliant sense of the power of narrative. What Modernism added was the power gained when you know what to leave out. Narrative is the ghost scaffolding that gives spine to the great works that haunt the twentieth century.
>
> A writer is caught by certain narratives, certain characters, and not by others. Prufrock is relevant to our sense of Eliot. He could be a

character in Pound's sequence "Hugh Selwyn Mauberley," but if he were, it would be without the identification, the sympathy and agony. Eliot had to go on to Gerontion and Sweeney and Tiresias, each trailing a ghost narrative. They are as crucial to the vision of Eliot as Bloom and Stephen Dedalus are to the vision, the sense of the nature of the world, of Joyce.

In my poem, "the creature smothered in death clothes" is Herbert White, the title character in the first poem in my first book; "the woman" two stanzas down is Ellen West, from the second.

Two more allusions. "The burning fountain" refers to this passage in Shelley's "Adonais," his elegy for Keats:

> He wakes or sleeps with the enduring dead;
> Thou canst not soar where he is sitting now.
> Dust to the dust: but the pure spirit shall flow
> Back to the burning fountain whence it came,
> A portion of the Eternal, which must glow
> Through time and change, unquenchably the same. . .

"The burning fountain"—the power that fuels, that generates and animates life—is the title of a book about the poetic imagination by Philip Wheelwright (generous, profound spirit), whose classes I took as an undergraduate (*The Burning Fountain*, Indiana University Press, 1954).

My poem's title comes from Shakespeare's *The Tempest*:

> Full fathom five thy father lies;
>   Of his bones are coral made;
> Those are pearls that were his eyes:
>   Nothing of him that doth fade,
> But doth suffer a sea-change
> Into something rich and strange.

My poem is about transformation, the bones of the poet made up out of the materials, the detritus of the world, that he or she has not only gathered but transformed and been transformed by.

"Poem Ending With a Sentence by Heath Ledger" (p. 586): The Joker (in *The Dark Knight*) and Ennis Del Mar (in *Brokeback Mountain*) are Ledger's greatest roles.

Thirst

"The Fourth Hour of the Night" (p. 622): The book that made me want to write about Genghis Khan, and that I've stolen most from, is René Grousset's *Conqueror of the World* (1966), translated by Marion McKellar and Denis Sinor.

(There is a space between stanzas at the bottom of each page of verse, except on pages 97, 104, 106, 126, 142, 154, 165, 170, 191, 197, 199, 202, 203, 238, 308, 328, 333, 570.)

Interviews

INTERVIEW WITH MARK HALLIDAY

Ploughshares, Spring 1983

MARK HALLIDAY: When I think about your two books, and the poems that I know will be in your third book, I seem to see a movement away from autobiographical material toward poems in which the characters are distinct from yourself—Nijinsky, Ellen West. Do you see a "story" of your choice of subjects for poems as beginning in family and autobiography and moving to something else? And if so, why has that happened?

FRANK BIDART: I've made a list of the subjects I hope we'll be able to take up in this interview: prosody; voice; "action"; punctuation; the relation of "personal" (or autobiographical) and "impersonal" elements in a poem; the struggle to make life *show* itself in a work of art.

It's hard to talk about any one of these things without talking about all of them—in my work at least, they seem to me so tangled, inextricable.

The heart of my first book was, as you say, autobiographical; but the story of how I came to this subject matter as the *necessary* subject matter for me at that time is bound up with discovering a prosody, figuring out (among other things) how to write down, how to "fasten to the page" the voice—and movements of the voice—in my head.

I wrote a lot of poems before the poems in my first book, *Golden State*, but they were terrible; no good at all. I was doing what many people start out by doing, trying to be "universal" by making the entire poem out of assertions and generalizations about the world—with a very thin sense of a complicated, surprising, opaque world outside myself that resisted the patterns I was asserting. These generalizations, shorn of much experience, were pretty simpleminded and banal.

Nonetheless, though the poems were thin, I was aware that what I heard, the rhythms and tones of voice in my head, I didn't know how to set down on paper. When I set the words down in the most "normal" ways, in terms of line breaks and punctuation, they didn't at all look to the eye the way I heard them in my head.

MH: Can you give an example from any of these poems?

FB: I remember a poem which ended with a sentence from Samuel Johnson, "The mind can only repose on the stability of truth." As I heard this sentence, it had a weight and grimness, a large finality it just didn't have as I first typed it. In the attempt to *make* the sentence look the way I heard it, I typed the words hundreds of different ways, with different punctuation and line breaks, for weeks. And I never did get them right; in the end, I realized the poem wasn't any good in the first place.

I never had a romance with writing *verse*. What caught me about writing poems was not the fascination of using meter and rhyme—I knew somehow, however gropingly and blindly, that there must be some way to get down the motions of the voice in my head, that somehow the way to do this was to write in *lines*. Lines, not only sentences or paragraphs. When I tried to "translate" the phrases in my head into formal metrical or rhymed structures, they went dead. It seemed that my own speech just wasn't, as so much English has always been, basically iambic. (There are lines of pentameter in my poems, but usually they represent some order or "plateau" of feeling I'm moving toward, or moving away from.)

What I *was* in love with was the possibility of bringing together many different kinds of thing in a poem. When I was an undergraduate, Eliot was probably my favorite (twentieth-century) poet; but Pound was the more liberating. *The Cantos* are very brilliant and they're also obviously very frustrating and in some ways, I guess, a mess. But they were tremendously liberating in the way that they say that anything can be gotten into a poem, that it doesn't have to change its essential identity to enter the poem — if you can create a structure that is large enough or strong enough, *anything* can retain its own identity and find its place there. *Four Quartets* is more perfect, but in a way its very perfection doesn't open up new aesthetic possibilities — at least it didn't for me then. *The Cantos*, and Pound's work as a whole, did; and do.

MH: As an undergraduate, did you already think of yourself as a poet?

FB: I *wanted* to be a poet as far back as I can remember, but I didn't think I could be. In college, many of my friends were far more fluent than I; they really knew how to shape something eloquently into a poem. My poems were always (with, maybe, one exception) awkward, bony, underwritten. My poems had vast structures of meaning and symbol, and about three words on the page.

MH: Could we go back now to your discovery of what you did have to do — the transition from those too abstract poems that were not successful, toward whatever it was that made you able to write the poems in *Golden State*. Could you talk about your years of graduate school, what you were reading and what you were thinking about, what you wanted to do?

FB: Really to answer that question I have to go back much further, because it's all bound up with wanting to be an artist when I was very young, and the different ways I imagined being an artist as I grew up.

When I was a kid, I was crazy about movies. In Bakersfield, I think movies were the most accessible art form, in terms of new things happening and being done in the arts—I mean, we didn't have the New York City Ballet or a great symphony orchestra, we didn't have a season of plays. But we did have, each week, surrounded by publicity, glamour, and controversy, these incredibly interesting movies. As early as I can remember, I wanted to be an artist; I certainly knew I didn't want to be a farmer, as my father was. Briefly, I imagined becoming an actor; but very quickly it was clear to me that the person who really *made* movies was the director. By the time I was in high school, I was determined somehow to become a director. I thought a lot, read a lot about movies; I graduated from fan magazines to reviews of contemporary films, to books like Paul Rotha's *The Film Till Now*. Because, in Bakersfield in high school, I could actually *see* almost none of the "serious," "art" films I was reading about, I ferociously held a great many opinions about things I had never experienced—the faith, for example, that the coming of sound had been a disaster to film as an art.

So, in college, I was determined to become a film director, and a *serious* film director. I wanted films to be as ambitious and complex as the greatest works of art—as Milton, Eliot, Joyce. I thought, at first, that I might become a philosophy major; but in the desolation of positivism and analytic linguistic skepticism that dominated American academic philosophy in the fifties, it seemed that the moral and metaphysical issues that had traditionally been the world, the province of philosophy, had been taken over by literature. *Ulysses* and *Absalom, Absalom!* and Yeats's "The Tower" seemed closer to Plato and Aristotle than what academic philosophers then were doing. One of my teachers at the University of California, Riverside, where I was an undergraduate, was a marvelous exception to this—Philip Wheelwright, who had written about literature and aesthetics, as well as translated Aristotle, Heraclitus. I was an earnest and clumsy freshman, and he was wonderfully humane and generous. (The first time I ever heard Maria Callas was in his living room, when he played to a final meeting of a class excerpts of her second recording of *Lucia*. I remember he was upset because he felt that it wasn't, compared to her first recording, nearly as well sung.)

MH: So you became an English major?

FB: I became an English major. Of course it's impossible to recapitulate all—or even the central—intellectual and emotional dramas of those years. But two books I particularly loved are relevant here.

First, Trilling's *The Liberal Imagination*: Trilling's sense, in "The Meaning of a Literary Idea," that one doesn't have to share "belief" in an author's "ideas," but has to feel their cogency, that the *activity* on the author's part has to be in a satisfying relation to the difficulty, the density of his materials. In "Art and Fortune," there is a long passage of great eloquence about "the beautiful circuit of thought and desire" (James's phrase), which culminates in this sentence:

> The novel has had a long dream of virtue in which the will, while never abating its strength and activity, learns to refuse to exercise itself upon the unworthy objects with which the social world tempts it, and either conceives its own right objects or becomes content with its own sense of its potential force—which is why so many novels give us, before their end, some representation, often crude enough, of the will unbroken but in stasis.

This image of the will "unbroken but in stasis"—after having "exhausted all that part of itself which naturally turns to the inferior objects offered by the social world"—and which has therefore "learned to refuse" . . . This image has haunted me: it seems to me a profound pattern, one of the central, significant actions that many works have, in different ways with different implications, *felt as necessary*. The passage also taught me, I think, one way a work of art can conclude without concluding—how it can reach a sense of "resolution," or completion, without "resolving" things that are inherently unresolvable. In college, I read these pages so many times I find I've almost memorized them.

The notion of "action" in Francis Fergusson's *The Idea of a Theater* is crucial to my understanding of poetry (and of writing in general)—so crucial, that I want to get polemical about it. Its source, of course, is Aristotle's *Poetics*, the statement that "tragedy is the initiation of an action." Fergusson cites Kenneth Burke on "language as symbolic action," and quotes Coleridge: unity of action, Coleridge says, "is not properly a rule, but in itself a great end, not only of the drama, but of the epic, lyric, even to the candle-flame of an epigram—not only of poetry, but of poesy in general, as the proper generic term inclusive of all the fine arts."

But the sense that the poem must be animated by a unifying, central action—that it both "imitates" an action and is *itself* an action—has been largely ignored by twentieth-century aesthetics. It was never an animating idea in the poetics of modernism. That doesn't mean that poets have ignored it in practice. When Pound, for example, writes that he has "schooled" himself "to write an epic poem which begins 'In the Dark Forest,' crosses the Purgatory of human error, and ends in the light," he is describing, of course, an action—a journey undertaken and suffered by the central consciousness of his poem, a journey that begins somewhere, goes somewhere, ends somewhere, a journey the *shape* of which has significance. But though Pound's poem was intended to imitate this action, the action that the actual poem he wrote inscribes is, we now all know, quite different. Its shape is tragic, and far more painful.

The notion that a poem imitates action, and *is* an action, seems to me so necessary now because it helps free poetry from so many dead ends—

"good description," the mere notation of sensibility, "good images," "good lines," or mere wit. Let me emphasize that an "action" is *not* a "moral," or merely something intended that the poet cold-bloodedly executes. Like Pound, a poet may *intend* that the action have a certain shape: but (again like Pound) any writer who is serious, as he moves through his materials, will inevitably find that what his poem must enact, what it embodies, is more mysterious, recalcitrant, surprising. (If only in detail, it's always, I think, at least *different*.)

What I've been arguing applies not only to long poems, but, as Coleridge suggests, to lyric. Kenneth Burke has a great essay called "Symbolic Action in a Poem by Keats."

MH: In your own work, have you found the "action" of a poem turning out to be significantly different from what you thought it would be, when you began the poem?

FB: I've just been through hell with a long poem in my third book, "Confessional." Six years ago, in the summer of 1976, I wrote the first part of the poem. I felt immediately that it wasn't complete, and wanted to write what I thought of as the second "half." And I knew what the last two lines of this second half must be. But that's all I had that was specific, that was concrete.

Well, it took me six years to discover what the second half must be. That was a time of immense frustration—I would have loved to consider the first part (which was four pages) "complete." But my friends kept telling me it wasn't finished, and of course *I* knew it wasn't finished, that from the beginning I had felt there must be more (though I tried to repress the memory of feeling this). I had an arc in my head, a sense— frustratingly without content—of the shape of the emotional journey that had to take place, and (because I had the last two lines) the words on which it would end. That was all!

The poem is about my relationship to my mother, though it begins with an anecdote about a cat that *didn't* happen to me (it's from the memoirs of Augustus Hare). I felt, for complicated and opaque reasons, that this story was right at the beginning—that I needed it. Everything else in the poem had to be "true."

Slowly during these six years the second part grew in me. I say "grew" (and it *did* feel that way), but the process wasn't at all orderly or continuous. I read in Peter Brown's wonderful *Augustine of Hippo*, the scene in the *Confessions* between Augustine and his mother at the window in Ostia. I felt immediately some version of this scene—as an embodiment of everything that between my mother and me *didn't* happen—should be in the poem. But *how* this could happen wasn't at all clear.

There is an "Elegy" for my mother in my second book. As I went back to it, I felt more and more dissatisfied with it—when "Elegy" was written, right around my mother's death, it was as true as I could make it, but it no longer represented what I felt about our relationship, the way (after several years had passed) I now saw it. I had to be, if not "fair" (who can know that?), *fairer*.

So the second part of the poem finally got itself written out of the desire to tell the whole thing again from the ground up, finally to get it "right." This desire in the end came to me clothed as necessity: I felt I *owed* it to my mother. The poem is still angry, just as "Elegy" was angry, but there's much more in it—among other things, much more sense of my complicity in everything that happened between us. What started out as the "second half" ended up three times as long (and was written six years later).

All art, of course, is artifice: words in our mouths, or our minds, don't just "naturally" happen on paper with focus, shape, or force. If, in a poem, we feel we are listening to a voice speak the things that most passionately engage it, it is an illusion. But I think that Frost's statement is also true: "No tears in the writer, no tears in the reader."

MH: Can you say more about "artifice" in a poem? In your own poems?

FB: There's a remarkable passage in a letter by Keats that for me stands for how genuinely mysterious and paradoxical this subject is. So often people use terms like "open form" or "closed form," or "sincere" or "artificial," as sticks to beat each other over the head. In the letter, Keats says that he is giving up "Hyperion" because it is too "Miltonic" and "artful": "there were too many Miltonic inversions in it—Miltonic verse cannot be written but in an artful or rather artist's humour. I wish to give myself up to other sensations." Then he suggests an experiment—that his reader pick out some lines from the poem, and put an X next to "the false beauty proceeding from art" and a double line next to "the true voice of feeling." There's something terrifically winning about Keats's desire to separate mere "art" (which led to falseness) from what he calls (in a great, beguiling phrase) "the true voice of feeling." Part of his greatness as a poet comes from the way he imagined the poet's job as discovering truth—from his sense (in the "Chamber of Maiden-Thought" letter) that his poems must "explore" the "dark passages" we find ourselves in after we see "into the heart and nature of Man"; from his impatient self-criticism of his poems, throughout his career, demanding that they "make discoveries."

So he asks his reader to put an X next to "the false beauty proceeding from art," and a double line next to "the true voice of feeling." Then there is an amazing passage: "Upon my soul 'twas imagination I cannot make the distinction—Every now & then there is a Miltonic intonation—But I cannot make the division properly." In other words, the distinction—so clear in "imagination"—cannot actually be made. There *are* things that seem only artifice ("Every now & then there is a Miltonic intonation"), but the *division* between what proceeds from "art," and "the true voice of feeling," cannot clearly or consistently be made.

I think "the true voice of feeling" is a necessary and useful ideal. So many poems seem *not* to be, at any point, "the true voice of feeling." We have to have the "imagination" of it. But in practice, I'm sure there is no one way—free verse or formal verse, striving for "originality" or "imitation"—for us to achieve it. It's certainly not the opposite of "art."

MH: That seems to lead us back to the question we began with—the discovery of the subject matter of your first book, and of your own prosody. At what point did that happen?

FB: I began graduate school in 1962, and the first poem that I've kept was written in 1965. Those were years of bewilderment, ferment, and misery. Why was I in graduate school? I wasn't at all sure. I thought I would like to teach; but I also felt that if I didn't become an artist I would die. By the time I graduated from Riverside, I'd ceased believing I must, or could, become a film director. Rather murkily I felt that if I really *were* a filmmaker I would have already, somehow, in however rudimentary a way, made a film. (I had shot a few feet, but they seemed stupid, arty, clumsy—and in any case, I couldn't connect them to a whole.) I felt the fact that this art could only be practiced if you convinced someone else to risk huge sums of money, the fact that movies were a business, would break me; Antonioni had said he spent ten years waiting in producers' waiting rooms before he was allowed to direct a film.

So I went to graduate school at Harvard—more out of the desire to continue the world of conversations and concerns I had found in an English department as an undergraduate, than out of any clear conviction about why I was there. I took courses with half my will—often finishing the work for them months after they were over; and was scared, miserable, hopeful. I wrote a great deal. I wrote lugubrious plays that I couldn't see had characters with no character. More and more, I wrote poems.

I began this interview by saying that discovering the subject matter of *Golden State*, as the *necessary* subject matter for me at that time, was bound up with discovering a prosody. This seems to me true; but I'm nervous that describing this process as a narrative, consecutive and chronological, will introduce far more order into it than existed. It was a time of terrible thrashing around.

So let me describe this period in terms of "problems." First, I felt how literary, how "wanting to be like other writers"—particularly like the Modernists, and Post-Modernists—the animating impulses behind my poems were. I said to myself (I remember this very clearly): "If what fills your attention are the great works that have been written—*Four Quartets* and *Ulysses* and 'The Tower' and *Life Studies* and *Howl* (yes, *Howl*) and *The Cantos*—nothing is *left* to be done. You couldn't possibly make anything as inventive or sophisticated or complex. But if you turn from them, and what you look at is your *life*: NOTHING is figured out; NOTHING is understood . . . *Ulysses* doesn't describe your life. It doesn't teach you how to lead your life. You don't know what *love* is; or *hate*; or *birth*; or *death*; or *good*; or *evil*. If what you look at is your *life*, EVERYTHING remains to be figured out, ordered; EVERYTHING remains to be done . . ."

However silly this speech may sound, "recollected in tranquillity," it was a kind of turning point for me. I realized that "subject matter"—confronting the dilemmas, issues, "things" with which the world had confronted me—had to be at the center of my poems if they were to have force. If a poem is "the mind in action," I had to learn how to *use* the materials of a poem to *think*. I said to myself that my poems must seem to embody not merely "thought," but *necessary* thought. And necessary thought (rather than mere rumination, ratiocination) expresses or acknowledges what has resisted thought, what has forced or irritated it into being.

Such an aim has huge implications, of course, for *prosody*—versification, how words are linked and deployed on the page. I needed a way to get "the world" onto the page (bits of dialogue, scenes, other voices, "facts"), as well as the mind *acting* on, ordering, resisting it. This sounds like the way I earlier described *The Cantos*—how Pound managed to create a texture which seemed to allow *anything* into the poem without changing its identity. Pound does this, predominantly, by using the "ideogram," the "ideogrammic method": by placing image next to image, quotation next to quotation, bit of cultural artifact next to bit of cultural artifact, allowing "meaning" to arise from the juxtapositions. The result is that the page often feels essentially static (though also often giving a sense of "sudden illumination" or "sudden liberation"). This static (though luminous) texture just did not feel like my experience of the mind, the way the mind acts upon and within the world. I needed a way to embody the mind moving *through* the elements of its world, actively contending with and organizing them, while they somehow retain the illusion of their independence and nature, are felt as "out there" or "other."

Slowly I stumbled toward "deploying" the words on the page through voice; syntax; punctuation. (By "punctuation" I mean not merely commas, periods, et cetera, but line breaks, stanza breaks, capital letters—all the ways that speed and tension and emphasis can be marked.)

MH: I've heard you talk, many times, about "voice" and "punctuation" in your work, but not "syntax." How is it connected in your mind with the others?

FB: Syntax—the way words are linked to make phrases, phrases to make sentences, even sentences to make "paragraphs"—has had a huge effect on the punctuation of my poems. Often the syntax is extremely elaborate. As the voice moves through what it is talking about—trying to lay out, acknowledge, organize the "material"—it needs dependent clauses, interjections, unfinished phrases, sometimes whole sentences in apposition. The only way I can sufficiently *articulate* this movement, express the relative weight and importance of the parts of the sentence—so that the reader knows where he or she is and the "weight" the speaker is placing on the various elements that are being laid out—is punctuation. In "Confessional," in the section based on Augustine, whole typed pages are single sentences (the sentences are longer than Augustine's own). Punctuation allows me to "lay out" the *bones* of a sentence visually, spatially, so that the reader can see the pauses, emphases, urgencies and languors in the voice.

The punctuation of my poems has become increasingly elaborate; I'm ambivalent about this. I feel I've been forced into it—*without* the heavy punctuation, again and again I seemed not to be able to get the movement and voice "right." The Nijinsky poem was a nightmare. There is a passage early in it that I got stuck on, and didn't solve for two years. Undoubtedly there were a number of reasons for this; the poem scared me. Both the fact that I thought it was the best thing I had done, and Nijinsky's ferocity, the extent to which his mind is *radical*, scared me. But the problem was also that the movement of his voice is so mercurial, and paradoxical: many simple declarative sentences, then a long, self-loathing, twisted-against-itself sentence. The *volume* of the voice (from very quiet to extremely loud) was new; I found that many words and phrases had to be not only entirely capitalized, but in italics.

Discovering punctuation that you haven't used before, because you need it, is *hard*. Probably the crucial instance of this, for me, was in

"Golden State" (the poem). The phrase I couldn't get right is in the eighth section: "The exacerbation / of this seeming *necessity* / for connection." The problem was the punctuation following "connection." The entire phrase (three lines long) comes as a kind of pained distillate or residue of everything above it on the page; it must seem itself both a *result*, and blocked; the next lines are about what in reality preceded it, and what is "beneath" it both on the page and as cause. I punctuated the lines differently for months, to the point where my friends winced when I pulled out a new version. The solution I finally found is "double-punctuation": a dash followed by a semicolon. Coming to it was so hard that I felt I had discovered this mark, this notation, all by myself. Later I found it in poems I had known very well — in "Grandparents" from *Life Studies*, for example. But because I hadn't understood it before, understood its necessity, I'd never seen it. (Finding the capitalized "MYSELF" in "Herbert White" was also a long drama — I couldn't get the word right until I saw a capitalized "MOI" in Valéry's "La Jeune Parque.")

James has a wonderful phrase: "the thrilling ups and downs of the compositional problem."

MH: And now your third term — "voice."

FB: Surely the logic — or self-serving calculation — of everything I've said now is clear. The nature of syntax and punctuation has to proceed from the demands, the nature, of the voice. (In the "Genesis" translation, for example — where whatever speaks the poem couldn't be more different from the voices usually in my poems — the punctuation is quite spare and simple, except for capitalization.)

A little more history is relevant here. The teacher I was closest to at Riverside was Tom Edwards — he is a great teacher. His sophomore survey course, "The English Literary Tradition," was the place that I feel I first learned how to pay attention to the details of a poem, to how it is made. The importance of "voice" and "tone of voice" was at the heart of what I learned. Edwards's teacher had been Reuben Brower, and Brower's teacher (or almost teacher) at Amherst was Frost. "Tone of voice" and "speaker" were crucial terms for Brower, and of course for Frost. Frost has the great statement about "voice":

> A dramatic necessity goes deep into the nature of the sentence. Sentences are not different enough to hold the attention unless they are dramatic. No ingenuity of varying structure will do. All that can save them is the speaking tone of voice somehow entangled in the words and fastened to the page for the ear of the imagination. That is all that can save poetry from sing-song, all that can save prose from itself.

I only read those sentences in graduate school, but I had absorbed them (or been absorbed by them), through Edwards, just at the time I was first seriously studying poetry. For Frost, this emphasis on "the speaking tone of voice" isn't separate from the importance of meter: "The possibilities for tune from the dramatic tones of meaning struck across the rigidity of a limited meter are endless." In Frost's terms, my poems—which rely so nakedly on voice, where everything in the prosody is in the service of the voice—just are "playing tennis without the net."

But he acknowledges how mysterious and peculiar these questions are: "the speaking tone of voice *somehow* entangled in the words and fastened to the page for the ear of the imagination." My work has been a long odyssey struggling to find ways to accomplish this "entangling" and "fastening"—a journey which starts in my own "ear of the imagination," and hopes to end there in the reader.

When I write, I always hear a "voice" in my head; and I always write in lines. I've never written a poem first as prose and then broken it into lines. The voice only embodies itself in words as the words break themselves in lines. (This movement is felt physically, in my body.) "Syntax" is dependent on this; the sentence can only take on a certain shape, have a certain syntax, as the voice finds that the sentence can be extended— can take on "new materials," and shape itself—across the lines.

But I find that *at the most intense moments* the line breaks are often not quite right. And the punctuation of the poem, including spaces between stanzas, initially is never right. The final punctuation is *not* an attempt to make the poem look the way I read it aloud; rather, the way I read it aloud tries to reproduce what I hear in my head. But once I finally get the typed page to the point where it does seem "right"—where it does seem to reproduce the voice I hear—something very odd happens: the *"being"* of the poem suddenly becomes the poem on paper, and no longer the "voice" in my head. The poem on paper suddenly seems a truer embodiment of the poem's voice than what I still hear in my head. I've learned to trust this when it happens—at that point, the entire process is finished.

MH: How does what you've said about prosody connect with the "subject matter" of *Golden State*?

FB: When I first faced the central importance of "subject matter," I knew what I would have to begin by writing about. In the baldest terms, I was someone who had grown up obsessed with his parents. The drama of their lives dominated what, at the deepest level, *I* thought about. Contending with them (and with the worlds of Bakersfield and Bishop, California, where I had grown up) was how I had learned—in the words of Bruno Walter about Bruckner and Mahler, which I quote in "Golden State"—to "think my life."

The great model for such poems was of course *Life Studies*. I had read it soon after it came out, and like so many others was knocked over. But I knew that Lowell's experience of the world he came from, and himself as an actor in it, was very different from *my* experience. Lowell's poems were written when he was around forty, and seemed to me to communicate an overwhelmingly grim, helpless sense that the dragons in his life were simply *like that*. At seven, he was "bristling and manic"—without any sense of *cause*. "Tamed by *Miltown*, we lie on Mother's bed; / the rising sun in war paint dyes us red": these poems are great glowing static panels in brilliant supersaturated technicolor, a world that refuses knowledge of the *causes* beneath it, without chance for change or escape.

But I was twenty-six, not forty—and *my* poems had to be about trying to figure out *why* the past was as it was, what patterns and powers kept me at its mercy (so I could change, and escape). The prosody of my poems could *not* reflect the eloquent, brilliantly concrete world of *Life Studies*; it had to express a drama of processes, my attempts to organize and order, and failures to organize and order. It had to dramatize the moments when I felt I had *learned* the terrible wisdom of the past (so I could unlearn it).

So rather than trying to replicate *Life Studies*, I was engaged in an argument with it. If *Life Studies* had done what I felt my poems had to do, I'm sure I couldn't have written them. Later, when I met Lowell—in 1966, after I'd written "California Plush" but before "Golden State"—I found that he shared this conscious sense of being engaged in an *argument* with the past. He liked to quote Edward Young: "He who imitates the *Iliad* does not imitate Homer."

MH: So he was not your teacher, then, in the sense of being the central guiding voice in your mind as you built that book.

FB: I didn't learn a prosody from him; and I certainly didn't want to write the poems he had already written. I somehow always knew that "what I had to say" was different from what he was saying; that's why, I think, though I got tremendously close to him and his work in later years, I never felt that as an artist I was about to be annihilated.

But much before I met him, I had known his work extremely well — I had admired it, and learned from it, in the way that I admired and learned from Eliot and Pound. And later, I sat and listened to him in class, for years; it would be impossible to listen to a mind that various and inventive and surprising and learned and iconoclastic and craftsmanlike, *without* learning things. The fact that later I could be useful, both as a reader of his poems and a friend, to someone I so much revered, was a profound event in my life: a *healing* event. I saw him in every kind of vicissitude, from insanity to suffering gratuitous humiliations; he *grew* in my eyes, the more intimately I knew him.

MH: When did you begin to write dramatic monologues?

FB: "Herbert White" begins *Golden State*, and was written at the same time as the family poems. I wanted to make a Yeatsian "anti-self" — someone who was "all that I was not," whose way of "solving problems" was the *opposite* of that of the son in the middle of the book. The son's way (as I have said) involves trying to "analyze" and "order" the past, in order to reach "insight"; Herbert White's is to give himself to a violent pattern growing out of the dramas of his past, a pattern that consoles him as long as he can feel that someone *else* has acted within it. I imagined him as a voice coming from a circle in Hell. The fact that he is an "anti-self" only has some meaning, I thought, if he *shares* something fundamental with me; I gave him a family history related to my own. He has another embodiment at the end of the book: the "MONSTER" who can only face his nature if he "splits apart," and who asks the "I" of the poem to help him to do so. I put "Herbert White" at the beginning because I felt the book had to begin "at the bottom"—in the mind of someone for whom the issues in the book were in the deepest disorder. He is the chaos everything else in the book struggles to get out of.

So "Herbert White" wasn't an escape from the world of the family poems—but I think the dramatic monologues I've written since are. *Golden State* did in fact do for me what I wanted it to do; I felt I had been able to "get all the parts of the problem" out there. I've never had to write about my father or Bakersfield again. (Will I?) It seemed to settle those issues for me. It drained those subjects of their obsessive power.

I think that it did this *because* I was able to "get all the parts of the problem" out there. My mother isn't at the center of *Golden State*, and as I've said, the poem about her in my second book didn't seem to me deep enough or true enough. I hope "Confessional" completes something.

MH: Can you say more about the dramatic monologues you've written since "Herbert White"? Are the concerns beneath them as "personal"?

FB: I've never been able to get past Yeats's statement that out of our argument with others we make rhetoric, out of our argument with ourselves we make poetry. At times that's seemed to me the profoundest thing ever said about poetry.

Williams said, "No ideas but in things"—but by that he *didn't* mean "no ideas." His work is full of ideas, full of "arguments with himself." By the end of another poem he manages to convince us that "The pure products of America / go crazy" (an idea), as well as that this most American of writers is riven to say it. The drive to conceptualize, to *understand* our lives, is as fundamental and inevitable as any other need. So a poem must include it, make it part of its "action." The ideas that are articulated in the course of the action don't "solve" or eradicate or end it, if the drama is true enough or important enough, any more than they do in the action of our lives.

So the dramatic monologues I've written since *Golden State*, insofar as they are animated by "arguments with myself," don't seem to me any less (or more) "personal." The books have been animated by issues: issues revolving around the "mind-body" relation in *The Book of the Body*; "guilt" (and ramifications) in *The Sacrifice*. No genuine issue, in my experience, has an "answer" or "solution." But the argument within oneself about them is still inevitable and necessary. In "Ellen West" and the Nijinsky poem, I didn't feel I was "making up" the drama—they were *there*, and I felt that to write the poems I had to let them (both the *voices* and the *issues* their lives embody the torments and dilemmas of) enter me. Of course they were already inside me (though I still had to let them in).

The most intense version of this that I've ever experienced happened with the Nijinsky poem. It was written in about a month, and during that month there was an independent voice in my head that insistently had things to say. I knew that I was, in effect, feeding it things, feeding it things I had thought about; but the voice had an identity and presence in my head that seemed independent of my conscious mind, and I was not simply telling it when to talk and when not to talk. On the contrary, the minute I would finish a section, the voice would begin making up new sentences and obsessing about the next stage of the drama. And one reason I felt certain that the poem *was* finished when it was finished, that the "action" was completed, was that at the end of the poem the voice just disappeared. The voice had no more to say: when I wrote the last line of the poem, the voice just ceased.

MH: At the beginning of this interview, you said something enigmatic about "the struggle to make life *show* itself in a work of art."

FB: There is a scene in "Herbert White" in which he is looking out the window of his room at home, and feels suffocated by the fact that everything is "just *there*, just *there*, doing nothing! / not saying anything!" He wants to see beneath the skin of the street, to see (in Wordsworth's terms) "into the life of things," and cannot. It's of course me feeling that. So much of our ordinary lives seems to refuse us—seems almost dedicated to denying us—knowledge of what is beneath the relatively unexceptionable surface of repeated social and economic relations.

The artist's problem is to make life *show* itself. Homer, Aeschylus, Vergil, Shakespeare—a great deal of Western art has made life *show* itself by dramatizing crisis and disaster. Lear, in his speech about "pomp," says that when he was king he saw nothing. Success, good fortune, power cut him off from seeing into the nature of things. Out of his blindness and vanity, he performs the stupid act that precipitates his "fall." But when he *does* fall, he sees much more than simply his former blindness, his stupidity. He can't stop from falling—from discovering our ineradicable poverty, and defying the heavens to "change or cease." In the course of the play, Lear "learns" things, but the play couldn't exactly be called the story of his education: Cordelia dies, and he dies.

When Lear "falls," the forces that before were present—but dormant, unseen, unacknowledged—then manifest themselves. (Only then.)

Many other works of art of course *are* "the story of an education." Wordsworth's "spots of time" and Joyce's "epiphanies" were moments they eagerly hoarded and clung to—for these moments seemed to them moments of true insight, with emblematic force, the story of the true education of their souls. They embedded these moments in narrative contexts, in actions, dramatizing their *access* to them.

Again and again, insight is dramatized by showing the conflict between what is ordinarily seen, ordinarily understood, and what now is experienced as real. Cracking the shell of the world; or finding that the shell is cracking under you.

The unrealizable ideal is to write as if the earth opened and spoke. I think that if the earth *did* speak, she would espouse no one set of values, affections, meanings, that everything embraced would also somehow be annihilated or denied.

Bookslut, June 2005

ADAM TRAVIS: So far you've published "The First Hour of the Night," "The Second Hour of the Night," and "The Third Hour of the Night"— what is the inspiration for this project? That is, what made you want to do this? Where is it going? Does the project have a name?

FRANK BIDART: The myth behind the series of poems is the Egyptian "Book of Gates," which is inscribed on the sarcophagus of Seti I. Each night during the twelve hours of the night the sun must pass through twelve territories of the underworld before it can rise again at dawn. Each hour is marked by a new gate, the threshold to a new territory.

Each poem in the series is an hour we must pass through before the sun can rise again. I don't know what will make moral and intellectual clarity and coherence rise again: I could never write twelve "hours." But were the sun to rise again, it would have to pass through something like these territories.

I've written only three "hours" over something like seventeen years. I'm sixty-six: I'll be lucky if I can write one more. I like the idea that I'm involved in a project that can't be completed: the project corresponds to how things are.

AT: What is your favorite hour of the night? (I mean literally. Not which poem.)

FB: It's easier to say which poem I like best! Of course, the way that I imagine each "territory" that the sun must pass through to rise again is different from the way someone else would imagine it. The "First Hour" is about the collapse of Western metaphysics, the attempt to make a single conceptual system that orders the crucial intellectual issues and dilemmas in our lives. At the end of the poem there is a dream that suggests the birth of something like phenomenology, the phenomenological ground out of which art springs, that survives the death of metaphysical certainty. The "Second Hour" is about Eros, how the "givenness" of Eros in our lives embodies the givenness of fate. The "Third Hour," which ends my new book, is about making, how "Making is the mirror in which we see ourselves." Making in the poem, and the book as a whole, proceeds from the twins within us, the impulse to create as well as not-to-create, to obliterate the world of manifestation, to destroy. (One of the many wars within us.)

I don't imagine the poems printed together as a series, one "hour" read after another hour. They are more like symphonies: you don't listen to Beethoven's symphonies consecutively, as you at least initially read the *Iliad* or even (perhaps) the *Duino Elegies*. But the fact that Beethoven's Fifth follows the Third and Fourth has meaning, as does the fact that the "Pastorale" follows the Fifth.

AT: From the readers' perspective, the project has the makings of what one could call your Great Work. Do you have that kind of ambition? The subjects and their presentation seem almost designed to inspire awe. Is that what you're after?

FB: I'm after something that will make some sense out of the chaos in the world and within us. The result should be something that is, well, "beautiful": but beauty isn't merely the pretty, or harmony, or equilibrium. Rilke says beauty is the beginning of terror: I feel this reading *King Lear*, or watching *Red Desert*.

AT: I like to memorize long poems (to show off). Would you think me a fool for memorizing an hour of the night?

FB: If the pulse of the poem is right, if the essential movement of the poem captures the essential pulse of the processes that the poem *sees*, one should be able to memorize it. At one time I could say the whole of "Second Hour" to myself, hearing the poem as I lay in bed.

AT: When "The Third Hour of the Night" (about Benvenuto Cellini) appeared in the October 2004 issue of *Poetry*, readers seemed to react only in one of two ways: awe or outrage. One common complaint was that the poem took up the entire issue (besides the "Comment" section). The logic here being that the poem is, supposedly, not good enough to have its own issue. Another complaint was that the poem read too much like prose, or was too obscure or esoteric or whatever. The final complaint was something like revulsion. The poem contains disturbing scenes of murder and some sort of ritual/sexual violence. These complaints beg a couple of questions: "How much of a long poem can actually consist of 'poetry'?" And: "These poems really are very violent. Why?"

FB: If a poem is any good, I don't think of some parts as "poetry" and other parts as "not poetry." Each line has to be written with a feeling for its place in the shape, the pulse of the whole: if it does that, it is authentically part of the *whatness* of the thing. It then has its own eloquence.

I think the question of violence is only a question because people think of poetry as lyric poetry. In lyric there is often a great deal of psychic violence, but usually little (say) murder. (Even in Browning's lyrics.)

A heart gets eaten in the first sonnet of Dante's "Vita Nuova," but that is the exception.

But violence is at the heart of Dante's long poem, as it is incessant in Shakespeare. Or Sophocles. It is offstage, but barely, in Racine. It is not offstage in Virgil.

AT: Can you explain what's going on in the last, very violent scene of "The Third Hour of the Night"?

> With my thumb over the end of the killing stick
>
> I jabbed her Mount of Venus until her skin pushed
> back up to her navel. Her large intestine
>
> protruded as though it were red calico.
>
> With my thumb over the end of the killing stick
> each time she inhaled
>
> I pushed my arm
>
> in a little. When she exhaled, I stopped. Little by little
> I got my hand
>
> inside her. Finally I touched her heart.
>
> Once you reach what is
> inside it is outside.

FB: This is from a four-page monologue that is based on the words of an Australian sorcerer, found in a book by Mircea Eliade on the history of religions. With an appalling neutrality and evenness of tone the speaker is describing a kind of rape. At first you think he is also describing a killing, that he has murdered the woman. (The anthropologist quoted in Eliade says that in his village he is known as a murderer.) Then he says that after touching her heart and covering up the signs of what he has done, she begins to breathe again. He tells her that she will live two days, that after two days she will die. She gets up, and two days later dies.

The passage is clearly about the will to power, to possess the woman by entering her, the fantasy of controlling her by determining when she will die. I have no idea what "actually" happened. Did a woman from his village simply die and the sorcerer imagine that he had control over this process? Or did he rape, and later murder her? On the literal level, his report cannot be believed: he could not have done what he reports doing. He has tried to master whatever happened by constructing a narrative that could not literally be true.

What is true is the will to power. He fantasizes that he has the same power that the third Fate, earlier in the poem, has: the power to determine when someone dies. He admits he cannot keep the woman alive forever: all he can do is determine when the thread of life is slit. In the poem he says this power is the same power the gods have: "Even the gods cannot / end death." After his psychic rape of the woman, which involves the attempt to touch and therefore know her "heart," all he can do is turn her into a kind of puppet: he tells her she will live two days, and she then enacts this. This is a terrible parody of what Cellini does earlier in the poem, when he saves the almost-ruined statue of Perseus and "what was dead [was] brought to life again." It is the terrible, negative version of the injunction the central consciousness of the whole poem hears after the monologue by the sorcerer: he "must fashion out of the corruptible / body a new body good to eat a thousand years." (Which is to say, echoing "Howl," that one must try to make what in despair one feels is impossible to make, a good poem.)

The whole book is about making, how the desire to make is built into us, its necessities and pleasures and contradictions. The impulse to make is itself neither good nor bad. It is a species of the will to power, which is inseparable from survival and creation. It is inseparable from the impulse to destroy. The most ferocious enactment of the will to power always must confront metaphysical and epistemological limits: in the poem (not in Eliade): "Once you reach what is / inside it is outside." Human beings constantly strive to reach the heart of something: when they reach it they find it is only another surface. Art strives to be that center that has reached the light, and remains the center: in Ashbery's brilliant phrase, the "visible core."

INTERVIEW WITH SHARA LESSLEY
National Book Foundation, October 2013

SHARA LESSLEY: In an effort to promote a literary event in Bakersfield, a woman once rented a billboard that read FRANK BIDART IS COMING HOME. Although you've been gone from California for some time, there are poems in *Metaphysical Dog* that return there. Is there a part of you that still inhabits the Golden State?

FRANK BIDART: The person who did that was a writer named Lee Mc-Carthy, who taught high school near Bakersfield. She was terrifically gutsy, independent, courageous. She was angry that I had been left out of a semiofficial anthology of California poets. She invited me to read in Bakersfield, and arranged for the billboard to startle anyone driving by.

Though I've now lived in New England much longer than my years growing up in Bakersfield, I've never thought of myself as a New Englander. I'm deeply someone made in California, in Bakersfield. Elizabeth Bishop has a wonderful line, "Home-made, home-made! But aren't we all?" But if you make yourself in California it's different than if you make yourself in Massachusetts. Class issues and assumptions, racial issues, manners are different. The things you argue about in your head are different. I think the things that are "Californian" about me have been modified as I've gotten older, but haven't changed in essence. Though everything I've written has been an argument with the world I'm from,

I'm no less a creature of it. This is an enormous, labyrinthine subject, as it probably is for any writer who felt wounded but made by the place he or she began. Think of Joyce and Ireland.

SL: Hunger in *Metaphysical Dog* is exhausting but persistent. "Words / are flesh," you write. The collection's speakers crave the soul, the absolute. Is desire for "the great addictions"—love, power, fame, god, and art—a flaw? Or, is it simply what drives what you call the "Ordinary divided unsimple heart"?

FB: I think they are what drive the ordinary divided unsimple heart. Though it's terrible to give in unqualifiedly to the desire for them, the notion that one has eradicated them from oneself—or that you should be ashamed you feel them—is naive, an illusion, one more chimera. No matter who or what you are, possessing whatever social or economic stature you've been born into or achieved, hunger is universal—hunger for something you don't possess, once thought important. Everyone feels grief for the unlived life. But not every addiction is equal. I tell my students that it's better to be addicted to Astaire and Rogers movies than to heroin. The notion that, short of death, one is going to be totally free of addictions is one more way of torturing oneself.

SL: "Writing 'Ellen West'" revisits your well-known poem on anorexia. Like Ellen, you claim, "*he* was obsessed / with eating and the arbitrariness of gender and having to / have a body" (emphasis mine). As a narrative strategy, why transform yourself into a character via the third person?

FB: It's a way of making fact available to art. To write about oneself as a character—to think about oneself as a character—opens up space between the "I" and the author. (In this sense, calling the *I* "he" is only a way of making inescapable this space. You can write as an "I" and still think of yourself as a character.) The space is necessary because the work isn't going to be any good if it is merely a subtle form of self-justification, if one is supine before the romance of the self. Not that self-justification is ever wholly absent.

SL: Image is often exploited as a means of generating feeling or propelling the contemporary poem's plot. *Metaphysical Dog*, in contrast, is stark — it draws its energy primarily from abstraction and pattern-making. Do ideas incite your work rather than concrete details?

FB: What's crucial for any writer is to understand how your mind apprehends meaning. How, in your experience, you apprehend significance. Understand it and find a way to embody it, make it have the force for the reader in a work of art that it has for you. Images, what the eye sees, is of course part of this for everyone. But I think tone of voice, situation, the look in an eye or on a face, are as much part of what make up for me "meaning" as what traditionally people think of as "images." When Williams said, "No ideas but in things," that's not an image. Pound's "Down, Derry-down / Oh let an old man rest," is not an image. Pound was of course right when he said, "Go in fear of abstractions." Abstractions can smother the quick of feeling in a poem. But reaching for abstractions and conceiving abstractions are not separable from feeling for a human being. When Williams said, "No ideas but in things," he didn't mean "no ideas."

SL: I'm struck by how precisely the last ten lines of "Poem Ending With a Sentence by Heath Ledger" characterize your life's work:

Once I have the voice

that's
the line

and at

the end
of the line

is a hook

and attached
to that

is the soul.

How are you able to imagine and sustain such varied voices—the sweep-
ing dramatic monologues of your early collections, for instance, versus
the more intimate lyric and philosophical poems that populate *Meta-
physical Dog?*

FB: First of all, that sentence really *is* by Heath Ledger. When I saw it
printed in an interview, it was printed simply as prose. But I thought there
was a movement in it, an iron logic if you will, that would be appre-
hended if it was set up in lines. I struggled over and over to do so. I found
that this movement was apprehensible if I used a form that I have more
and more used the longer I've written: a single line followed by a two-
line stanza, followed by another single line followed by a two-line stanza.
One followed by two followed by one followed by two. I've found this
form tremendously flexible; it reveals the anatomy of many (but not all)
sentences that, for me, are eloquent. One magazine that printed the
poem—a magazine that did not send me proofs—eliminated all the
stanza breaks, in an attempt to save space. The poem was reduced to
drivel. It's how the words exist in space that allows them, on the page,
their eloquence.

    Crucial to getting a character to speak in a poem is hearing in your head as you write the way the character talks. Because a poem is made up of words, speech *is* how the soul is embodied. (Ledger asserts, of course, that even in a movie this is true.) What's crucial is that how the words are set down on the page not muffle the voice. When I first began writing, writing the voice down in the ways conventional in contemporary practice seemed to muffle or kill the voice I still heard in my head. If I lost that voice, I knew I had lost everything. I'm grateful to Ledger for saying more succinctly than I have ever been able to what I had felt since I began writing.

SL: "I don't know the value of what I've written," said Robert Lowell, "but I know that I changed the game." Your poems—with their typographical innovations, mining of the paradoxical, psychological complexity—have been game changers for so many of us. What about your own work or the process of making poems continues to surprise you?

FB: Nothing is better about writing than the passages about writing in Eliot's *Four Quartets*. "A raid on the inarticulate / With shabby equipment always deteriorating"; "the intolerable wrestle / With words and meanings." The solutions that I felt I found aren't going to be the solutions that work for someone else. But I'll be happy if my poems seem to say to younger writers that you still can be as bold about setting a poem down on the page as Wordsworth was or Mallarmé was or Ben Jonson was or Pound was or Ginsberg and Lowell and Bishop were. Getting the dynamics and voice down are what's crucial. Whatever it takes to get the whole soul into a poem. An emphasis on voice isn't fashionable in contemporary practice. I hope my poems make people reconsider that.

Index of Titles